Edith Wharton

EDITH WHARTON'S WOMEN

FRIENDS & RIVALS

SUSAN GOODMAN

UNIVERSITY PRESS OF NEW ENGLAND
HANOVER AND LONDON

The University Press of New England
is a consortium of universities in New England dedicated to
publishing scholarly and trade works by authors from
member campuses and elsewhere. The New England imprint
signifies uniform standards for publication excellence
maintained without exception by the consortium members. A
joint imprint of University Press of New England and a
sponsoring member acknowledges the publishing mission of
that university and its support for the dissemination of
scholarship throughout the world. Cited by the American
Council of Learned Societies as a model to be followed,
University Press of New England publishes books under its
own imprint and the imprints of

Brandeis University   Brown University
Clark University   University of Connecticut
Dartmouth College
University of New Hampshire
University of Rhode Island   Tufts University
University of Vermont   Wesleyan University

© 1990 by University Press of New England

Quotes from Edith Wharton are courtesy of the Collection of
American Literature, Beinecke Rare Book and Manuscript
Library, Yale University.

Printed in the United States of America

∞

Library of Congress Cataloging-in-Publication Date

Goodman, Susan.
    Edith Wharton's women : friends and rivals / Susan Goodman.
        p.   cm.
    Includes bibliographical references.
    ISBN 0-8745-521-1 (alk. paper). — ISBN 0-87451-524-6 (pbk. :
alk. paper)
    1. Wharton, Edith, 1862-1937—Characters—Women.   2. Women in
literature.   I. Title.
    PS3545.H16Z653   1990
813′.52—dc20   89-40617
                                                      CIP

1 2 3 4 5

TO
GREGORY GOODMAN

CONTENTS

ACKNOWLEDGMENTS

E*dith Wharton's Women* first began to take shape during my conversations about Edith Wharton and literature with the late Gary H. Lindberg. It owes much to the thoughtful readings of Michael DePorte, Sarah Sherman, Barbara White, David Leary, Alan Gribben, and D'lila Terracin. Carl Dawson's insightful and often provoking comments have made this a better book. Above all, I am indebted to Melody Graulich, my dissertation director at the University of New Hampshire, for her support, encouragement, and criticism during the text's evolution.

Gratefully, I acknowledge the invaluable research assistance extended to me by the staffs of the Beinecke Rare Book and Manuscript Library at Yale University, the University of New Hampshire, the Houghton Library at Harvard University, the Lilly Library at Indiana University, and California State University, Fresno. Without the financial support for travel and research provided by the Graduate School and the Central University Research Fund of the University of New Hampshire, this work might still be in process. I want to express my appreciation to Gloria Loomis, the literary agent for Wharton's estate, for permission to quote from the author's published texts and to the Collection of American Literature, the Beinecke Rare Book and Manuscript Library, for permission to quote from the Wharton Archives.

S. G.

Fresno, California
January 1990

The Alliance between Artist and Woman

> *[I]t was always the imagina-*
> *tive side of my work that*
> *helped me over the ugly details.*
> —*THE FRUIT OF THE TREE*

For decades the mosaic that most readers had of Edith Wharton was designed by Percy Lubbock in the memoir *Portrait of Edith Wharton* (1947).[1] Consisting of a series of sketches and personal reminiscences contributed by her friends and linked by his commentary, it seems informed, as William Tyler has observed, by "a systematic personal hostility."[2] In it he presents a woman who is imperious, insensitive, and belligerent to other women, one who liked and repeated the remark that she was a "self-made man."[3] Lubbock heard those words said with a certain self-satisfied pride, but another, more sympathetic listener might have detected in her inflection an ironic undertone or—to borrow a line from *Ethan Frome*—"depths of sad initiation."[4] This book attempts to determine the many meanings—social, artistic, and personal—that the phrase "a self-made man" had for Wharton.

Considered an anomaly as a woman pursuing intellectual

and artistic interests and as a woman writer publishing ironic, unsentimental stories, Wharton has been largely defined by a series of absences: lack of love, lack of children, lack of compassion, lack of social sensitivity, lack of "femaleness."[5] Those critics who have credited her work with a "woman's sensibility" have for the most part failed to examine the implications of that judgment. In a 1906 review of *The Touchstone*, for example, Henry Dwight Sedgwick states that "her talents and capacities are not only intrinsically feminine, but also, despite her cleverness, which, generally speaking, is a neutral trait, they are specifically feminine."[6] The dilemma that Wharton presented to early critics was this combination of femininity and cleverness that—to use Q. D. Leavis's phrase—relegated her to the role of Henry James's "heiress."[7] I examine how she balanced these traits in a society that tended to see them as mutually exclusive.

Wharton was able to appeal to both critical and popular audiences because she employed an ironic tone, so highly prized by twentieth-century academics, and because she never wholly divorced herself from a female literary tradition. Lily Bart's final vision of Nettie Struther's baby daughter, Undine Spragg's vocation as a billionaire's wife, and Anna Leath's disillusionment with George Darrow are rooted in that tradition. Wharton's heroines, like those of *Godey's Lady's Book*, know that conflict with men, if not unthinkable, is self-destructive. At the same time, they seek greater knowledge of the world and of themselves through the only means available to them, bonding with another woman. In this way, Wharton's texts incorporate and in a sense reverse the pattern that David Leverenz traces in the works of Thoreau, Emerson, Melville, and Whitman. Leverenz argues that male rivalry exists under the seemingly fraternal bond between these authors' narrators and their implied audience, a "you" who "is accused and appealed to, as double, potential convert, and comrade for the self-refashioning 'I' " of the narrative.[8] Wharton, however, locates that "you" within her text by pairing her heroines and making them rivals for the same man. Sorority flourishes under the women's competition, as they become allies in the process of reshaping themselves.

Best known as a novelist of manners, dealing exclusively with the upper classes, Wharton was vulnerable to charges of literary elitism. The novelist Robert Herrick, for example, wrote in 1915 that "her talent, a defining, analyzing, and subtilizing talent, has found little that was really congenial or suggestive in the common run of our coarsely accented national life."[9] This accusation would haunt her all of her career, as did the other criticism embedded in Herrick's statement—that she had little passion. It was more than half a century before Cynthia Griffin Wolff noticed a decided emotional change in the novelist's work after 1910, a change that we now know resulted partially from Wharton's affair with the journalist Morton Fullerton.

In 1965 Millicent Bell's study of the literary and personal relationship between James and Wharton took the latter out of the master's shadow and helped her to cast her own.[10] By the 1970s there was a resurgence of critical interest in Wharton prompted by the 1969 unsealing of the author's papers at Yale. Writers such as Wolff and R. W. B. Lewis attempted to answer the question that Blake Nevius had posed in his 1953 study: What was the relationship between Wharton's life and her art?[11] Feminist critics in particular noticed the author's consistent concern with women's issues. Margaret McDowell, Elizabeth Ammons, Wendy Gimbel, Carol Wershoven, and Annette Zilversmit have written at length about Wharton's heroines in studies that tend to see her women in isolation and as primarily competitive.[12] In contrast, I see her heroines struggling to define themselves through connections with other women. Using biographical, feminist, and to some extent psychological methods, I ana-

lyze the relationships between women in the major novels
while highlighting those interesting intersections of the author's life and what she called her "making up." I discuss
why Wharton's professional identity, so irrevocably intertwined and at odds with her sexual identity, made her relationships with other women and with women writers difficult. Wharton was not, as Shari Benstock argues, so much a
woman among men as a woman who sought value for her life
and her work in relationships with women.[13]

Previous discussions of the author's work have tended to
neglect the importance of female relationships in part because she has for so long been characterized as a woman who
did not really care for women. Although R. W. B. Lewis's biography of Wharton has helped to correct this image, and
the work of Cynthia Griffin Wolff has increased our understanding of the forces that shaped her, the image persists
still. In a 1986 review in *The New York Times*, Janet Malcolm states that in *The Custom of the Country* Wharton's dislike of women is taken "to a height of venomousness previously unknown in American letters, and probably never
surpassed."[14] The writer she describes bears no resemblance
to the one whom Elizabeth Ammons sees as consistently having shown a regard for the circumstances of all women.

The seemingly incompatible readings of Malcolm and
Ammons reflect Wharton's own conflict about her roles as
woman and author. In her guise as author, the novelist
claimed that she had little difficulty stilling the critics. The
"best safeguard," she advised, is to put out of one's mind "the
quality of the praise or blame bestowed . . . by reviewers
and readers, and to write only for that dispassionate and
ironic critic who dwells within the breast."[15] As a woman,
though, she found it more difficult to quiet the inherited and
internalized voices of her childhood. The volume and resonance of those voices were generations in the making,
stretching back three hundred years. They were also pre-

dominantly male and always associated with the old New York of her youth, in which a woman's charm provided the background and her quiet labor supplied the expertise necessary for the smooth working of the community's great social and civic machine. During the first years of her marriage, when Wharton tried to conform to this tradition, she felt as if she had no identity: "I had as yet no real personality of my own, and was not to acquire one till my first volume of short stories was published—and that was not until 1899" (*ABG*, 112). That volume's title, *The Greater Inclination*, points to her future course.

The multiple names given to Edith Wharton in her childhood, "Lily," "Pussy," and "John," highlight the problem of determining the real Wharton, as does a 1925 photograph that presents one image but two portraits. It is her most reproduced likeness and the one she herself chose to greet the readers who opened the covers of her autobiography, *A Backward Glance*. At first one sees an obviously wealthy society matron: her hair woven with a strung crown of cameos, her shoulders smokily swathed in furs, and her columnar throat adorned by a finely wrought choker. The gaze is unblinking, imposing, intimidating. On closer inspection, however, a shadow portrait emerges: she still staunchly faces the camera, but smudges hollow her sad eyes; her right shoulder, turned delicately and barely raised, recedes into the darkened background; and the choker checks her pulsing throat. The jaw is strained, set, controlled. The first portrait presents the traditional view of Wharton; the second is more in keeping with recent revisions of that view, which see her as a successful Lily Bart, a survivor of a suffocating and insensitive society. Yet, belonging to and joining both portraits are wisps of hair that poignantly escape their pins and the sheerly veiled *décolletage*. Wharton, as Virginia Woolf would have said, was neither "this" nor "that," and it is in these more ambiguous, hard-to-pigeonhole details that a fuller picture of a complex woman begins to emerge. Underneath her picture are two words "THE AUTHOR," and they stand there at attention as if to reassure the reader that this elegant, gentle-browed woman is indeed the Edith Wharton who, as one reader complained, has never known "a respectable woman" (*ABG*, 126). The label is needed because in any of these portraits of Wharton, the artist, as well as the artist's alliance with the woman, is obscured.

To survive she had to be as flexible as her created Lily, "a water-plant in the flux of the tides,"[16] and as inflexibly driven as Undine Spragg. Her portrait suggests that Edith Wharton was a woman of many paradoxes: the painfully ignorant bride and the middle-aged adulterous lover; the stilted, shy guest and the brilliant conversationalist; the society matron and the professional artist; the unmotherly woman and the mother of countless Belgian refugee children; the rebel, like Charity Royall, and, like Newland Archer, the compromising upholder of the status quo. She was able to forge at best only an uneasy truce with the past, and that turbulent, delicate relationship was a limitless imaginative catalyst.

Wharton liked to think of herself as dealing with "eternally human" themes and feelings, and she grumbled in her essay "Permanent Values in Fiction" (1934) that "the novel in its most serious form is tending to become a sort of anthology of the author's ideas."[17] Her own work, however, cannot escape being such an anthology. In trying to find her own place in the past by piecing together her personal history within a broader cultural context, she analyzed and commented on the roles of women in society and their responsibilities to each other and to themselves by working principally with two often interwoven plots. The first is expressed in "Souls Belated" (1899), the tale of a woman who escapes a conventionally stifling marriage only to discover that she and her lover have no choice but to duplicate the union she has just fled. "Souls Belated" shows how Wharton challenged the concept of marriage but was never able to escape the imperative that women must marry. The following year she wrote "Friends," a story that articulates the second plot that I trace in her fiction. Having passed her childhood and early adulthood starved for good conversation and "cultivated intelligence" (*ABG*, 92), the author knew how transfiguring the meeting of like minds could be, and the story's key themes inform almost all of her novels.[18] Women who seem to be opposites are in reality more similar than dissimilar. Each begins to see from the other's perspective, and their expanded consciousness is both painful and enriching. The supposed rivals become the means for each other's moral growth, as they realize that being true to another woman means being true to oneself. What appears to be a sacrifice is in reality a touchstone that imbues life with meaning.

Penelope Bent and Vexilla Thurber are the friends of the early story. Unlike most of Wharton's heroines, they are not rivals for a man but for a job. Both are the sole supporters of their families, though Vexilla's cares are greater because her household includes a grandmother, a younger sister, and a paralyzed brother. Penelope has earned a meager but comfortable living for herself and her mother as a distinguished teacher in the local school, and although she has tried to ease her friend's burden by persuading the board to hire her, they have remained obdurate: Miss Thurber is not "smart enough."[19] They change their minds, however, when Penelope resigns to marry.

After spending all of her money on a trousseau and being deserted by her fiancé, Penelope returns to her hometown, desperately hoping to regain her old position. At first she feels only anger at Vexilla's good fortune, but on learning that her friend is willing to resign, she finds the courage to begin a new life in New York. The example of Vexilla's loyalty has once again made "life comprehensible and duty a joyful impulse."[20] From Fulvia in *The Valley of Decision* (1902) to Laura Testvalley in *The Buccaneers* (1938), almost all of Wharton's heroines must decide whether to flee or to embrace a similarly crucial moment. "Friends" outlines the novelist's concern with analyzing where the temptations and the benefits reside in relationships between women, and as the ending illustrates, the chief benefit is to oneself.

Wharton continued to explore, test, and refine this plot throughout her career in short stories, such as "Autres Temps . . . ," "The Lady's Maid's Bell," "Her Son," "Bewitched," and "Roman Fever," as well as in her novellas, *The Touchstone, Bunner Sisters, Madame de Treymes,* and *Sanctuary.* In *The Reef* and *The Age of Innocence* the pattern varies, when Anna Leath and Sophy Viner, in the former, and May Archer and Ellen Olenska, in the latter, protectively conspire to keep Owen Leath and Newland Archer ignorant of what they have fought to learn. The novelist never looked at women's relationships in isolation, and her bleakest books, *The House of Mirth* and *The Custom of the Country*, illustrate what results when women adopt their society's values and play by its rules. Wharton's most repeated symbols reflect her analysis: the frozen tableaux, enchaining adornments, stifling veils, unvoiced words, and the precarious thresholds that lead to rooms of all types—dangerous, lonely, and locked.

Without ever rejecting the inevitablity and the rightness of marriage, her heroines resemble their author. Their wish for a perfect soulmate, coupled with their inability to envision other structures for their lives, necessitate painful compromises. Stripped of romantic illusions, these women are now "grown-up." They have graduated beyond "the exercises of the Montessori infant."[21] As Wharton continues in *French Ways and Their Meaning*, "real living . . . is a deep and complex and slowly developed thing . . . ; it has its roots in the fundamental things, and above all in close and constant and interesting and important relations between men and women."[22] No matter how hard her heroines struggle, they are almost always denied "important relations" with men, which makes relationships between women, though sometimes strained or crippled, of additional importance. In particular, *The Reef* (1912), *The Age of Innocence* (1920), and *The Buccaneers* (1938) examine their potential power.

Wharton's use of the marriage plot and the plot outlined in "Friends" cannot be isolated from the context of her other concerns, including the development of personal consciousness, the allure and danger of romanticism, the possibilities of female artistry, and the continuation of personal and literary traditions. From different angles of vision, she examined and reexamined these issues. Her thoughts do not follow a clear linear progression, but they do tend to fluctuate between two paradoxical poles, one marking female competition and the other marking female cooperation. Wharton's relationship with her mother, Lucretia Jones, falls under the shadow of the first pole, and her friendship with Sara Norton illuminates the second. Her fiction incorporates both. In "Roman Fever," for example, Mrs. Slade and Mrs. Ansley's girlhood rivalry continues well into middle age, perversely feeding their intimacy; and in *The Reef*, *The Age of Innocence*, and *The Buccaneers* women deliberately choose to aid each other, even at the expense of their own best interests.

The form and content of my study attempts to reflect the complexity of Wharton's thinking as it fluctuates between these two poles. For that reason, its structure is less linear and chronological than circular and textured. In designing my format, I have tried to avoid imposing an interpretive overlay that would mute the tenor of the texts' intricacies or veil their ambiguities. Rather, I have attempted to give a sense of the accumulative effect of reading Wharton's novels.

Chapter 1 analyzes the writer's antagonistic relationship with her mother as presented in her autobiography, *A Back-*

ward Glance (1934) and provides the background for succeeding discussion, and Chapter 2 describes her supportive
relationship with Sara Norton by examining their 1899–1922
correspondence.

Focusing on *The House of Mirth* (1905) and *The Custom of
the Country* (1913), Chapter 3 provides the social context for
Wharton's work, and Chapter 4 probes the "buried fables" or
stories of "inward rescue" in *Ethan Frome* and its companion
work, *Summer* (1917).[23]

From her friendship with Sara Norton, Wharton knew the
benefits—as examined in Chapter 5's discussion of *The Reef*
(1912) and *The Age of Innocence* (1920)—that women missed
when they viewed each other as rivals.

Chapter 6 addresses the question of marriage and the
conundrum of "mother" in *The Mother's Recompense* (1925),
and the last chapter argues that in *Hudson River Bracketed*
(1929) and *The Gods Arrive* (1932) Wharton symbolically
embraces the part of herself that she saw as the "self-made
man" and the part that she saw as purely female. Like
Emerson before him, Vance Weston learns that "man-making words"—to quote Leverenz—yield to "mother-made temperaments."[24] This insight preceded Wharton's most concise
statement about adult identity and the merits of female alliance. By never "going back on each other" (to paraphrase
Lily Bart) the girls of her last and posthumously published
novel, *The Buccaneers* (1938), vanquish older and more experienced rivals and win the chance to buy their own experience. Wharton's answer to the New Woman, Nan St.
George, buys hers with an unhappy marriage to the Duke of
Tintagel, and it promises to transform her into the grown-up
woman described in *French Ways and Their Meaning*.

For the first time in a Wharton novel, one character does
not try to protect another from seeing what she termed the
Gorgon, and the change implies that the author had reevalu-
ated the cost of that vision. An early autobiographical story,

"The Fullness of Life," shows the ultimate price she imagined:

> I have sometimes thought that a woman's nature is like
> a great house full of rooms: there is the hall, through
> which everyone passes in going in and out; the drawing
> room, where one receives formal visits; the sitting room,
> where the members of the family come and go as they
> list; but beyond that, far beyond, are other rooms, the
> handles of whose doors are never turned; no one knows
> the way to them, no one knows whither they lead; and
> in the innermost room, the holy of holies, the soul sits
> alone and waits for a footstep that never comes.[25]

At the end of her life the price was not as extravagant as
the image implies. Like Vance Weston, Wharton learned
that her solitary quest into the darkened corners of that innermost room fed her art and made it hers—hers alone. Not
many people could follow her to that sanctum's threshold,
but there were those whose feet found the path and whose
lips found the right word. As readers we are still trying to
determine that word, to which perhaps only the soul sitting
in "the holy of holies" can give breath.

CHAPTER ONE

The Continuing Contest in *A Backward Glance*

> *Mothers and daughters are part of each other's consciousness, in different degrees and in a different way, but still with the mutual sense of something which has always been there.*
>
> —*THE MOTHER'S RECOMPENSE*

In an age when critics tend to focus more on the text than the person who produced it, Edith Wharton offers an important instance of the connection between a writer's life and the work that grows from it. Wharton, who never wanted to be heard shrilling her tale,[1] would object to the suggestion that there was any connection, but her memoir stands as a rebuttal. *A Backward Glance* (1934) shows her processing the same issue that dominates her fictional treatment of mothers and daughters: is it possible to have separate but compatible identities?

The autobiography does not resolve this question, but it does highlight the factors that influence and limit Wharton's thinking about their relations. From its pages her mother, Lucretia Jones, emerges as the most influential person in her life. The novelist literally cannot author her own story without authoring her parent's.[2] If she is to reconcile the past and its values with those of the present, validate her history within a larger social context, and become concurrently woman and writer, she first must recall, reevaluate, and re-create her mother's life. Wharton does much the same when writing about mothers and daughters (or mother and daughter figures). In *The Mother's Recompense*, for example, she establishes Anne Clephane's identity by telling the story of her heroine's mother, Kate.

A Backward Glance likewise has a split perspective. As autobiographer and biographer, Wharton has two sometimes opposing roles. Unlike her subjects Henry James, Vernon Lee, and Bernard Berenson, her parents are of significance only in connection to her. The empowering stuff of every child's dream, this situation also establishes a curious tension between author and subject. The urge to protect, rescue, and lionize is particularly strong when writing about someone of the same sex because coming to terms with another's life involves coming to terms, at least for a time, with one's own.[3] Wharton experienced this dilemma when discussing the mother who she felt had crippled and misdirected her life.[4] Although Cynthia Griffin Wolff empasizes the life-and-death struggle for autonomy that the child had to fight against such a mother and from which she sees the novelist emerging battle-scarred but triumphant,[5] *A Backward Glance* shows the war still being waged. Only the positions of the generals have shifted.

Warning her readers that she had to make "the best of unsensational material,"[6] Wharton consciously limits her memoir almost entirely to what Georges Gusdorf defines as "the public sector of existence."[7] In this way she attempts to continue in the tradition of male autobiographers, as defined by Susan Stanford Friedman.[8] However, her need to ground her individual identity in relation to a chosen other and in the context of a culture that defines "woman" as a group makes her similar to the female autobiographers originally described by Mary Mason.[9] *Bios*, or the historical course of

Wharton's life, dominates the surface text of *A Backward Glance*, but emerging memories threaten to deform that narrative.

In Wharton's version of the Freudian drama, her father would have been a far different man, less "lonely," less "haunted by something always unexpressed and unattained" (*ABG*, 39) if he had married someone less like his wife and more like his daughter. Wharton's description of her father contains many of the elements explored in her fiction. First, there is a weaker but nobler nature checked by one less sensitive. Second, there is the prison of inarticulateness, what she calls in the "Love Journal" "the poor shut-in soul," "*Ah! pauvre âme close!*"[10] Critics have always complained about the novelist's weak, dilettantish men, and one does not have to look much farther to find Newland Archer's archetype. By defining George Frederic Jones as a thwarted artist with a familial role much like her own, Wharton clearly aligns herself with him. In this way she establishes "the separateness that is threatened by identifying with her mother,"[11] while refusing to grant Lucretia the power of having circumscribed her own development.

Lucretia Jones was her child's supporter and enemy, the granter and denier of selfhood, and Wharton felt her mother's fearful power in the alternately comforting and terrifying world she ruled.[12] As Wharton wrote in the first draft of her autobiography, "Life and I," "I was never free from the oppressive sense that I had two absolutely inscrutable beings to please—God & my mother—who, while ostensibly upholding the same principles of behavior, differed totally as to their application" ("Life," 6).

From the beginning the identities of mother and daughter were interdependent.[13] Rather than denounce her own will in the service of home and hearth, Lucretia exercised it, and like God she framed the world. Her presence colors even one of Wharton's earliest and most pleasant memories about her

father. Wharton recalls walking with him and meeting a little boy, who suddenly "put out a chubby hand, lifted the little girl's veil, and boldly planted a kiss on her cheek" (*ABG*,
3). She describes that experience as being "wakened to conscious life by the two tremendous forces of love and vanity"
(*ABG*, 3), and although that awakening mimics the myth of
"Sleeping Beauty,"[14] it clearly aligns daughter with mother.

Once roused, Wharton outwardly became her mother, "the
best-dressed woman in New York" (*ABG*, 20), a woman
whose greatest raptures were for the trunk of Parisian
dresses that arrived each year: "for the first time she woke to
the importance of dress, and of herself as a subject for
adornment—so that I may date from that hour the birth of
the conscious and feminine *me* in the little girl's vague soul"
(*ABG*, 3).[15] The simultaneous birthing of consciousness and
femininity marks Wharton's recognition of her own separateness (consciousness) and her connection to a group identity
(femininity). The awareness forever divides the girl from her
father by making him "other." It also left her nowhere to
turn. Perceiving her mother as unnurturing, Wharton de-
fensively objectified her, or—to paraphrase Jessica Benjamin—she substituted rationality for affective exchange with
the other.[16]

Wharton, however, also identified with her mother as a
woman, and it led to her awareness of femininity and consciousness as separate and independent entities, characterized by gender. The former she defined as a feminine need to
please ("Life," 1-2) and the latter as a masculine need to control and to dominate ("Life," 45). Knowing that she had
"more will" and "more strength" than her childhood compan-
ions, Wharton did not care to use it or know to what use to
put it because, as she writes, "I did not want to dominate—I
wanted to be adored!" ("Life," 36). This yearning grows from
three related sources: if adored, Wharton could dominate
without censure, she could ally the "masculine" and "femi-

nine" parts of her nature, and she could fulfill the aims, ambitious and erotic, that Freud sees as part of the "family romance."[17] Adoration offered a legitimized way of exercising both power and desire, but Wharton's need for domination shows her also wanting the privilege and power of agency that Benjamin assigns to males.[18] This conflict partially explains Wharton's often ambiguous treatment of her female characters, in which she appears to relegate them to object, rather than subject, status. It is not surprising, therefore, that Wharton's paired heroines often find that satisfying either the need for power or the need for affection excludes the other.

Wharton never felt adequately loved, either by her mother or by her several suitors. Despite her expression of bitter regret, one must question whether she indeed truly desired that kind of intimacy or felt it deserved. For example, Wharton complained that Emelyn Washburn, the girlhood friend who reportedly inspired the writing of *Fast and Loose*, was "morbidly [perhaps homosexually] attached" to her ("Life," 29–30).[19] This conclusion reveals Wharton's discomfort with adoration and suggests that she was suspicious of those who did not mirror either her mother's disapproval or her father's benign neglect.

In the memoir Wharton expresses pity for "all children who have not had a Doyley—a nurse who has always been there, who is as established as the sky and as warm as the sun, who understands everything, feels everything, can arrange everything, and combines all the powers of the Divinity with the compassion of a mortal heart like one's own" (*ABG*, 26). Wharton probably owed her strong sense of self to Doyley and the women who followed her as surrogate mothers, Anna Bahlmann and Catherine Gross, yet Doyley's very perfection and her unconditional love made her easy to take for granted. In Wharton's case the creative mind not only thrived on a reduced diet, it also perhaps needed one.[20] Her stance of emphatic autonomy, or what Benjamin calls "false differentiation," may have been won at the expense of "real recognition and attunement,"[21] especially with her mother, but it also allowed her to become a player in a profession that idealized masculine individuality.

The pattern was established early. When Wharton felt un-replete, she would "make up" stories. Coupling the manipu-lation of language with the manipulation of people and events, she would grab one of her father's favorite books, Washington Irving's *The Alhambra*, and, holding it upside down, imperiously travel the terrain of some secluded room reading aloud her own spontaneous stories.[22] Wharton's choice of reading material, which shows a desire to emulate her father's behavior while gaining his attention, implies that George Frederic's emotional withdrawal or absence from the family was potentially as painful as his wife's presence.[23]

"Making up" served three purposes for Wharton: as Freud argues in "Creative Writers and Daydreaming" (1908), it corrected an unsatisfying reality; it gave her an identity dis-tinct from the other members of her family; and it gave her an instrument for keeping them—like *The Alhambra*—at arm's length. The format of the autobiography attempts to do the same. Readers learn about her genealogy, the old New York of her childhood, her travels, and her friendships, but they learn little of her feelings.

Wharton's motives and her attendant feelings, though, are never far from the surface of *A Backward Glance*. For some-one who had been "swept off full sail on the sea of dreams" (*ABG*, 34), she had a remarkably accurate and detailed mem-ory of those she left on shore: "Parents and nurses, peeping at me through the cracks of doors (I always had to be alone to 'make up'), noticed that I often held the book upside down, but that I never failed to turn the pages, and that I turned them at about the right pace for a person reading aloud as passionately and precipitately as was my habit" (*ABG*,

34–35). She obviously did not "always have to be alone to 'make up,' " and, in fact, the child who had an audience of parents and nurses enthralled as she strode the floor reciting was much more an actress than an author. Decades later she recalled: "The fact that I could not read added to the completeness of the illusion, for from those mysterious blank pages I could evoke whatever my fancy chose" (*ABG*, 34).

What she chose to construct was a self-centered kingdom in which she ruled by virtue of her presence (the performance) and her speaking (the "making up"), and that creation was both an imitation of and a challenge to her mother's feminine and polite reign in the drawing room. When Wharton told her mother, "Mamma, you must go and entertain that little girl for me. *I've got to make up*" (*ABG*, 35), she was neatly reversing their roles, and tellingly, the room to which she fled was her mother's bedroom ("Life," 12).

The story of Wharton's "making up" highlights the appeal that writing fiction would have for her, but it also underscores the difficulty she would always have trying to integrate her roles as woman and author. Wharton began life learning that it was acceptable to act—instead of be—the author. As the example of Lily Bart in *The House of Mirth* illustrates, she later more clearly identified acting as a feminine skill regrettably necessary for a woman's prescribed public role. When Wharton no longer wanted to mimic an author, she had to leave the stage.

Wharton later responded to this situation by developing distinct identities, author and hostess. Mornings she reserved for writing and afternoons for entertaining. For the second half of the day, her mother's example of dressing up offered a far more typical and socially accepted form of "making up." Because each new costume had its attendant identity, a woman could—without disapproval—author a public identity. Wharton's afternoons and the frontispiece in *A Backward Glance*, which shows her hands hidden in a muff and her shoulders teased by stray wisps of fur, illustrate the duration and the source of her dilemma. To discard, integrate, or redefine this one of her many selves, she would have to acknowledge the mother she did not reject and accept the one she imitated. Only "radical surgery," to paraphrase Adrienne Rich, could keep the daughter's personality from dangerously blurring and overlapping with the mother's.[24] Not unexpectedly, Lucretia's sculpted image in *A Backward Glance* retains some traces of the surgeon's scalpel.

Wharton saw her mother with double vision: she was part of old New York's "prosaic" society and part of another tradition waiting to be "made up": "I know less than nothing of the particular virtues, gifts and modest accomplishments of the young women with pearls in their looped hair or cambric ruffs round their slim necks, who prepared the way for my generation. A few shreds of anecdote, no more than the faded flowers between the leaves of a great-grandmother's Bible, are all that remain to me" (*ABG*, 15).

Although these foremothers' gifts to her were less substantial than the fort named in honor of Great-grandfather Major General Ebenezer Stevens's military exploits, their ghostlike voices and muted presence affected Wharton's own upbringing.[25] No better educated than the young women with pearls in their hair, Lucretia and her sisters "were taught needle work, music, drawing and 'the languages,' . . . They suffered, like all young ladies of their day, from chilblains and excruciating sick-headaches" (*ABG*, 16–17). Wharton, in turn, experienced the same deprivation (and the same sick-headaches), and it prompts her to characterize Lucretia more sympathetically before she becomes a mother. For example, she imbues her father's courtship of "the eldest of 'the poor Rhinelander' girls" with romance when he transforms an oar into a mast and a bed-quilt into a sail and crosses the Sound to "his lady's feet" (*ABG*, 18). "False Dawn" preserves the family story.

Although the young martyr elicited Wharton's empathy, motherhood soon transformed Cinderella into the wicked step-mother.[26] Nowhere is Lucretia more insensitive than when responding to her daughter's first prose effort:

> My first attempt (at the age of eleven) was a novel, which began: " 'Oh, how do you do, Mrs. Brown?' said Mrs. Tompkins. 'If only I had known you were going to call I should have tidied up the drawing-room.' " Timorously I submitted this to my mother, and never shall I forget the sudden drop of my creative frenzy when she returned it with the icy comment: "Drawing-rooms are always tidy." (*ABG*, 73)

This story, which shows a direct relationship between Wharton's creativity and her mother's judgment, functions on many levels: it is an expression of anger and humiliation, a retrospective justification of the child, and a tribute from a successful novelist of manners. Underlying the telling is Wharton's lifelong appreciation of irony and a good joke— this time on herself. No doubt the phrase "Drawing-rooms are always tidy" never ceased to rankle, but the lesson had merit because later readers, who faulted details concerning factory work in *The Fruit of the Tree* (1907), demanded the same standard.[27] The author's insistence on "the exact dates when Mme. Christine Nilsson sang *Faust* at the old Academy of Music, when Delmonico's moved north to Twenty-sixth Street, and the times of the first Patriarchs' Balls, the Assemblies, and the Friday Evening Dancing Classes"[28] helped to forestall similar criticisms about *The Age of Innocence*.[29] Internalizing her mother's censure, Wharton made certain that her own drawing rooms were always tidy and that all passions and tumults, whether personal or fictional, occurred offstage.

A Backward Glance gives Wharton the opportunity to transform her mother into one of "those mysterious blank pages" that she evoked when pretending to read *The Alhambra* upside down (*ABG*, 34). The author depicts herself as the model of ladylike repression, much as she describes Anna Leath, but her retelling places her mother at a distinct disadvantage and is revealing about herself. As in any first-person narration, how the story is told tells most about the teller.

With her father Wharton may have been Sleeping Beauty, but with her mother she was a second-generation Cinderella, her role repeating a matrilineal pattern. According to Wharton, Lucretia was the least pretty and least indulged of the Rhinelander girls (*ABG*, 17). In turn, Wharton saw herself as the least attractive member of her family, and the self-loathing that perception generated can be read in her life-long inability to overcome an "abhorence" for "ugly" people ("Life," 3). The story of Lucretia Jones and her daughter is similar to those of many nineteenth-century women writers who suffered loss of or alienation from their mothers and identified with and were dependent on their fathers.[30]

As the heroine of her own drama,[31] Wharton perceived that the fault lay outside herself, and for that reason the drama was more empowering than disabling. "Life and I" reveals just how empowering when she makes her mother both "dumb" and "blank": "My mother took an odd inarticulate interest in my youthful productions, & kept a blank book in which she copied many of them" ("Life," 38). The mother has no words and no identity other than what she can "copy" from the daughter. But if Wharton saw her mother's actions as a form of stealing her identity, she more than retaliates by turning her into a nonentity.

Their battle, symbolic of the much greater one Wharton fought with the societal definitions of womanhood that her mother represented, isolated Lucretia from the intimate parts of her daughter's life. After her mother's death Wharton discovered that she had kept *"brouillons"* (rough copies)

of letters that her daughter had written to aunts and god-
mothers ("Life," 15). The long-kept copies poignantly suggest
that Lucretia had her own untold story.

There is no one to tell how much of the daughter's "making
up" and the mother's copying down were inarticulate and in-
effectual efforts by both to make up. Just as we must feel
compassion for the child who had to scribble her stories on
used wrapping paper, we must feel some compassion for the
mother whose daughter reduces her to inarticulateness.
Wharton remembers her mother reading for hours, and the
early desire to "make up" might easily have originated from
a wish to occupy, impress, and entertain her. The atmosphere of the Joneses' home may have starved heart and soul,
yet it provided the backdrop against which Wharton could
see herself as special and apart.

The uneven characterization of Lucretia in *A Backward
Glance* results in a continually amended text. Although
Wharton invariably begins to tell her mother-daughter story
the way she always told it to herself—the insensitive mother
of the sensitive daughter, the prosaic mother of the lyrical
daughter, or the indifferent mother of the eager daughter—
she ends by modifying or correcting the narrative, and those
changes often conjure the image of the young woman George
Frederic clandestinely courted. Describing her mother's
character much as she would later (but more sympathetically) describe Mrs. St. George's in *The Buccaneers* (1938),
Wharton initially writes: "My mother, perplexed by the discovery that she had produced an omnivorous reader, and not
knowing how to direct my reading, had perhaps expected
the governess to do it for her" (*ABG*, 65).[32] She then elabor-
ates:

> Being an indolent woman, she finally turned the diffi-
> culty by reviving a rule of her own schoolroom days,
> and decreeing that I should never read a novel without

> asking her permission. I was a painfully conscientious
> child and, conforming literally to this decree, I submit-
> ted to her every work of fiction which attracted my
> fancy. In order to save further trouble she almost al-
> ways refused to let me read it—a fact hardly to be won-
> dered at, since her own mother had forbidden her to
> read any of Scott's novels, except "Waverly", till after
> she was married! (*ABG*, 65)

Until the dash, this anecdote is congruous with the picture of
the mother who said, "Drawing-rooms are always tidy!" In
its entirety, however, the story embodies Wharton's ambivalence, for what follows the dash in that final sentence is an
explanation and a justification for her mother's behavior.
The very tone of the sentence reflects this change, shifting
from cynicism to understanding and sympathy.

The same two voices sound a whole note in the following
passage:

> At all events, of the many prohibitions imposed on me—
> most of which, as I look back, I see little reason to
> regret—there is none for which I am more grateful
> than this, though it extended its rigours even to one of
> the works of Charlotte M. Yonge! By denying me the
> opportunity of wasting my time over ephemeral rub-
> bish my mother threw me back on the great classics,
> and thereby helped to give my mind a temper which
> my too-easy studies could not have produced. (*ABG*,
> 65–66)

One voice speaks for the part of Wharton that would always
remain the misunderstood, unappreciated, and abandoned
child, forever angry and competitive with her mother. The
other speaks for the more assured and successful adult able
to sympathize with the mother who was never able to overcome the cultural disabilities her daughter surmounted.

The excerpt shows Wharton first ruminating on and then evaluating the past. The surface text reads that "all turned out for the best," but the thinly disguised subtext implies that the lazy mother did what the daughter could not, waste her time over ephemeral rubbish. It taxes the imagination, however, to believe that Wharton never peeked between the covers of those forbidden books or that their mystique was not the subject for secret musing, because in later life she apologized to the "decorous shade" of Grace Aguilar, "loved of our grandmothers, for appropriating and applying to uses so different the title of one of the most admired of her tales."[33] Her repeated and almost strident insistence on her careful and obedient avoidance of most novels authored by women reads as an attempt to avoid all charges of influence. It is another assertion of her difference and a variation on the theme of the brilliant child of lusterless parents.

Wharton's fictional treatment of mother-dauther relationships is delicately structured on the same pattern of competing visions that underlie *A Backward Glance*. The novels also have two voices. Although Wharton does not forget to address the plight of a single mother like Carry Fisher of *The House of Mirth* (1905), the voice of the deprived child dominates that book and other early books, such as *The Fruit of the Tree* (1907) and *Ethan Frome* (1911). Mothers in these works represent a threat to their daughters' development as if they have the psychic power to reabsorb them. After *Summer* (1917), in which Charity Royall matures by claiming the mother she has feared and despised, it grows fainter. In later novels, such as *The Mother's Recompense* (1925) and *The Buccaneers* (1938), Wharton defines mothers and daughters more by gender than by role as each tries to fashion an identity that is consistent with societal defintions of womanhood. In *The Mother's Recompense*, for example, Kate Clephane and her daughter are antagonists because they are in many ways twins. *Hudson River Bracketed* (1929) and *The*

Gods Arrive (1932) find the two voices no longer contending, for Wharton in a sense returns to mother by metaphorically locating the source of creative power in motherhood itself.

Wharton's ambivalence toward her mother affected her relations with older, established women writers, such as Mary Wilkins, Sarah Orne Jewett, and Rhoda Broughton. Broughton, for example, was the author of *Not Wisely but Too Well* and one of the writers prohibited in her youth. Wharton visited her in England, and though Percy Lubbock says their meeting was unsuccessful, his word cannot necessarily be trusted.[34] As a sensation novelist of the 1870s, Broughton made (according to Elaine Showalter) a "genuinely radical female protest against marriage and women's economic oppressions."[35] She may have treated her subjects "still in the framework of feminine conventions that demanded the erring heroine's destruction,"[36] but the subjects themselves as well as Broughton's pioneering efforts must have interested the author of *The House of Mirth* and *The Custom of the Country*. Viola Hopkins Winner contends that the young Wharton did in fact read at least one of Broughton's novels, *Goodbye, Sweetheart!*, which she used as a model for *Fast and Loose*.[37] An observer other than Lubbock might have seen Wharton either paying her respects to a literary predecessor or repeating her behavior toward her mother—wanting to embrace and to deny.

Uncomfortable with literary techniques that broke down the barriers between life and fiction, Wharton did not believe—to quote Ellen Glasgow—that the emotional and the intellectual life "formed a single strand, and could not be divided."[38] Valuing her mother's premise that "you could do what you liked with the language if you did it consciously, and for a given purpose" (*ABG*, 51), she instead saw herself living in two "totally unrelated worlds . . . side by side, equally absorbing, but wholly isolated from each other" (*ABG*, 205). Nevertheless, these two worlds often become tangled in her fiction; for example, *The Reef*, with or without its author's conscious intent, "takes up the same [autobiographical] material in complete freedom and under the protection of a hidden identity,"[39] as Wharton projects her own internally warring aspects of the self as separated individuals: Anna, the repressed lady; Sophy, the unconventional, exiled woman; and George, the privileged aesthete.

The fictional transformations of the secret story-world of Wharton's childhood function in a similar manner and subtly serve as an index of the distance that she was able to achieve from the past. First appearing in "The Fullness of Life," the space is overtly sexual; the author compares a woman's nature to a house full of unused rooms, "the handles of whose doors are never turned."[40] Later the image is repeated in Ralph Marvell's secret cave (*The Custom of the Country* [1913]), Newland Archer's inner sanctuary (*The Age of Innocence* [1920]), and Nan St. George's imprisonment in the Tintagel castle (*The Buccaneers* [1938]). The function of this enclosure may vary from Archer's necessary haven to Marvell's narcissistic kingdom, but inevitably its safety is tenuous and dependent—as was Wharton's usurpation of her mother's bedroom—on the goodwill or indulgence of another. By the time of *Hudson River Bracketed* (1929) and *The Gods Arrive* (1932), the space has also become protected, cherished, and inviolate. "I believe I know the only cure," Wharton advised Mary Berenson during her nervous collapse in 1918, "which is to . . . decorate one's inner house so richly that one is content there, glad to welcome any one who wants to come and stay, but happy all the same in the hours when one is inevitably alone."[41]

As Wharton's metaphor of the innermost room suggests, she was able to find a design in the novels that she did not realize in the autobiography. Nevertheless, the shape of autobiography, its form and approach, bears directly on the shape of her fiction. *A Backward Glance* seeks the same truth, but its design, the vacillations and rationalizations that give the novels their delicately balanced tension, is more apparent.

To borrow Roy Pascal's phrase, design—in all of its many meanings—and truth become synonymous in Wharton's portrayal of her mother.[42] In addition to testifying to the magnitude of Lucretia Jones's influence, the memoir also substantiates the author's adolescent prediction that opportunity was "in the narrow present close at hand" ("Life," 39) because Wharton's choice of genre, the novel of manners, is an attempt to fuse the two seemingly antithetical forces that ruled her early life: God and mother. God she associated with "truth" and mother, with "politeness." Her fiction, which studies manners as a means of testing truths, reconciles the two. It reveals that literature is—as Wharton herself defined it—a "contemplation of life that goes below its surface."[43]

CHAPTER TWO

A Safe Forum: Edith Wharton's Correspondence with Sara Norton

How quickly fall the hours!
It needs no touch of mind or rime
To loose such facile flowers.

—*"USES"*

Edith Wharton's relationship with her mother—complex, contending, insoluble—affected but did not inhibit her relationships with other women. In particular she valued the friendship of Sara Norton, the younger daughter and helpmate of Charles Eliot Norton, with whom she corresponded from 1899 to 1922. Although the frequency of their correspondence varied, especially during the war, the two communicated a little less than twice monthly for many years. By 1901 Wharton was writing, "It was so pleasant to find that we're *d'accord* on the more inaccessible subjects that one doesn't get at in the ordinary course of acquaintance, & that form either a barrier or a bridge to real friendship—such as I should like ours to be."[1] Norton concurred and left the following instructions in 1906: "In case of my death—I wish all Edith Wharton's letters to me returned to her. . . . She may burn the letters, I can't." Neither could Wharton, who found herself and her "dear Sally" once more *d'accord*.

The dialogue of letter writing encouraged confidences in a relatively unthreatening manner and provided a safe forum in which Wharton could articulate and achieve a fuller understanding of herself personally and professionally.[2] The letters are some of her most intimate; and although their tone, style, and intensity do not match the often fulsome and impassioned exchanges between the nineteenth-century correspondents whom Carroll Smith-Rosenberg has studied, they are often emotionally similar in substance.[3] "Don't ever regret having cried out your pain to me," Wharton wrote her friend in 1908, during Charles Eliot Norton's last months, "or how shall *I* feel over my self-abandonment? Let us rather be glad that such outcries do help a little, sometimes—."[4]

As Wharton's two trailing qualifiers ("a little" and "sometimes") suggest, there were boundaries beyond which one could only help oneself. The letters show her desire for close communication tempered by her need for distance. She never wrote, for example, to Norton about her affair with Morton Fullerton, although as R. W. B. Lewis notes, her 1907 letters are uncharacteristic in their playful enthusiasm about her new acquaintance.[5] She did, however, write about her mother's death, her own mental and physical problems, and her increasing worries about her husband's growing erratic behavior, her desire to believe that it resulted from "gout" in the head, and her small hope that a change of scene would refresh him. Wharton and her husband had little to say to each other, but each valued the haven of structure and the force of habit. Their marriage resembled "the deaf-and-dumb asylum" that May and Newland Archer shared in *The Age of Innocence*, and Norton helped to make the union more tolerable for the author by partially making up for Teddy Wharton's emotional and intellectual deficiencies. In this respect, the friendship was possibly a model for Wharton's fiction, in which relationships between women sustain the marriages that are the foundation of an ordered civilization. With slight variations the pattern is repeated in works such as *The Touchstone, The Fruit of the Tree, The Reef, The Age of Innocence, The Mother's Recompense,* and *The Buccaneers.*

Wharton's friendship with Sara Norton was less susceptible to the ambivalences common to Wharton's relationships with other women, and the letters can be read as the author's rebuttal to her decades-long characterization as a woman "who doesn't really care for women."[6] Marion Bell's testimony in Percy Lubbock's *Portrait of Edith Wharton* (1947)— "many women who only knew her slightly have said to me, 'She looks at me as if I were a worm' "[7]—is still quoted as evidence of the author's "cold dislike of women."[8] Bell is also the woman who said, "Being a very normal person she preferred men to women, and often terrified the latter with a cold stare";[9] and this statement, coupled with her first, exposes some of the reasons Wharton's relationships with women seemed problematic.

Marion Bell, Sara Norton, and Edith Wharton did live at a time when it was considered normal to prefer men to women, and this belief had a divisive and inhibiting effect on women's relationships. As Nancy Sahli says in "Smashing: Women's Relationships before the Fall," the network of intimate, supportive relationships between women that existed for many American women in the eighteenth and nineteenth centuries was "subjected to increasing stress after about 1875."[10] By the turn of the century "the female world of love and ritual" that Carroll Smith-Rosenberg records was under attack. Relationships between women, having "a high degree of emotional, sensual, and even sexual content," were later seen as "abnormal."[11] Born in 1862, Wharton came to maturity during this change of attitude. In her later years, as previously mentioned, she wondered if a very close childhood friend, Emelyn Washburn, had had a "streak of 'degeneracy'—that is, lesbiansim."[12]

The post-Freudian introduction of evaluative words, such

as "homosexual" or "lesbian," to describe close relationships
between women in part contributed to the dramatic change
in how women defined themselves and related to each other.[13]
No longer as comfortably at home in a cooperative female
world, they more frequently sought tenancy in the competitive prevailing culture that saw them as "other" and encouraged them to do the same. Wanting recognition as an artist,
not as a woman artist, Wharton often felt it necessary to distinguish herself from others of her sex.

Wharton certainly had a great deal at stake, emotionally
and artistically, in seeing herself as the "extraordinary woman" in a fraternity of male writers.[14] Discussing *Ethan
Frome*, for example, she made a deliberate point of separating herself from two other regional women writers, Sarah
Orne Jewett and Mary Wilkins, who, Wharton says, saw
New England "through rose-coloured spectacles." Instead,
she aligned herself with Nathaniel Hawthorne.[15] Unlike Virginia Woolf, she did not proclaim her indebtedness to all of
her ordinary predecessors; and in this sense Wharton is as
vulnerable as is her heroine Lily Bart to the speculation that
"a great many dull and ugly people must, in some mysterious way, have been sacrificed to produce her."[16]

This feeling underlies the reminiscences of Wharton's female acquaintances and in part explains their ambivalent
tone. Wharton was privileged, socially, economically, and
creatively, and those meeting Edith Wharton "the author"
saw her in that context. Her natural reserve was frequently
read as snobbishness or lack of interest, and it catalyzed
crises of confidence that prompted people self-protectively to
look for flaws and sources of resentment. Marion Bell again
provides an example: "I remember once when I first knew
her, looking up and finding her staring at me with what
seemed an unfriendly gaze. I said, 'What have I done to be
looked at so disapprovingly?'—and she said, 'Oh no, I was
just thinking that I like your hat.' "[17] The anecdote, which
both excuses and condemns, illustrates the tensions inherent

in many of Wharton's female relationships. Her extraordinary success was a challenge and a reproach to other women, and, as even Henry James knew, it could have a demoralizing effect.[18] It also had the potential for making her pass her life like one of the rare books encased behind gilt trellising in Elmer Moffat's seldom-visited library.

Someone like Marion Bell—to borrow the metaphor from "The Fullness of Life"—never got past the author's drawing room, the place "where one receives formal visits." Sara Norton, however, approached her innermost room, "the holy of holies," where the soul sits alone.[19] Although Wharton had extended correspondences with a number of men (such as John Hugh Smith) and women (such as Margaret Chanler and her sister-in-law Mary Cadwalader Jones), Norton provided the perfect audience for a developing writer. No other relationship fulfilled a similar function. Wharton's relationships with most other women and with women writers were troubled by the difficulties mentioned, and though she frequently talked with Walter Berry, Henry James, and Morton Fullerton about her work, Berry was the man who taught her how to write; James, the literary father she had rejected but held dear; and Fullerton, the enigmatic lover.[20]

All of those friendships were implicitly less egalitarian than her friendship with Norton. As the daughter of Harvard's distinguished fine arts professor, Sara had been at home in intellectual and literary circles since Carlyle had held "his little sweetheart" on his knee and given her a gold locket that contained his own hair.[21] Known as a cellist, she acted as her father's hostess and affectionately counted Annie Fields, Sarah Orne Jewett, and Henry James as friends. In many ways she and her father provided Wharton with the ideal family. There was no Mrs. Norton to withhold love or to be critical and competitive in the ways that Wharton remembered her own mother being, and Charles Eliot Norton was the perfect substitute father for a literary daughter.

The friendship began in 1899, a crucial time for Wharton.

That year she published her first book of short stories, and as she recalled in *A Backward Glance*, "The publishing of 'The Greater Inclination' broke the chains which held me so long in a kind of torpor. For nearly twelve years I had tried to adjust myself to the life I had led since my marriage; but now I was overmastered by the longing to meet people who shared my interests" (*ABG*, 122). Those interests included a special empathy for dogs and an unbounded love of literature. The similarities between the women were as superficial and class-bound as a horror of Roman teas ("they are too *awful*, & I don't wonder you shrink from them") and the new moneyed "invaders" of established society: "the Vanderbilt entertainment was just what you say—but for a novelist gathering documents for an American novel, it was all the more valuable, alas!"[22] More important, though, the two strongly identified with European values as a result of having spent part of their early lives abroad: "the contrast between the old & the new, between the stored beauty & tradition & amenity over there, & the crassness here" made Wharton feel they were like "wretched exotics produced in a European glass-house."[23] Wharton's fiction is full of "wretched exotics," such as Ellen Olenska and Fanny de Malrive; but as critics have demonstrated, not many Americans were sympathetic to their point of view. Sharing conflicted feelings about their nationality made the friends feel akin to the man in one of Wharton's favorite Schopenhauer analogies: "the intelligent person in the world," she wrote in a 1901 letter, "is like a man whose watch keeps the right time in a town where all the public time-pieces are wrong. *He* knows what time it is; but what good does it do him?"[24]

Besides belying the image of Wharton as a misogynist, the letters reveal no split between woman and artist. The diligent writer who, after a full morning's labor, descended at the stroke of noon, transformed into the perfect but belligerently inartistic hostess, is nowhere in view. Wharton wants and needs to explain herself:

> I am so afraid of encouraging vague emotions about art
> or literature—so sure that it is better to let them die if
> they are not strong enough to fight their own way to the
> front—that I had my doubts about the wisdom of doing
> anything [for a joint acquaintance]. I hope this doesn't
> sound brutal to you. I have so much incipient art & po-
> etry & fiction brought to me, which might so much bet-
> ter have been plain hem-stitching or pumpkin-pie or
> double-entry book-keeping, that I suppose I have grown
> rather callous.[25]

The passage shows Wharton as author and critic of her own
text. The author articulates a belief ("vague emotions about
art and literature" should be discouraged) about which the
critic recognizes a need for qualification. The process of
writing involves the reading and rereading of one's text, and
this quotation indicates that Wharton was not satisfied with
what she read because she attempts to make the speaker of
the letter congruous with her image of herself. Her recognition that literary and domestic arts originate from the same
artistic impulse, for example, makes her aware of the callousness she would like to deny. Not succeeding, she asks
Norton to deny it for her ("I hope this doesn't sound brutal to
you") and in this way treats her as a mirror of her own conscience. Wharton may well expect the asked-for answer,
"No, the discouragement of inferior art is ultimately more
humane," but she is still risking an alternative and morally
censoring reply. The letter shows Wharton's strong identification with Norton (the mirror) while concurrently crediting
her differentiation (moral critic).

Wharton's awareness of her own bias does not mean that
she sees literary and domestic arts as equivalent, for she has
internalized her culture's evaluation of the relative importance of the two activities; nevertheless, her hierarchical
evaluation causes her some discomfort and again highlights
the dilemma of the extraordinary woman, who must validate

her efforts by devaluing other forms of women's work. The woman artist, forced to suppress her connection to and appreciation of female artistic traditions, is one step away from seeing herself as a self-made man, originating from and continuing a genderless, universal art form. Wharton's resistance to the dominant literary tradition can be seen in the characterizations of Lily Bart and Ellen Olenska, who are artists in their own spheres; but, like Henry James, she could be a severe critic when literary values were at stake.[26] Thirty-three years later she would write authoritatively in *A Backward Glance*, "the greatest service a writer can render to letters is to follow his conscience" (*ABG*, 140). In 1901, though, she struggles to articulate her position and asks for Norton's understanding and validation of that stance.

During this period (1901) of artistic resolve and definition, Wharton lost her mother, Lucretia Jones. At the time of Lucretia's death, mother and daughter were effectively estranged after years of misunderstanding, competition, and recriminations. Cynthia Griffin Wolff characterizes their relationship as the major inhibiting force in Wharton's life and argues that she would never have emerged as an artist without winning independence from her mother's influence.[27] With such a history, Wharton could only be expected to write, as Lewis notes, "conventionally" to Norton about the event,[28] but what the letter does not say is unconventional. There is no expression of grief or regret or (as Sara was later to express on the death of her father) guilt.

> I must begin by saying that this paper [black-edged notepaper] signifies that my poor mother died suddenly and unexpectedly the day after you left. She had been hopelessly ill for fourteen months, paralyzed & unconscious for nearly a year—but it was one of the cases in which it seemed that life—that kind of life—might go on for years; and there is no room for anything but thankfulness at this sudden conclusion of it all.[29]

Wharton had a horror of that kind of suspended existence to the extent that in 1908 she would write of a dying friend: "But, oh, if I had morphia in reach, as she has, how quickly I'd cut the knot."[30] Norton was of like mind and did not find anything peculiar in Wharton's almost gushing her relief at the death of Sally's aunt in 1916: "First of all, thank heaven your poor aunt is dead! I am so glad to think that the misery is over for her, & the long cruel strain for you."[31] Knowing her audience, Wharton directed Norton's response to prohibit conventional expressions of sympathy. Lucretia's condition made relief at her death appropriate, and her daughter's words, "there is no room for anything but thankfulness at this sudden conclusion of it all," function equally well as an expression of conscious and subconscious feelings.

The tone of Wharton's news and her removed stance mask the emotions that she must have had difficulty in trying to control at this time: grief and regret for the past, self-pity for her mother's emotional abandonment, a longing to atone, and despair that the history of mother and daughter could never be amended. Wharton's inevitable confusion about her own feelings would have made it painfully difficult for her to react comfortably to expressions of sympathy. Her sparse communication tells Norton in what manner and degree of sympathy she should respond and shows that good reading skills were one of the keystones of this friendship.

Wharton, in turn, was the logical confidante for Norton as her father became progressively ill. The author was able to see each of her friends' points of view, and though she felt great distress at the father's discomfort, she sympathized more with the difficulties his condition created for the daughter. Sally wanted to do what pleased her father and would make him most comfortable, but there was no ideal action that could do both. Wharton helped her cope with feelings of inadequacy and guilt:

> Now that you tell me the Doctor is on your side, I can't

help advising you to go to Ashfield when the next "hot
spell" comes. It will cost a struggle, but the struggle
will really be worse for you than for your father. After
a certain age it becomes necessary now & then to
"*passer outre*" in dealing with old people, even the most
intelligent & reasonable—& it is often a relief in the
end to *them* to be "dealt with" & over-ruled. I think it
wd be in this case, & I am sure the moral effect of getting to Ashfield, especially the new & improved Ashfield, would be of great good, & probably soon dispel
the nervous apprehensions.[32]

The letter strikes just the right tone by clearly aligning the
writer with Norton without showing her father any dis-
respect.

During times of extreme emotional distress and breakdown, the letters provided comfort, sympathy, and reassurance. At the beginning of their correspondence, Wharton
wrote: "Don't I know that feeling you describe, when one
longs to go to a hospital & *have something cut out*, & come out
minus an organ, but alive & active & like other people, instead of dragging on with this bloodless existence!! Only I
fear you & I will never find a surgeon who will do us that
service."[33] In Sally, Wharton finally found the understanding
of a fellow sufferer, which the following phrase again emphasizes: "but I know so well the state of mind & body in
which the things one likes are precisely those that seem to
use one up most severely."[34] Because Norton experienced the
same symptoms, Wharton did not have to suppress or deny
her own. Rather, she now had a place where she could discuss them, and as modern psychology will attest, that is
crucial for the beginning of the "talking cure."

Wharton had a serious breakdown in 1902, described in
the following March 9 letter:

Last week is a kind of night-mare to me. I am just com-

> ing back to the realities, & yesterday I was seized by a
> sudden fear that I had not sent you word when I found I
> should have to give up my Boston visit—I remember
> scrawling a line in pencil last Monday, to say that I had
> postponed my departure; but I can't recall writing or
> telegraphing that it was definitely given up. . . . I
> mean it was rather confusing—If, therefore, I failed to
> let you know, please, please forgive me! I have not for a
> long time had such a bad breakdown. You, who know
> what such things are, will make allowances, I am sure.

Norton experienced a similar state in 1905, and Wharton
responded:

> It seems so strange to think of you at Newport, all alone
> in Catherine St.! I wish just this once that I were back
> at Land's End & could take you in. I am so sorry that
> you have had this break-down. No one knows better
> than I do (at least few know better) the unutterable
> weariness of pulling out of the tide of life into a drydock
> for repairs. The first time one does it there comes a cer-
> tain refreshment; after that, though no doubt the physi-
> cal effect is good, the mental & moral results are less
> exhilarating.[35]

Often characterized as "reserved," Wharton was readily
unreserved about herself when she could help "repair" a
friend, as the case of Norton's sister, Elizabeth ("Lily"),
illustrates:

> What a detestable year [1908] you have all had, you
> poor dear Shady Hillers, & how I wish I could wave a
> wand & lift all the clouds!—Tell Lily, if it's any com-
> fort, that for *twelve* years I seldom knew what it was to
> be, for more than an hour or two of the twenty four,
> without an intense feeling of nausea, & such unuttera-
> ble fatigue that when I got up I was always more tired

than when I lay down. This form of neurasthenia consumed the best years of my youth, & left, in some sort,
an irreparable shade on my life. *Mais quoi*! I worked
through it, & came out on the other side, & so will she,
in a much shorter time, I hope.[36]

Wharton, herself caring for an emotionally disabled husband, had the greatest sympathy for her friend's comparable
position.

As the friendship progressed, Wharton became an increasingly prolific, well-known, and self-assured author; and Norton had her own authorial success in editing her father's letters. The correspondence with Norton in part chronicles the
development of Wharton's critical voice, heard in *A Backward Glance* (1934) and *The Writing of Fiction* (1925) and
shows how the friendship's flexibility and its ability to tolerate each partner's individuality provided a forum for the
testing of that voice.

When Wharton wrote her first novel, *The Valley of Decision* (1902), she actively sought her friend's criticism: "Here
I am, like a mother rushing to the defense of her deformed
child! I hoped, when I sent you the advance sheets, that you
might be interested enough to tell me just where you thought
I had made mistakes—& I rather expected you to put your
finger on what is undoubtedly the weak spot from the novel-
reader's point of view."[37] Wharton is asking Sally to articulate and to corroborate what she herself suspected was the
novel's "weak spot," its characterization. The degree of her
chiding is a measure of her reliance on Norton's criticism at
this time. When the book was published, the reviews were
generally positive, but the one that justified the novel's emphasis on period rather than character particularly delight-
ed Wharton, who wrote: "I am childishly pleased by a review of my book in 'The Mail Express,' in which the writer
says that the book should be regarded as the picture of a pe-

riod, not of one or two persons & that Italy is my hero—or heroine, if you prefer."[38]

With Sara, Wharton did not have to affect a well-bred lack of interest in the critical reception of her work, and she could safely venture opinions before asserting them in more professional and competitive company. In this way, writing to Norton helped Wharton further articulate her own aesthetics. The following excerpt from a 1902 letter about Henry James's *The Wings of the Dove* illustrates this process:

> Alas, alas! One doesn't know what to say. The book seems to me, in a sense, quite ignoble; & you know I don't think this simply of what are called "unpleasant subjects." This is an unpleasant subject, but chiefly so, to me, because the author hasn't seen beyond it, has accepted it without a revolt. And then the style! It is *délirant*. . . . I can't reconcile myself to such an end for the mind which could conceive Roderick Hudson, The Portrait of a Lady, & how many of the earlier short stories.[39]

As Millicent Bell aptly demonstrates, Wharton was never James's apprentice. She mourns what she sees as his decline, but to justify her feeling about Merton Densher and Kate Croy's courting of Milly Theale and her fortune, she is compelled to analyze its source. Rejecting the idea that her dislike of the novel is simply personal and particular, she must attempt to define again the source of her feeling.

Her second definition is more theoretical: "This is an unpleasant subject, but chiefly so, to me, because the author hasn't seen beyond it, has accepted it without a revolt." She says much the same years later in *A Backward Glance*: "There are but two essential rules: one, that the novelist should deal only with what is within his reach, literally or figuratively (in most cases the two are synonymous), and the other that the value of a subject depends almost wholly on what the author sees in it, and how deeply he is able to see *into* it" (*ABG*, 206). This idea originates from Wharton's own psychological history. She would not have been Edith Wharton, the author, if she had not seen beyond, revolted, and escaped the prison cell of her background and its inherited obligations. Like their author, Newland Archer, Lily Bart, Charity Royall, and Ethan Frome all see possibilities for self-expression beyond their restrictive environment, possibilities that reveal to them the dignity and meaning in accepting and maintaining certain traditions and loyalties. Unfortunately, readers who think that the endings to novels such as *The Age of Innocence* and *The Mother's Recompense* seem unfair and forced also have been known to revolt. Why should Newland Archer not have Ellen Olenska and "the world beyond"? Why should Kate Clephane have to give up her respectability and her daughter a second time? The answer is related to the standard of judgment Wharton applies to James: the author must revolt against his or her subject by seeing beyond the autobiographical. Wharton had done so, and her protagonists, who resignedly accept compromise, denial, and loss, do the same. In turn they are rewarded with the perception that life has a moral significance beyond individual concerns.

As Wharton articulates her feelings about James's novel, she transforms a personal insight (why it is an unpleasant subject) into a standard that determines literary merit, while denying she has done so. James, however, could not resolve emotional and spiritual complexities this neatly in his portrayal of Kate Croy. The lack of censure and closure in *The Wings of the Dove* annoys Wharton because she wants a philosophical solution to emotionally chaotic circumstances, and such a solution makes the ending of a novel like *The Age of Innocence* seem almost formulaic. Her criticism may fault James's novel, but ironically two of her own, *The House of Mirth* and *The Custom of the Country*, show its influence:

Lawrence Selden's belated awareness of his love for Lily Bart matches Merton Densher's reverence for Milly Theale, and Undine Spragg could be Kate Croy's less subtle American cousin.

Almost a year after Wharton expressed her opinion about *The Wings of the Dove*, she mailed Sara and her father a typewritten copy of a letter that Henry James had sent her. It contained his now famous advice to "do New York," itself a muted criticism of Wharton's treatment of the subject in *The Valley of Decision*. Prompted by pride in James's recognition of her talent, the gesture was also an assertion of independence and authorial identity.[40]

The benefits of the relationship were not all on Wharton's side. Norton herself wrote poetry and in 1916 published a collection of jingoistic verse called *New Nursery Rhymes on Old Lines By an American*.[41] In 1905, when a mutual friend's sister died after a long illness, Wharton proved how much she valued the consoling power of Norton's verses:

> I am very glad you sent me the lines on Ethel, dear Sally, not only because of my own interest in reading them, but because I know how deeply they will touch Henriette's heart. I am not even going to ask your leave to send them to her, feeling sure that you will understand my wish to do so.—They are charmingly done, & I am now wondering why you have kept this gift so long a secret from me.[42]

In this passage Wharton expressed something she would probably not have voiced elsewhere: her admiration for obituary verse, a custom that by 1905 was beginning to strike many educated people as sentimental and mawkish. Considering Wharton's own use of irony and her efforts to separate herself from other women writers, her acknowledgment of the value and power of Norton's lines seems all the more remarkable.

The published novelist, displaying a sound understanding
of the basis of modern poerty, responds to Norton's work as
to a fellow professional in the following excerpt from a 1906
letter:

> I was sorry you would not let me re-read your poems
> while I was with you yesterday. I did not want to write
> about them because I wanted to show you, in detail, just
> how & where I think they need to be changed. I don't
> know that I can sum up my meaning on paper, unless
> by saying that, where you say that you have tried not to
> be "poetic"—by which, of course, you mean ornate, rhe-
> torical, *imagée*—I think you are trying to skip a neces-
> sary *étape* on the way to Parnassus.—Such bareness as
> "she neither feels nor sees" is the result of a great deal
> of writing, of a long & expert process of elimination,
> selection, concentration of idea & expression. It is not
> *being simple* so much as being excessively subtle; &
> the less-practised simplicity is apt to have too loose a
> "weave." That is the criticism I wanted—with much
> more explicitness & illustration—to make on your lines,
> which I should like to re-read with you some day in that
> light. Personally, I think a long apprenticeship should
> be given to form before it is thrown overboard—& I
> don't see why, with your bent, you don't give it. Here is
> as much as I can make clear without a talk—but that, I
> hope, will come soon.[43]

Wharton's prose drafts, themselves studies in the process of
"elimination, selection, concentration of idea & expression,"
indicate how seriously she took her own advice.

In turn, Wharton good-naturedly accepted criticism from
Norton; for example, in a 1906 letter, she chides Norton for
praising *The House of Mirth* when her first response to the
book was to implore its author "to abstain from the writing
of fiction."[44] The friends' disagreements were part of their

ongoing literary discussion: Wharton expressed her admiration for James's prefaces, and Norton wrote about her pleasure in Turgenev. By 1912, however, they had been corresponding for thirteen years and felt safe enough to address the times when they did not feel exactly the same:

> I don't know why you ever think it necessary to buy my books. Don't you trust to my sending them to you? The order to send you "The Reef" went to Appleton over a month ago. Nor do I know where you get the idea that I don't care to have my friends talk to me of my books. Nothing gives me greater pleasure—naturally—than their being sufficiently interested to do so. But I'm never surprised, or disappointed, if they don't, because their liking, or not liking, what I write, seems so unimportant a part of the general pleasure of the relation.[45]

Wharton sees Sally's gesture as critical. Her friend should know that she would never consciously act inconsiderately toward her. Wharton's hurt stems from Norton's lack of trust, but her irritation most likely stems from guilt: the implied criticism has some truth in it. Wharton's question ("Don't you trust my sending them to you?") is designed, whether consciously or unconsciously, to unnerve Norton before she gets to her real grievance: "Nor do I know where you get the idea that I don't care to have my friends talk to me of my books." Obviously, Wharton feels defensive. She would like to see herself as naturally accepting criticism, but the unnatural insertion of the adverb "naturally" belies her contention that nothing gives her greater pleasure.

The excerpt is full of double-messages: I want you to read my books but treat them as a gift; I want your opinion, but I don't value it; I appreciate my friends' comments but not in comparison to their other attributes. In Wharton's defense, she probably did not fully recognize the tone of this 1912 letter because during this period she bemusedly wrote: "I am

puzzling my head to know why my last letter held you 'at
arm's length.' *In* arms' length is where I hold my friends, &
as I have long strong arms they ought to feel secure there!"[46]
Wharton sought similar reassurance the next year when
Henry James hotly refused her efforts to present him with a
birthday remembrance from his American friends.

Although other obligations and physical and emotional
weariness often made it difficult to write during the war
years, Wharton assumed that such communication was unnecessary, knowing, as she wrote in 1914, that Norton would
feel the same and be in the same state of mind.[47] Unfortunately, that bond was subject to time, and to borrow Wharton's own words from an earlier 1907 letter, she could "only
look on & feel unavailing sympathy" when Norton was found
to have a cancerous tumor in 1922.[48] By May 2, Norton didn't
need a scribe, and Wharton answered: "When I saw those
closely-written pages of yours yesterday I was almost as
cross as I was pleased, & 'applauded with both hands' the little scolding that your admirable Doctor gave you when he
caught you in the act! Still, it *was* a great satisfaction to read
this report of yourself in your own hand—as firm & beautiful as ever it was—& I'm glad he didn't catch you till you'd
nearly done." Wharton rejoiced in Norton's progress, but her
euphoria was not to last—that summer her friend suffered a
relapse and died.

By offering an alternative model to Mrs. Bell's for female
relations, Norton left a legacy that enriched Wharton's fiction. In it, men and women seldom find the right word to say
to each other. For that reason women's relationships with
other women have added significance. Even in *The House of
Mirth* (1905), *Ethan Frome* (1911), and *The Custom of the
Country* (1913) women are not "natural" enemies. When
women are competitive with or cruel to each other, the
blame clearly belongs to society. In *The Reef* (1912), Wharton
redefines relationships between women and between women

and men by showing how women can grow through their relationships with each other, instead of under a lover's tutelage. Her last work, *The Buccaneers* (1938), depicts the advantages of cooperation between women, as well as the similarities between women as disparate as the young American, Nan St. George, and the Duchess of Tintagel. These fictional relationships do not deny that women's relationships have problems and jealousies, as the examples of Bertha Dorset, Undine Spragg, and the case of May Archer and Ellen Olenska illustrate, but they do offer a reasoned way to recover from the fall that Nancy Sahli describes. Honest communication, such as Anna Leath and Sophy Viner experience, necessitates seeing with another's eyes, and that expanded vision is the first step toward revising inherited myths about our own natures. Being true to another woman can mean being true to oneself. Wharton's friendship with Sara Norton challenged assumptions that women's relationships had to be either unnatural or competitive; and although women's partnerships in her fiction are not an alternative to male-female relationships, they can have, as Wharton wrote Norton in the poem "Uses," their own "sweet content."[49]

CHAPTER THREE

The Context of Women's Relationships

> *"After all, what's the meaning of 'self-realization' if you're to let your life be conditioned and contracted by somebody else's?"*
>
> —*"JOY IN THE HOUSE"*

The *House of Mirth* and *The Custom of the Country* are maps that chart the range and scope available to most of Wharton's characters. Because the novels expose society's ruthlessness, they have been used to illustrate the lack of female community in her work. For example, Joan Lidoff faults Wharton for placing, in *The House of Mirth*, the "blame for the inadequacies of the whole socializing process" on "the women who teach and enforce social paradigms," and she sees "the primary motivations that determine the plot" as being "feelings of resentment and revenge among women."[1] Janet Malcolm goes a step further by stating that the "symbolic world of Edith Wharton's fiction is a world where 'strange experiments' (that is deviations from the social norm) inexorably lead to tragedy, and where the callousness and heartlessness by which this universe is ruled is the callousness and heartlessness of women."[2] Certainly, Bertha Dorset exemplifies the cruelties that women are capable of committing against each other, but Wharton uses her to focus on the forces that inhibit their relationships. By making Bertha the source of Lily's salvation, Wharton reveals the potential power inherent in the most unlikely of alliances. Lily's economic and social descent—from Mrs. Peniston's parlour to Gus Trenor's study to Mrs. Hatch's hotel suite to the boardinghouse's common room—marks her closer identification with her own sex; and though her world is restricted, it offers more opportunity for emotional and spiritual growth.

The Trenor set assumes that merciless competition is "the custom of the country," and this assumption naturally fosters distrust and jealousy among women.[3] Yet they resist to the best of their ability. Lily resists until death, and her death is Wharton's plea that no more women suffer her fate. For that to happen, however, society must rethink and relax its strict and divisive definitions of women into categories, such as "nice" and "not nice." It must make room for children whose parents teach them to be both beautiful and useful. If the world persists in turning a deaf ear, Wharton warns, future Lily Barts will grow up to be Undine Spraggs, women who seek the new and stylish as relentlessly as Ahab sought his whale, women who, claiming their rightful place in the lobby of the Nouveau Luxe, have an apocalyptic effect on every culture they encounter.

Undine appears to set her own course; still she is rudderless without a first mate. In a novel that Wharton considered "a neglected masterpiece," *Susan Lenox: Her Fall and Rise* (1917), David Graham Phillips describes the dilemma: "None of these women, none of the women of the prosperous classes would be there but for the assistance and protection of men."[4] Married off to an ignorant and brutal farmer, Susan learns what Lily suspects: not much separates the business of marriage from the business of prostitution. Preferring to earn an honest living, Susan chooses the latter, for, she reasons, a prostitute sells her time, not her soul. Her thinking is a logical extension of Lily's and is assigned by Wharton to Mrs. Hazeldean in *New Year's Day* (1924). It is also more honest because Lily wants to play on this knowledge and still remain respectable; for example, she sexually manipulates Gus Trenor to invest her small funds for her at great profit, thinking that "surely to a clever girl, it would be easy to hold him by his vanity, and to keep the obligation on his side."[5]

Lily knows that she must eventually pay for the favors of her crassly materialistic world on its terms, but she balks at paying the required pound of flesh.[6] Her society, believing that any woman disobedient of its rules has collaborated in her own destruction, deems Lily's punishment deserved. By making Lily's nature a composite of the women, "nice" and "not nice," who people *The House of Mirth*, Wharton exposes how this thinking harms them all. Lily eventually and logically bonds with other women because it is in a sense her nature to do so. After Lily, Wharton's heroines are less male-identified, and they more readily recognize their connection and responsibility to others of their gender.

Lily defies classification, although her moral appeal stems from her persistent refusal to define herself as a commodity comparable to Percy Gryce's Americana, "the one possession in which he took sufficient pride to spend money on it" (*HM*, 49). Lily knows that the ladylike barter she must effect would necessitate her giving up the little sense of self she possesses, and that is a form of living suicide to which she cannot contract. Already she too often forgets the specter of her inner self imprisoned behind one of her mind's carefully avoided "closed doors" (*HM*, 82). Rebelling against being consumed as greedily as the pastry with which her last name rhymes, she nonetheless sees some justification in Gus Trenor's reasoning: "Hang it, the man who pays for dinner is usually allowed to have a seat at the table" (*HM*, 145). Lily defines herself most clearly at her final tea with Rosedale when she asserts: "I have lived too long on my friends" (*HM*, 239). Rosedale's affectionate response to Carry Fisher's child makes him the only other character besides Lily linked with the next generation, and as such it is fitting that he is the one witness who can testify to Lily's nobler impulses. The future belongs to him, and it is just possible that someday he will disclose to Selden the history of Bertha's letters, making it possible for Lily vicariously to voice the final word.[7]

Wharton agrees that economic independence is necessary for identity. Selden correctly thought that Lily "must have cost a great deal to make, that a great many dull and ugly people must, in some mysterious way, have been sacrificed to produce her" (*HM*, 5). In the pages of *The House of Mirth* we cannot avoid their acquaintance—the Miss Kilroys in Mme. Regina's workroom, "the sallow, preoccupied women, with their bags and note-books and rolls of music" (*HM*, 302), the thouands and thousands of women like Miss Silverton "slinking about to employment agencies, and trying to sell painted blotting-pads to Women's Exchanges" (*HM*, 267), the "shallow-faced girls in preposterous hats and flat-chested women struggling with paper bundles and palm-leaf fans" (*HM*, 5). Without their sacrifices and cheap labor there would be no Judy Trenors, no poetical Ned Silvertons, and no Lily Barts. Phillips makes the same point more overtly in his story of Susan Lenox: respectable women maintain their honored position because other women are exploited. Each step Lily descends on the social ladder marks her increasing awareness of this point and brings her into closer relationship with all women regardless of class. In this way, her spiritual growth and her identification with her own sex are interdependent.

Lily first detects the full measure of economic exploitation in Regina's workroom, where others more competent than she arrange Mrs. Trenor's "green Paradise" and Mrs. Dorset's "blue tulle" (*HM*, 285) and where her inability to sew spangles on straight is humiliatingly self-revelatory: "Since she had been brought up to be ornamental, she could hardly blame herself for failing to serve any practical purpose; but the discovery put an end to her consoling sense of universal efficiency" (*HM*, 297). Her present demands a reevaluation of the past. Then she had always felt a sympathy for those who served her: "She had been long enough in bondage to other people's pleasure to be considerate of those who depended on hers, and in her bitter moods it sometimes struck her that she and her maid were in the same position, except that the latter received her wages more regularly" (*HM*, 28). Her empathy, though, was of the same kind as Judy Trenor's: "the daily nibble of small temptations to expenditure, were trials as far out of her experience as the domestic problems of the charwoman" (*HM*, 77). Just as Judy could not truly understand Lily's pecuniary difficulties, it was impossible for Miss Bart to understand the depth of her maid's frustrated longing, anger, and self-pity as she hung up a crumpled dress before returning to her rented room.

Lily's own experience subsequently educates her. After her dismissal from Regina's, Lily can claim "the same position," but driven to make use of Mrs. Dorset's letters, she more resembles the charwoman at the Benedick, Mrs. Haffen, than the maid. In retrospect, Mrs. Haffen's actions seem less despicable. As she explains to Lily, "I brought 'em to you to sell, because I ain't got no other way of raising money, and if we don't pay our rent by tomorrow night we'll be put out. I never done anythin' of the kind before," (*HM*, 105). Mrs. Haffen probably never did, because she proceeds to ask Lily to use her influence to have her and her husband reinstated at the Benedick. An embarrassed Lily, however, only hears the implied threat in "I seen you talking to Mr. Rosedale on the steps that day you come out of Mr. Selden's rooms—" (*HM*, 105). Like Lily, Mrs. Haffen would prefer to support herself without resorting to blackmail.[8] By making parallels between Lily and other working women, such as Mrs. Haffen, Carry Fisher, Gerty Farish, and Nettie Struther, Wharton is asking her readers to reexamine the entire fabric of society, not just the upper-class world of Bellomont. She is also stating that society—to differing degrees and in different ways—exploits all women. Only learned attitudes and social training separate the women wearing silk from those wearing homespun.

The twice-divorced Carry Fisher, who supports herself and her daughter parenting the nouveau riche, has the most insight into Lily's predicament. Taking Lily under her wing, Carry counsels that the world is "not a pretty place; and the only way to keep a footing in it is to fight it on its own terms—and above all, my dear, not alone!" (*HM*, 252). Lily accepts the fact that men's money assists and protects; but she mistakenly assumes that it also naturally empowers,[9] for in the Trenors' and Gormers' worlds of "conspicuous consumption," the wives rule with a ruthlessness that Rosedale would appreciate on Wall Street.[10]

The novel opens with these women trying to include Lily in their world by the only means available to them—securing her marraige to Percy Gryce and his Americana:

> . . . Lily found herself the centre of that feminine solicitude which envelops a young woman in mating season. A solitude was tacitly created for her in the crowded existence of Bellomont, and her friends could not have shown a greater readiness for self-effacement had her wooing been adorned with all the attributes of romance. In Lily's set this conduct implied a sympathetic comprehension of her motives, and Mr. Gryce rose in her esteem as she saw the consideration he inspired. (*HM*, 46)

Although appreciative of their efforts, Lily feels that Mr. Gryce's doing her the honor of "boring her for life" is not honor enough (*HM*, 25). She would prefer an elegant and richly appointed room of her own. Selden is the only person in Lily's circle who seems incapable of furthering her material ascendancy, and as a result, he is her logical confidant: "I shouldn't have to pretend with you or be on my guard against you" (*HM*, 9).

Lily never rejects the world that Percy Gryce represents. She is like Rappaccini's daughter, whose beauty and delicacy are nourished by her exotic, poisoned environment: "her whole being dilated in an atmosphere of luxury; it was the background she required, the only climate she could breathe in" (*HM*, 236). Everyone at Bellomont, male and female, accepts the premise of male authority and female submission, and that system eventually corrupts all. Economically dependent on last year's dresses or this season's opera tickets, Lily must always be on guard, and it taints every relationship. The only goods she can offer in exchange are her charm and affability, two traits often antithetical to honesty. Lily's lack of honesty, what Jennifer Radden calls her "self-deception," makes her in part responsible for her plight.[11] Whether lying is done "with words" or "with silence," as Adrienne Rich notes, it widens the gulf between the public and the private selves and puts women in the untenable position of lying to and trivializing themselves.[12] *The House of Mirth* illustrates—as do all Wharton's novels—that lying thwarts the development of an emotionally and intellectually rich inner life. Refusing to lie to oneself is the means of becoming empowered. As Elaine Showalter observes, in Lily's world women are "spoken for" and unable to speak for themselves.[13] Consequently, when Lily tells Rosedale her story, she fixes her identity and assumes responsibility for herself: "She made the statement clearly, deliberately, with pauses between the sentences, so that each should have time to sink deeply into the hearer's mind" (*HM*, 292).

Usually Lily is seen as being of finer stuff than those around her, but her behavior to Judy Trenor belies the point and loses her a most powerful and needed ally. Wharton's description of Judy is developed from the stereotypical assumption that women are most likely to "go back" on each other.[14]

> The collective nature of her interests exempted her from the ordinary rivalries of her sex, and she knew no more personal emotion than that of hatred for the woman who presumed to give bigger dinners or have more amusing house-parties than herself. As her social talents, backed by Mr. Trenor's bank-account, almost always assured her ultimate triumph in such competitions, success had developed in her an unscrupulous good nature toward the rest of her sex, and in Miss Bart's utilitarian classification of her friends, Mrs. Trenor ranked as the woman who was least likely to "go back" on her. (*HM*, 41)

Lily is decidedly self-serving and disloyal when she follows Carry Fisher's example and takes money from Gus Trenor, fully knowing Judy's feelings about such behavior: Carry Fisher's "a perfect vulture, you know; and she hasn't the least moral sense. She is always getting Gus to speculate for her, and I'm sure she never pays when she loses" (*HM*, 86). Judy tells Lily, "There's nothing I wouldn't do, you poor duck, to see you happy!" (*HM*, 46); but of course there is: she is not willing to be made a fool.

Bertha Dorset frequently wins distinction as the villain of *The House of Mirth*; however, even her behavior has some previous justification.[15] Fully intending to marry Percy Gryce, Lily callously contemplates playing with Lawrence Selden: "If Selden had come at Mrs. Dorset's call, it was at her own that he would stay" (*HM*, 53).[16] In this way, she behaves as her society expects women to behave. Lily draws the original battlelines, and Bertha never trusts her again.

When Lily exhibits more integrity, she is ruined. Forgetting Judy's accurate analysis of Bertha's nastiness, she assumes a relationship, even though the two, who have been cruising the Mediterranean for months, have never been on confidential terms. Lily's possession of Bertha's love letters to Selden gives her a mistaken and unshared sense of their intimacy: "If she had destroyed Mrs. Dorset's letters, she might have continued to hate her; but the fact that they remained in her possession had fed her resentment to satiety" (*HM*, 119). Bertha has not had a similarly uplifting experience, and when she must desperately hide any knowledge of her affair with Ned Silverton, Lily becomes the logical scapegoat.

Having already staked Bertha, Lily mistakenly expects that "the barrier of reserve must surely fall" (*HM*, 205). Bertha expects Lily to respond as before; yet owning and not employing the means of Bertha's demise enhances Lily's sense of moral superiority and allows her to feel compassion for the former rival, whom she now tragically misreads as "a friend in need." Ironically, Lily is unable to profit from her keen social sensibilities. Blind to Bertha's point of view, Lily ascribes her own to Bertha, and it nearly bankrupts her. In the past Lily aligned herself with Gus Trenor, forsaking his wife, but here she does not hesitate to support Bertha. The response marks the beginning of Lily's closer identification with her own sex as well as her moral rise. The flux of the tides has changed when Lily sees Bertha as what she will later in truth be: the symbolic representation of her youthful desire to exercise a "power for good" (*HM*, 35). As the temptation to use the letters increases, they function much as Penelope's desire for her old job does in the story "Friends." They become the characters that Lily uses to spell out her identity. Significantly, the means of Lily's spiritual salvation comes from another woman (the most unlikely one of her acquaintance) and reverses plot expectations that Selden will come to her rescue.

The source of Lily's rescue has been foreshadowed by her relationship with Gerty Farish. Although Gerty does not understand her friend's true position or its temptations, she proves to be the one friend who never "goes back" on her; and Lily, unaware that Gerty views her as a rival for Selden, instinctively flees to her embrace after Gus Trenor's attempted rape. When Gerty pulls Lily across her threshold, she rescues them both from the "dingy" moral wilderness outside.

The moving picture of Gerty holding Lily belies stereotyped images of both the scorned and the beloved woman. Because readers know the exact frequency, measure, and duration of Selden's seldom heroics, Gerty's gesture becomes the novel's moral measure:

> "Hold me, Gerty, hold me, or I shall think of things," she moaned; and Gerty silently slipped an arm under her, pillowing her head in its hollow as a mother makes a nest for a tossing child. In the warm hollow Lily lay still and her breathing grew low and regular. Her hand still clung to Gerty's as if to ward off evil dreams, but the hold of her fingers relaxed, her head sank deeper into its shelter, and Gerty felt that she slept. (*HM*, 167)

By re-befriending and sheltering Lily, Gerty saves her own soul and Lily's sanity; and if Lily were not so much the product of "the civilization which had produced her" (*HM*, 7), Gerty might even have saved her life. In this way, *The House of Mirth* seems an alternative answer to James's *Bostonians* (1886), which ends with Basil Ransom effectively separating the two friends Verena Tarrant and Olive Chancellor. Occurring near the narrative's center, the image of the embracing women is the novel's moral and emotional heart.[17]

The image of Lily and Gerty grows in significance as it is elaborated and repeated at the novel's end with Lily and Nettie Struther's imagined child:

> . . . she felt the pressure of its little head against her shoulder. She did not know how it had come there, but

she felt no great surprise at the fact, only a gentle pene-
trating thrill of warmth and pleasure. She settled herself into an easier position, hollowing her arm to pillow
the round, downy head, and holding her breath lest a
sound should disturb the sleeping child. (*HM*, 323)

Nettie's kitchen, where one woman can speak plainly to
another, is a living example of the Republic of the Spirit.
There female continuance and matriarchal heritage are emphasized. Lawrence Selden envisions his own version of this
land but always evades it because he views Lily as Vander-
bank views Nanda in Henry James's *The Awkward Age*
(1899): too knowledgeable to be marriageable. Selden's thinking dictates that his Republic of the Spirit must be a kingdom of one.

Named after an actress who reminded the mother of Miss
Bart, the baby represents the potential of what Lily herself
could have become with the love and protection of a mother.'
The comfort Lily receives from her dream of Nettie's daughter is all the more poignant when one considers Lily's own
orphancy.[18] When Lily holds the child, she feels "the soft
weight sink trustfully against her":

> The child's confidence in its safety thrilled her with a
> sense of warmth and returning life, and she bent over,
> wondering at the rosy blur of the little face, the empty
> clearness of the eyes, the vague tendrilly motions of the
> folding and unfolding fingers. At first the burden in
> her arms seemed as light as a pink cloud or a heap of
> down, but as she continued to hold it the weight in-
> creased, sinking deeper, and penetrating her with a
> strange sense of weakness, as though the child entered
> into her and became a part of herself. (*HM*, 316)

The featureless child is like an earlier Lily, "as malleable as
wax" (*HM*, 53), and the baby's "tendrilly motions" are remi-

niscent of Wharton's description of Lily as "a water-plant in the flux of the tides" (*HM*, 53). Their identification becomes complete when Lily feels the child penetrate and enter her body.

All of her life, Lily has fled intimacy and kept others at a distance, but here she absorbs another, as the imagery suggests, into her womb. When Lily sleeps that final time, the child she cradles is herself. Through a painful process of establishing limits, by saying no to Gus Trenor, no to Mrs. Hatch, no to George Dorset, no to Sim Rosedale, no to blackmail, and no even to the well-intentioned Gerty Farish and Lawrence Selden, Lily gives birth to herself. Although she transcends her fate when her "poor little tentacles of self" cling to the baby on her arm (*HM*, 319), the struggle kills her and suggests, as did *The Story of Avis* (1877), that it may take three generations to make an independent woman artist.

Hope for the future lies with the daughters of women like Nettie Struther, who have the chance of growing up to be useful as well as ornamental. Showalter observes that the *The House of Mirth* ends with a death that offers "a vision of a new world of female solidarity, a world in which Gerty Farish and Nettie Struther will struggle hopefully and courageously,"[19] and Elizabeth Ammons writes that the lady of the leisure class holding the infant of working class parents promises the hope of the New Woman.[20] The images of mother and child also imply, though, that Lily's death is unnecessary and that the lady and the New Woman are not mutually exclusive. Instead, the novel shows their sisterhood and seems to plead for a time when there is a less divisive definition of "woman" so that a lady such as Lily will know how to respond to the sympathy of a Miss Kilroy. Previous definitions of "woman" have proved inadequate and unreliable: by the novel's end Lily has become unmarriageable, and Gerty, with the "points" Selden observes, promises to be marriageable: "really, some good fellow might do worse" (*HM*, 154). Lily's own experience has taught her to have compassion and to feel a sense of kinship with even her flesh-and-blood Fury, Bertha Dorset. Wharton's indictment of society is not a comprehensive criticism of the lady, for Lily has many admirable qualities. Rather than banish the "lady" to another land, like the "lost lady" of Willa Cather's fiction, or lose her to insanity, as in Ellen Glasgow's *The Sheltered Life*, Wharton believes society should redefine her.[21] The image of Lily and child, which represents the grafting of the artistic (the "purely decorative" [*HM*, 301]) with the utilitarian, embodies Wharton's definition of "woman." It can also serve as a metaphor for her art, which both delights and instructs. In addition, it suggests what will happen to the child if attitudes do not change: she will be laid to rest on a bed of lilies.

In *The Custom of the Country* (1913), Wharton continues to explore societal restrictions on women by showing what Lily could have become if she had not had the tenacity to say no. Undine's keen sense of business, her lack of emotional coloration, her ability to plan and focus on long-term goals, her social instinct, imitative ability, and singular lack of altruism should guarantee her the type of success and power her father chases on Wall Street. But Wall Street is as closed to her as it was to Miss Bart, and her energy and ambition must be contained within the embossed walls of the drawing room—the only deals she can hatch are on the marriage market.[22]

The Wharton heroine with the fewest self-illusions, Undine is also the one with the least self. Her private life finds expression in the hackneyed vocabulary of romances, like *When the Kissing Had to Stop*, and her public life is summarized by tabloid headlines such as "New York Beauty Weds French Nobleman."[23] Undine is never any more real than the story her publicist can manufacture for the morning paper. From first to last she displays "a kind of epic effrontery" (*CC*, 254) toward any spiritual, intellectual, aesthetic, historical, or cultural values.

When *The Custom of the Country* was published in 1913, Wharton was in full command of her powers as a writer and as a woman. Her passionate affair with Morton Fullerton, which by now had cooled to friendship, made her even more acutely aware of and angry at the lessons of suppression she learned and practiced in her mother's drawing room. A child of Wharton's shadow side, Undine took five years (1908–1913) to see the light of day, perhaps because her ferocity, her frenetic intensity, and her association with glittering and blinding light all point to her creator's own fury. There are obvious similarities, as Lewis notes, between heroine and author: Wharton has given Undine her own nickname of "Puss," her love of dressing up, her ambivalence about marriage, her disdain for "fossilized" modes of conduct, and her incredible, all-consuming energy.[24]

The genuineness of Wharton's own anger in this text also explains, in part, readers' fascination with Undine. We may not share her values, but it is hard not to admire her as she goes about getting exactly what she wants. Her appeal is two-sided: she is the outsider in the Marvell and the de Chelles sets who makes it inside; and once inside, she thumbs her nose at them. Wharton wants us to feel incensed for Undine, who, like Lily, is the product of her civilization, a perfect blank screen on which Ralph Marvell can project his romantic and sexual ideals: "He had been walking with a ghost: the miserable ghost of his illusion. Only he had somehow vivified, coloured, substantiated it, by the force of his own great need—" (*CC*, 221–222). Justice is served when the ornament becomes a retributive tool of destruction.

At the same time that we identify with Undine, we also feel a certain superiority toward her shallowness; and the more successful she and Elmer Moffatt are, the more self-congratulatory we become on our superior taste. In this way the reader, like Undine herself, who goes from Moffatt to Moffatt, is brought full circle and realigned with Ralph Marvell's values. However, our sympathy for Undine lets us see those values from a fuller perspective after understanding the pathos of her situation when she meets Moffatt at St. Desert: "Here was some one who spoke her language, who knew her meanings, who understood instinctively all the deepseated wants for which her acquired vocabulary had no terms; and as she talked she once more seemed to herself intelligent, eloquent and interesting" (*CC*, 536). Because society has always denied Undine an individualized vocabulary, it is not surprising that she is either inarticulate or can only repeat phrases from "Town Talk." Just as Lily Bart is "manacled" by the links of the bracelet "chaining her to her fate" (*CC*, 7), Undine is tragically limited by a society that does not value intelligence or eloquence in women until after they are safely married. Moffat's example shows the cost of this system is not limited to women, for the man who wants only the best gets Undine.

The Custom of the Country is rightly viewed as an indictment of American marriages, but it is overlooked as an indictment of irresponsibly permissive child-rearing practices. The Spraggs' indulgence of Undine ironically supports Wharton's belief about her own upbringing, "the creative mind thrives best on a reduced diet."[25] Mrs. Spragg is presented as "a partially-melted wax figure" (*CC*, 4) who "had no ambition for herself—she seemed to have transferred her whole personality to her child—but she was passionately resolved that Undine should have what she wanted" (*CC*, 11). As a result, Undine learned to rule by making the house "uninhabitable" until she had exactly "what she wanted" and has matured into an overgrown child, who believes that "if only everyone would do as she wished she would never be unreasonable" (*CC*, 266). But if she had been taught how to "think" instead of how to "look" (*CC*, 86), Mr. Dragonet's prediction, "My child, if you look like that you'll get it" (*CC*, 96), might not have been so ironically true.

The Spraggs' passive devotion makes them Undine's most pathetic victims. They have touchingly sacrificed to give her a chance but have not made her aware of any reciprocal obligation. They have no more substance for their daughter than Mr. Bart had for his, who "seemed always to have seen him through a blur—" (*HM*, 33). Undine is annoyed when her mother, who has waited up for her after the Marvell dinner, pleads, "I just *had* to, Undie—I told father I *had* to. I wanted to hear all about it" (*CC*, 104). At the same time she cannot imagine her parents as existing apart from her: "She had never paused to consider what her father and mother were 'interested' in, and, challenged to specify, could have named —with sincerity—only herself" (*CC*, 92). Undine manipulates both, expecting her mother to be her advocate ("If she and her mother did not hold together in such crises she would have twice the work to do") and expecting her father to cough up "extras" on the strength of her charms (*CC*, 45). Resembling Mrs. Bart, she has been taught to believe that men go "down town" "to bring back the spoils to their women" (*CC*, 44), and if they do not, they are being perverse.

Because the Spraggs have abdicated their parental roles, it is no wonder that Undine's forgery of her mother's signature, Mrs. Leota B. Spragg, shows her garbled conception of her mother's identity or that when her father asserts his authority and orders Undine to return Peter Van Degen's pearls, his daughter sells them and pockets the money. At the novel's conclusion the Spraggs are effectively excluded from their child's life and will see less of their grandson, who now has no father to bring him to the sitting rooms of their hotels. Mr. Spragg's betrayal of Mr. Rolliver (and his resulting financial decline) has also been in vain because it was prompted by his desire to separate his daughter and Moffatt.

Undine has no knowledge of herself, so it follows that she

experiences no real intimacy with others. Sexually active by Wharton's standards, she is neither "sexual" nor loving. Lacking both education and sensibility, Undine is a horrific version of the New Woman, described by Carroll Smith-Rosenberg, as "Androgyne."[26] Rejecting domesticity but not destiny, she is willing to sell low, as in her relationship with Peter Van Degen, if the return promises to be high. Undine's willingness to trade on her physical attractiveness is one reason for her success, but in fact she owes much of her success to the support and mentorship of other women—a group that she manipulates with more expertise and more crude honesty than Lily Bart.

In a modern sense, Mrs. Heeny, Mabel Lipscomb, Madame de Trézac, Princess Estradina, Indiana Frusk, and even Claire Van Degen are her network. They are willing to help her if she in turn helps them and plays square. Indiana tells her up front that she will not tolerate Undine's ingratiating herself with Mr. Rolliver in the same way she did with Millard Binch back in Apex, but once that is understood, she is her ally. Later her confidante, Madame de Trézac, instructs her on the finer points of French etiquette toward mistresses and flagrantly flaunts her "in the face of the Faubourg like a particularly showy specimen of her national banner" (CC, 484). And all the while—from the Stentorian to Washington Square to St. Desert to Paris—Undine keeps Mrs. Heeny's advice in mind: "Go steady, Undine, and you'll get any-wheres" (CC, 25). That advice echoes Judy Trenor's to Lily Bart, "Oh, Lily, do go slowly" (HM, 45). Undine, though, differs from the more impulsive Lily in her self-protective ability to parlay present failure into future glory. Planning her strategy with Peter Van Degen, Undine reasons: "Already in her short experience she had seen enough of the women who sacrifice future security for immediate success, and she meant to lay solid foundations before she began to build up the light superstructure of enjoyment" (CC, 234–

235). These traits are not endearing, but—better than Lily's plasticity—they allow her to survive.

Undine and her best friend, Indiana Frusk, are two of a kind, disdainful like Daisy Miller of anything "poky" (*CC*, 8) and believing that an American woman doesn't need to know a lot about Europe's "old rules" (*CC*, 162). Belonging to the future, to the "showy and the promiscuous" (*CC*, 193), they concur that "if a girl marries a man who don't come up to what she expected, people consider it to her credit to want to change" (*CC*, 96). Their relationship, based on lifelong rivalry and competition for the "new and stylish," resembles that between Mrs. Ansley and Mrs. Slade in "Roman Fever." Although it is less sentimental and more pragmatic than the bond between Penelope and Vexilla in "Friends,"[27] there is no denying that Undine and Indiana understand each other as no one else in the novel can. As a result, they are most intimate with one another and because each accepts "the custom of the country," most wary. The tragedy of *The Custom of the Country* (as in all but Wharton's later works) can be read in the final and frightening loneliness of all of its characters.

Like Lily Bart, Undine has the power to save and to redefine herself; but having squandered it getting and spending, she is in danger of looking in the mirror and seeing a blank glass. By misusing her intelligence and creativity, Lily also lays waste her powers. Her death and Undine's spiritual and emotional barrenness are the end results of participating— even successfully—in a corrupt and immoral system.

The House of Mirth and *The Custom of the Country* urge women not to squander their talents. Susan Lenox, the heroine who combines Lily's sensitivity and Undine's drive, is a good example. She survives with her self-respect intact because she creates her own image of her mother, Lorella Lenox, as brave, loving, and resistant to the tyranny of marriage: "My mother never let any man marry her. They say she was disgraced, but I understand now. *She* wouldn't stoop to let any man marry her."[28] True or not, that image becomes the daughter's personal grail. Susan's predecessor, Lily, looks for her grail elsewhere and finds it in Nettie Struther's warm kitchen. It too is of her own making.

All three books speak to the artistic and imaginative power of women. Wharton was able to harness her own creative power, and its force enriched her life. Undine is an example of the pathological implications of that force, misguided and unchecked, and Lily is an example of its wasted potential. Wharton knew from her own experience that each of us is alone in "the flux of the tides" and that the only sure rescuer is oneself. Lily's and Undine's cases show the need for women to abandon models of female behavior that emphasize self-destructive competition. Lily's experience in particular mirrors the magnitude of the risk; nevertheless, Wharton is adamant: mothers need to nurture and spiritually mentor their daughters, and women need to direct their energies inward. If one behaves with honesty and openness, other women can be a source of help, a reef in "the flux of the tides." Only then can there be a "new" woman and a new world.

CHAPTER FOUR

The Buried Fables in *Ethan Frome* and *Summer*

> *"[O]ne way of finding out whether a risk is worth taking is not to take it, and then to see what one becomes in the long run, and draw one's inferences."*
>
> —*"THE LONG RUN"*

Edith Wharton's New England novels, *Ethan Frome* (1911) and *Summer* (1917), proclaim her psychological and artistic emancipation from the internalized voices of the past. In them she attempts to do—personally and asthetically—what she demanded of Henry James in *The Wings of the Dove*: to see "beyond" an "unpleasant subject."[1] On the surface, these texts seem straightforward and familiar. *Ethan Frome* extends regional writing beyond "the rose and lavender pages of Sarah Orne Jewett and Mary Wilkins,"[2] and *Summer* makes a tradition of seduced-and-abandoned plots her own.[3] Beneath the surface, however, each contains "a story of inward rescue" or a "buried fable" about an unpleasant subject: incest.[4]

In the author's first New England novel, this theme is tied to a second buried fable, Wharton's rescue of herself from impoverished and tradition-bound ways of seeing. "It was not until I wrote 'Ethan Frome,' " she recalls in her autobiography, "that I suddenly felt the artisan's full control of his implements" (*ABG*, 209). Wharton felt that she could now claim her place in American letters because *Ethan Frome*'s narrative structure shows her seeing beyond the narrator's simple tale of two women and one man to her own larger categories, in this case the difference between prosaic imagination and artistic vision. Before *Ethan Frome*, as Blake Nevius states, "the narrators employed in Edith Wharton's early stories are *always men*."[5] It seems significant, therefore, that Wharton's next novel, *The Reef* (1912), is the story of a woman's growing consciousness, told primarily from her point of view, that undermines men's symbolic constructs of female behavior. The change in narrative perspective suggests that the writing of *Ethan Frome* helped to prepare its author to assume and sustain a voice closer to her own.

Wharton's unnamed narrator is an example of what she saw herself becoming if she could not find new ways of using old plots. He is a self she sheds, for as Carroll Smith-Rosenberg observes, "the act of adopting another's language can be tricky and costly, even if one does so with a self-conscious, ironic intent."[6] Arguing that male plots are inadequate for describing a female writer's experience, Joanna Russ asks who ever read a short story about a girl going off into the wilderness alone, killing a bear, and returning a woman.[7] Wharton is grappling with the same issue in *Ethan Frome*. Her narrator sees what he has been primed to see culturally and literarily. By undercutting his authority and reliability, she dissociates herself from his error: telling the wrong story. As the ghostly landscape of the novel suggests, she saw that road ending in frozen creativity.

The tale the narrator tells of two women and one man is a story that Wharton told all of her life, but unlike her, he does not challenge its convention, nor does he highlight the falsity of categorizing and stereotyping the rivals.[8] To him, the phrase "two women and one man" is explanation enough for why the Frome farmhouse is not a home. If Wharton had seen only as much as her narrator saw, she would have lost her individual identity as a writer in much the same way that Frome becomes a part of "the mute melancholy landscape, an incarnation of its frozen woe."[9]

The narrator's identification with Ethan determines his point of view. From Ethan he envisions a tale of triangular passion. It is, however, only one of many possible ways of telling the story; for example, Mattie Silver could speak for all poor relations, who have no choice but to suffer a cousin's querulous tongue and the advances of her husband. Wharton goes to excessive length, or, one could say, to excessive ellipsis, to make this point. Forced to take shelter from a blizzard in the Frome farmhouse, the narrator informs us: "I found the clue to Ethan Frome, and began to put together this vison of his story. . . . ." (*EF*, 25). The extended fade-out emphasizes that what follows is just what the narrator has said, a vision of Ethan Frome; and it grows from the narrator's initial response to him: "the sight pulled me up sharp. Even then he was the most striking figure in Starkfield, though he was but the ruin of a man" (*EF*, 3). When the narrator crosses the threshold of the Frome farmhouse, he fleshes out this original fragment, which might be titled "The Ruin of a Striking Man."

Ethan is the narrator's creation just as surely as the narrator is Wharton's, and, in fact, Ethan the character appears to the narrator in much the same way that Wharton describes her characters intruding upon her consciousness: "I may be strolling about casually in my mind, and suddenly a character will start up, coming seemingly from nowhere. Again, but more breathlessly, I watch; and presently the character draws nearer, and seems to become aware of me, and to feel the shy but desperate need to unfold his or her tale."[10] As she explains in her introduction, his function mirrors her own:[11]

> Each of my chroniclers [Hamon Gow and Mrs. Ned Hale] contributes to the narrative *just so much as he or she is capable of understanding* of what, to them, is a complicated and mysterious case; and only the narrator of the tale has scope enough to see it all, to resolve it back into simplicity, and to put it in its rightful place among his larger categories. (*EF*, ix)

The narrator is not as reliable as the quotation first appears to suggest, for his "larger categories," in part Aristotelian and gender-bound, are not Wharton's.

Wharton believed that books that shed "a light on our moral experience" result from the author's ability to see beyond his or her characters (*WF*, 28–29). Above all, she valued—without questioning the concept—the "human significance" of the universal.[12] The narrator, however, never sees beyond the personal, and he mistakes such superficial likenesses as an interest in popular science and joint sojourns in Florida for deeper similarities between himself and his subject.[13] By describing the protagonist and the narrator as if they were puppets (Ethan's lameness checks each of his steps "like the jerk of a chain" and his observer is "pulled up sharp" [*EF*, 3]), Wharton underscores her own distance from them.

In an allegorical reading of the novel, the narrator is a pilgrim, traveling to a critical junction. Like the speaker in the Robert Frost poem, he must choose between two roads. One is known and leads to his desired destination, the Corbury power plant, but a blinding snowstorm has swallowed its track. If he is to reach his goal, if he is to be empowered, he must continue by forging a second, original path. Wharton articulated the narrator's challenge in *The Decoration of Houses* (1898): "Originality," she said, anticipating T. S. Eliot's "Tradition and the Individual Talent" (1917), "lies not in discarding the necessary laws of thought, but in using them to express new intellectual conceptions."[14]

Instead, the narrator chooses a road that leads into an infertile and frozen landscape, past "an orchard of starved apple-trees writhing over a hillside among outcroppings of slate that nuzzled up through the snow like animals pushing out their noses to breathe" (*EF*, 19–20). This road ends at the Frome farmhouse, but like the road to Corbury Junction it too could lead—as it did for Wharton—to an original story on familiar lines. However, the forumla of two women and one man dictates that the tragedy results from competition for Ethan.

By calling attention to the limits of this vision, Wharton manages to have her narrator tell an old story while suggesting a new one; for example, Ethan sees Mattie no more clearly than when Zeena's "volubility was music in his ears" (*EF*, 69):

> She laughed at him for not knowing the simplest sick-bed duties and told him to "go right along out" and leave her to see to things. The mere fact of obeying her orders, of feeling free to go about his business again and talk with other men, restored his shaken balance and magnified his sense of what he owed her. Her efficiency shamed and dazzled him. (*EF*, 70)

By the novel's end this dynamo is transformed into a ghoul, whose "pale opaque eyes" reveal nothing and reflect nothing (*EF*, 173). The reason is obvious: Ethan is more child than husband. Silent and remote, he offers her no choice but to endure like his mother, Endurance Frome. Not only has he broken the promise to move to a larger city, but he has done so on the pretext that there "she would have suffered a complete loss of identity" (*EF*, 72). In passive retaliation, Zeena assumes a new identity as a hypochondriac. She is like one of her geraniums with the faded, yellow leaves that "pine away when they ain't cared for" (*EF*, 138). Whether her illnesses result from a need for attention or from suppressed anger, they are symptomatic of the Fromes' marriage, and in that sense Ethan is also diseased.

Zeena's characterization makes one particularly aware of what the narrator said at the beginning of his tale: "the deeper meaning of the story was in the gaps" (*EF*, 7). Wharton asks the reader to fill them in. Despite the narrative point of view, Zeena has a right to berate Mattie for breaking the red glass pickle dish that was a present from her Philadelphia relatives: "You're a bad girl, Mattie Silver, and I always known it. It's the way your father begun, and I was warned of it when I took you, and tried to keep my things where you couldn't get at 'em—and now you've took from me the one I cared for most of all—" (*EF*, 127). That neither the narrator nor her husband credits her point of view again shows Wharton's distance from them and her criticism of their shared perspective. Mattie and Ethan have shattered Zeena's heart as thoroughly as they have the dish; and although Wharton's choice of dish humorously puns on Mattie and Ethan's situation (they're in a pickle), sympathy must extend to Zeena, whose own romantic fantasy has materialized into hours of unappreciated drudgery. The narrative's masculine perspective excludes her story, which could be one of unbearable loneliness, emotional and economic deprivation, or physical and psychological abuse.[15]

Herself a realist and a realistic writer, Wharton knew the dangers of romantic notions and of romance plots obscuring the actual. Ethan's failure really belongs to his author, the narrator, who has not succeeded in characterizing either Mattie or Zeena in the round. The women's pairing throughout the story reinforces how little individuality they have in the narrator's mind. Mattie comes to the Frome house to help as Zeena came to care for Ethan's ailing mother seven years before. The women merge first in the narrator's imagination when he enters the Frome kitchen and then in the vision he attributed to Ethan: "She stood just as Zeena had stood, a lifted lamp in her hand, against the black background of the kitchen. She held the light at the same level, and it drew out with the same distinctness her slim young throat and the brown wrist no bigger than a child's" (*EF*, 81). Wharton simultaneously exposes the distortion of Mattie's characterization and the self-serving nature of romantic visions by having Ethan's desire affect his perception, as before his eyes she becomes "taller, fuller, more womanly in shape and motion" (*EF*, 82).

Although lovely, Mattie is possibly the most inarticulate heroine in American literature, and her name is indicative of her position and treatment in the Frome household. She is indeed, as Ethan notes, a "serviceable creature" (*EF*, 33)— either as Zeena's doormat or Ethan's dream lover; for example, when she responds to the sunset by saying, " 'It looks just as if it was painted!' it seemed to Ethan that the art of definition could go no farther, and that words had at last been found to utter his secret soul" (*EF*, 34). Ethan first sees Mattie as an extension of himself. Finally, they become one on that winter night's ride down Corbury Road when "[a]s they flew toward the tree . . . her blood seemed to be in his veins" (*EF*, 169–170). In the narrator's telling, Ethan has been the author of this fiction; and as the quotation illustrates, it ends with the appropriation of Mattie's identity.[16]

The lovers' vision of dying wedded in each other's arms resembles the deaths of Tom and Maggie Tulliver in George Eliot's *The Mill on the Floss* (1860). In Eliot's novel, Maggie and Tom Tulliver die in a flood, and their embrace joins them in a way that the brother and sister never could be or were in life. All of their training and schooling worked to separate them, and their deaths are partly Eliot's criticism of a system that persists in treating men and women differently. Eliot was one of Wharton's favorite authors, and her ending to *Ethan Frome* is in some ways a tribute to and a comment on that novel. Like Tom and Maggie, Ethan and Mattie are two parts of one whole, representing maleness and femaleness. Their botched suicide is Wharton's comment on the real-world impossibility of wedding male and female aspects of the self in 1911.

Everyone on the Starkfield farm is a victim of the romantic plot's inadequacy for dealing with life's day-to-day plodding and day-to-day boredom. No rescuer will appear, and no fortunes will be reversed after Ethan wakes to the sound of Mattie making a noise "like a field mouse," "a small frightened *cheep*" (*EF*, 171).[17] The lovers' crippling shows the danger of cheap romantic fantasies: "The return to reality was as painful as the return to consciousness after taking anesthetic" (*EF*, 95). Doomed to pass all of this life and the next in each other's company, Mattie, Zeena, and Ethan's predicament predates Sartre's vision of hell in his 1945 play *No Exit* (*Huis clos*). In this way Wharton's stark realism triumphs over the narrator's tragic romanticism.[18] Mattie's arms may encircle Ethan on that fateful ride just as Maggie Tulliver hugs her brother Tom, but she and Ethan are predestined to be torn apart. The fiction of their union cannot be sustained.

In "The Criticism of Fiction" Wharton made a point that summarizes *Ethan Frome*: meaning, she wrote, is not to be found in "the fate of the characters, and still less in their own comments on it."[19] Instead, it results from a story's "atmosphere." The decidedly unsettling atmosphere of *Ethan Frome* emanates from its other buried fable. If we take the story from Wharton instead of from Ethan, the narrative becomes a Gothic one, in which Wharton explores her own struggle for independence from a demanding and overbearing mother. Although she may show her indebtedness to Hawthorne by appropriating the name Ethan from "Ethan

Brand" and Zenobia from *The Blithedale Romance*,[20] her tale is more akin to Eugene O'Neill's autobiographical *Long Day's Journey into Night* (1941); for a narrator, whether the created narrator of *Ethan Frome* or Wharton herself, cannot escape from telling at least a part of his or her own narrative. The very selection, arrangement, and interpretation of events are all self-revealing.

Feeling that her mother, Lucretia Jones, withheld love and approval, Wharton frequently characterized her as "cold," "disapproving," and "distant"—all adjectives that could be applied to Zenobia—while also appreciating her wit, style of dressing, and care in demanding a strict standard of spoken English in the house. A story in the first draft of her autobiography, "Life and I," demonstrates how these conflicting feelings made the author's struggle for independence difficult and complex. Wharton remembers being sent to a small dancing class taught by Mlle. Michelet. The teacher's "small shrivelled bearded mother" observed all the classes, and Wharton could not look at her "without disgust."[21] She revealed her disgust to a classmate, which he delightedly repeated: Mlle. Michelet's mother was *"une vieille chevre"* ("Life," 4), an old goat. Feeling guilty for saying something about Mlle. Michelet's mother that she "would not have said *to her*, & which it was consequently 'naughty' to say, or even to think" ("Life," 4), Wharton decided to atone by making a public confession to all of the members of her dancing class. She was disappointed, however, "when, instead of recognizing & commending the heroism" of her conduct, Mlle. Michelet delivered a furious scolding for her impertinence ("Life," 6).

Wharton's behavior was in an indirect way aimed at herself because the real victim of her childhood unkindness was not Mme. Michelet but Mlle. Michelet. The child's frustration with herself for not being able to confront her mother was covertly directed at another daughter in what she per-

ceived to be a similar situation. At the same time, Wharton
obviously expected more sympathy and support from the
daughter she was misguidedly defending. Mlle. Michelet's
example predates Mattie Silver's, but the lesson has not
changed: the alternative they choose—not to leave mother—
ends with living in or being buried under a mother's "icy"
shadow.[22] The final scene in the Frome kitchen, where a
"slatternly" Zenobia tends her witchlike twin, confined to a
chair—which, like herself, is "a soiled relic of luxury" (*EF*,
174)—exposes the horror inherent in that option.

Wharton's relationship with her mother is a useful context
for analyzing her statement about the composition of *Ethan
Frome*: "For years I had wanted to draw life as it really was
in the derelict mountain villages of New England, a life even
in my time, and a thousandfold more a generation earlier,
utterly unlike that seen through the rose-coloured spectacles
of my predecessors, Mary Wilkins and Sarah Orne Jewett"
(*ABG*, 293). Her evaluation of both authors and of Mary
Wilkins in particular is self-serving and incorrect, but it ac-
complishes its purpose of separating her work from that of
women local colorists. Her statement stands as an aggressive
defense of her singular vision, but it is also a declaration of
power; for, unlike the narrator of her tale, she did not choose
the predictable path. It reveals the novelist's competitive
drive and need for autonomy by effectively casting Jewett
and Wilkins in the role usually reserved for her own mother,
Lucretia Jones.

In *Ethan Frome*, Lucretia's role is assigned to Zeena and
those of Wharton and her father to Mattie and Ethan, who
resemble Hansel and Gretel more than they do Paolo and
Francesca. The orphaned Mattie's tenancy is dependent on
Zeena because Ethan cannot stand up to the mother who re-
placed his own. Mattie worries that she "won't suit" (*EF*, 47),
for her abilities to "trim a hat, make molasses candy, recite
'Curfew shall not ring to-night,' and play 'The Lost Chord'

and a pot-pourri from 'Carmen' " (*EF*, 59) are not sufficient to provide her with economic independence. Although she is of adult age, twenty-one, her household skills prove that she is incapable of caring for herself. She is more suited to be the childless Zeena's daughter than her replacement, and her gold locket and fairy princess looks pair her with the only other child mentioned in the novel, the daughter of a man who left his wife to go West "with the girl he cared for" (*EF*, 131).

As the only adult in the story, Zeena does her best to give Mattie a chance to make a home of her own. It is her idea that Mattie attend the young people's dances, and she wants to encourage the idea of Denis Eady as a suitor. When Mattie stands on the threshold of the Frome kitchen, "with all its implications of conformity and order" (*EF*, 93), she has a choice: to be like Zeena or to be herself. Mattie's decision, symbolized by the broken red glass of the pickle dish, disrupts social order and shows the self-destructiveness inherent in incestuous fantasies. If a woman remains too closely bound with her mother's life, she can count on spending eternity in a chaste single bed in the family graveyard.[23] Mattie's confinement and Zeena's martyrdom articulate those dangers for both daughter and mother.

Ethan Frome demonstrates that the failure to gain independence results in death—or worse, maiming. That realization may have been a literal life-saver for Wharton, and she restated it more overtly and strongly the next year in a verse play (not to be confused with a story of the same title), "Pomegranate Seed" (1912). In her rewriting of the Demeter–Persephone myth, Persephone does not make Mattie Silver's mistake. Instead she chooses to leave her mother and return to Hades,[24] and that return foreshadows Charity Royall's return to her guardian's house in Wharton's other New England novel, *Summer* (1917).

Wharton dubbed this tale of a young woman's burgeoning

sexuality and its attendant responsibility the "Hot Ethan."[25] The daughter of a prostitute and a drunken convict, Charity has been raised as a Christian by Lawyer Royall and his late wife. She knows she should be thankful, but instead she hates everything—her guardian; the small, sleepy town of North Dormer; the moldy and seldom frequented Hatchard Memorial Library, where she works as a librarian as few hours as possible; most of all, she hates the part of herself that comes from the Mountain, that bad and shameful place from which she was thankfully rescued and about which she must hold her tongue.

When Bernard Berenson expressed his admiration for Royall, Wharton exclaimed, "Of course *he's* the book."[26] He is also the key to the novel's buried fable, which attempts to anwer two questions: What would George Frederic Jones have been like without his "matter-of-fact" wife; what would the consequences have been for his daughter? The answers show the impossibility of Ethan Frome's fantasy. A wife's death may leave one free to marry a child bride, but the ending is not unqualifiedly happy—charity does not necessarily begin at home.

Summer opens with the mother figure effectively banished. Mrs. Royall is dead, but unlike Zeena Frome's absence, hers has not made her house any cheerier. Resembling the Frome farmhouse in a different season, it is decorated with its own "wraithlike creeper," "a sickly Crimson Rambler," and its yard is being devoured by "traveler's joy" and the encroaching "wilderness of rock and fern."[27] The yard symbolizes Charity's nature. Eager for sensation, she is a precursor of Faulkner's Dewey Dell, more at home under the ceiling of the open sky: "She was blind and insensible to many things, and dimly knew it; but to all that was light and air, perfume and colour, every drop of blood in her responded" (*Summer*, 13).

In comparison, her guardian has spent his summers and tries to deny his ward the squandering of her own. Royall's

sexual advances to Charity several years earlier and his subsequent shame and dumb need assure that the man who
rules in North Dormer is mastered by his foster daughter at
home. Lewis observes that this novel "gives off intimations of
something darker, stranger, more ominous—a domain of experience she [Wharton] normally approached only in her
ghost stories."[28] He sees the Mountain as the source of these
disturbing intimations and argues that "it is by artful contrast with the Mountainfolk that Lawyer Royall appears so
basically humane."[29] Although right about the novel's unsettling undercurrent, Lewis is mistaken about its source. As
Royall's actions illustrate, not much separates the Mountain
and its outpost of civilization, North Dormer. The dark current emanates from Royall himself, just as Zeena Frome "se-
creted" "an evil energy" (*EF*, 117–118), and it prefigures
Wharton's overt treatment of incest in the Beatrice Palmato
fragment (c. 1919).

Wolff discovered Beatrice's story in the Wharton archives
at Yale and suggests that it is a rehearsal for a longer piece.
It consists of three parts, the cover sheet, a summary of the
story, and a piece of fiction titled "unpublishable fragment
of Beatrice Palmato."[30] In the graphically erotic story of an
incestuous relationship between a father and his daughter,
Wharton perhaps defines in sexual terms what she felt missing from her childhood, the need for adoration: "I want you
all,"[31] Mr. Palmato whispers to "his little girl."[32] The sex between father and daughter has a positive allure. When Mr.
Palmato draws his daughter to "the deep divan," "his touch
had never been tenderer," and "[a]lready she felt every fibre
vibrating under it, as of old, only now with the more passionate eagerness bred of privation, and of the dull misery of
her marriage."[33] Although the fragment begins with the father's implied admonition, "I have been you see . . . so perfectly patient," the daughter, through her submission, exercises mastery. Mr. Palmato is literally on his knees as he
tirelessly devours Beatrice with his lips and his eyes. The

tale shows Beatrice's needs for adoration and domination being concurrently gratified, and in this respect Wharton perhaps envied her character. At the same time, Wharton qualifies the surface text. Mr. Palmato is unappealing in his
gluttony, and his seduction of his daughter precipitates madness and death.

Summer's surface and subtexts are the reverse of those in
the Beatrice Palmato fragment, and the novel's dark intimations grow mostly from the text working against itself. On
the surface, as Elizbeth Ammons observes, the incestuous relationship between father and daughter is identified as un-
healthy;[34] yet it also has its unconscious fascination. *Summer*'s
concurrent and contradictory texts in part explain the dis-
puted interpretations of Charity's return to North Dormer.[35]
Wharton never satisfactorily resolves the conflict. In a disturbing reversal at the novel's conclusion, incest is condoned
by the community, and Charity and Harney's love is the
thing not named.

Fictionally, the dilemma is partly resolved by pairing the
two men in Charity's life. Together they form a whole. Charity, for example, naturally sees Harney, a visiting architect,
as a younger version of Royall: she "divined that the young
man symbolized all his ruined and unforgotten past" (*Summer*, 49). As his name promises, Harney embodies the lus-
cious sweetness of first love. Class, education, and sensibility
separate him from Charity, but passion and youth are the
common denominators. The couple tryst in a deserted house,
"as dry and pure as the interior of a long-empty-shell" (*Summer*, 122). It cradles them just as Charity's womb will soon
cradle their child. The illusion of comfort is shattered when
the two, forced to seek shelter from the rain, visit its night-
marish twin. Set in a swamp, the house resembles their own
in a later season, and its frame holds a weak-minded old
woman, ragged children, an unkempt, fearful mother, and a
man "sleeping off his liquor" (*Summer*, 60–61).

Contrary to the standard seduced-and-abandoned plot, Charity ultimately rejects Harney as a husband because she has never been able to picture herself as his wife. With relief she urges him to honor his engagement to her rival, Annabel Balch (*Summer*, 163): "Behind the frail screen of her lover's caresses was the whole inscrutable mystery of his life: his relations with other people—with other women—his opinions, his prejudices, his principles, the net of influences and interests and ambitions in which every man's life is entangled" (*Summer*, 145). Charity knows enough about herself to know that she will feel uncomfortable and inadequate in his world, and she is not willing to be powerless.

Marriage to Royall offers power and protection within the respectable bounds of lawful domesticity while fulfilling unconscious incestuous fantasies. To choose Royall consciously, though, Charity must first define herself in relation to her own mother and to the child she carries. Projected motherhood has made her more keenly aware of her own motherlessness, and her journey to the Mountain, prompted by desperate need, is itself a quest for identity. Charity's first impulse was to support her child in the only way available to her—as a prostitute in Nettleton—but her soul recoiled from it. Her mother, who "could hardly help remembering the past, and receiving a daughter who was facing the trouble she had known" (*Summer*, 178), is an alternative.

Once on the Mountain, Charity awakens from this dream, as she sees the consequences of ungovernable passions and the squalor of moral isolation in the inhuman figure of her mother, who resembles a "dead dog in a ditch" (*Summer*, 186). Across her mother's corrupted body, she sees her own face reflected in her nameless half-sister. Charity rejects this image, and Wharton shows that even from the worst possible mother (whether a Zeena Frome or a Lucretia Jones), one can learn, if only by rejecting her example.

Charity, however, does not simply deny her similarities

with her mother. She also embraces them, and her split perspective mirrors Wharton's rejection of and identification with her mother. When she puts herself in her mother's place, when she sleeps where "her dead mother's body had lain" (*Summer*, 192), she experiences a second awakening more powerful than the one she had with Harney in the deserted house. The mother in Charity responds to and bonds with the dead woman, whom she no longer blames for abandoning her: "was her mother so much to blame? . . . What mother would not want to save her child from such a life?" (*Summer*, 193).[36] Charity both buries and resurrects her mother when she realizes that for her own child she is willing to do anything, whether it is stealing food to feed the developing embryo or walking the streets of Nettleton. Assuming responsibility for her baby thrusts her across the threshold of adulthood and eventually across the threshold of Laywer Royall's house as his bride.

The ability to see *into* and beyond a subject that Wharton thought so necessary for the creation of "literature" is equally vital for the creation of a mature, autonomous self. Free from the curse of the Mountain, Charity is now free to embrace herself without feeling ashamed of the part of her that is her mother. The minister's words at her mother's funeral have come to fruition: "*In my flesh shall I see God!*" (*Summer*, 187). In her mother's flesh Charity has found redemption; and in her own, salvation. Yet she will people worlds, not create them.

Wharton's second look at New England differs from her first by suggesting that within realtistic parameters the imagination has the potential for healing. The novel comes full circle when Charity sees Royall's old proposal—still shadowed by what Lewis calls "intimations of something darker, stranger, more ominous"[37]—in new terms. A more mature, more whole vision demands this kind of qualification, however; and, as Charity's visit to her mother illustrates, the shadow side can also be a source of illumination.[38] As her new husband pretends to sleep on their wedding night, for example, Charity begins to envision an alternative ending to her story in which "Mr. Royall's presence began to detach itself with rocky firmness from this elusive background" (*Summer*, 204). Charity cares far less about love than she does about having somebody belong to her, "the way other folks have" (*Summer*, 35); and for this reason, her marriage may provide something she values and needs more than romance. Charity's future child is as symbolic as Lily Bart's vision of Nettie Struther's infant girl. It represents the self she will continue to create. The future of that middle-class baby promises to be more hopeful than that of Lily Bart's less advantaged namesake.

Although Charity's pattern of growth is far less retrogressive than Ethan and Mattie's, she still never learns that independence is a sweeter sensation than dependence. In this way the novel's ending is eerily reminiscent of *Ethan Frome*. There the result was graphically illustrated by Mattie's twisted spine. Here the maiming is more subtle. Royall's praise, "You're a good girl, Charity" (*Summer*, 216), seems the equivalent of Mattie's broken back. Both result in neverending girlhood, for as she tells Harney, "Things don't change at North Dormer: people just get used to them" (*Summer*, 89). If one interprets the novel as ending in her imprisonment (she passively awaits "a fate she could not avert" [*Summer*, 159]), then things don't change, and one can even get used to an incestuous marriage. This reading shows Wharton reiterating the point she made in her previous New England novel: the failure to leave home thwarts the growth of identity.[39] Father's house is no safer than Mother's.

Wharton thought that all readers asked themselves, "What am I being told this story for? What judgment on life does it contain for me?" (*WF*, 27). *Ethan Frome* and *Summer* also raise a third question: "Why is this particular writer telling this particular story?" Wharton was not able to achieve peace with her mother, except the peace established by distance, and her work is in part a record of her own efforts to hammer out an equitable truce. The later novels in particular show her weighing and often balancing the two sides of mother-daughter relationships. The progression of her thinking about this issue from the child's point of view moves back and forth from anger to dismissal to a qualified acceptance, while it acknowledges—as in *The Fruit of the Tree* (1907) or *Summer*—the need to find or create one's own mother if the original seems as inadequate as Mrs. Bart in *The House of Mirth* (1905), Mrs. Spragg in *The Custom of the Country* (1913), or Mrs. Manford in *Twilight Sleep* (1927). After *Summer*, Wharton was increasingly able to reflect the belief that mothers and daughters (or mother and daughter figures) are capable of seeing from the other's perspective. Instead of emphasizing conflicts between women of different generations and backgrounds, she makes their similarities apparent to the reader, if not to themselves. Whether from distinct classes, like Anna Leath and Sophy Viner of *The Reef* (1912), or possessing different sensibilities, like Bessie Westmore and Justine Brent in *The Fruit of the Tree* (1907), her heroines in general struggle to resist rivalry, and often their cooperation is mutually beneficial. In this way the fiction expresses a wish unrealized in its author's life.

Wharton's treatment of the mother-daughter theme shows a recognition of the competition between them and suggests—as in *Ethan Frome* and *Summer*—a way to transcend it: scrupulous self-analysis or a sympathetic imagination can lead to personal insight and growth. In Wharton's case it led, as Janet Flanner wrote, to two careers, "that of a great woman of the world and a great novelist," who in some ways "is her works."[40]

CHAPTER FIVE

Female Partnerships in the Business of Living

Now she perceived that to re-
fuse the gifts of life does not en-
sure their transmission to
those for whom they have been
surrendered.
  —"BUNNER SISTERS"

W‌harton's heroines await, sometimes passively, sometimes eagerly, a fate they cannot avert. That fate is marriage, and Wharton's acceptance and advocacy of it for the continuation of civilization inevitably leads to the same dead end, the sacrifice of one woman for another, who represents the status quo. In *The Reef* and *The Age of Inno-cence*, Wharton struggles to rewrite the marriage plot, but it ultimately holds her captive.[1]

The reasons for Wharton's failure are multiple: her gender, her Victorian childhood, her guilt about her own un-happy marriage, and above all, her inability to side with either of the novels' paired heroines. These split heroines symbolize the author's own uncertainty about the desirabil-ity of both intimacy and marriage. Her letters to Morton Fullerton, for example, disclose an impassioned and vulner-able woman, often asking and sometimes demanding more considerate treatment. At the same time, they reveal an acceptance of and even an emphasis on the transitory nature of their affair. Wharton's ambivalence, which gives her novels their exquisite tension, was not limited to Fullerton.[2] It characterizes her relationship with Walter Berry, who himself had a history of beginning and terminating strong attachments. Wharton may have truly believed, as she writes in *A Backward Glance*, that he was an expansion and interpretation of her own soul,[3] yet she seems never to have regretted their not marrying. The independence of her position suited her personality and made it impossible for her to disown her exiled heroines. Critics debate the tone of her novels in part because she systematically and sometimes ruthlessly exposes the dangers of romanticizing without ever entirely relinquishing a belief in the perfect soulmate and the happy ending.

Except for *The Buccaneers* (1938), *The Reef* (1912) is Wharton's most concise statement about the possibilities and the limitations of women's partnerships. The lives of its heroines, Anna Leath and Sophy Viner, are irrevocably intertwined. The factors that would normally distinguish them, such as age, education, and class, are purposefully blurred until Anna's fair and Sophy's dark hair becomes their most distinguishing feature. Though each loves George Darrow, their relationship is further complicated by the fact that Sophy became engaged to Anna's stepson Owen while employed as a governess for her daughter Effie. Sophy is now Effie's surrogate mother, and in the future Anna will be Sophy's mother-in-law. Wharton minimizes the differences that would normally cast them as mother and daughter.[4] Instead their likenesses indicate a figurative sisterhood.[5]

The characterization of Anna and Sophy marks a change in Wharton's thinking about mothers and daughters. No longer must they be—like Zeena Frome and Mattie Silver— enemies for all eternity.[6] Gender and its attendant, perhaps unavoidable, roles make them partners. Because they are not exclusively mother and daughter substitutes, Anna and Sophy can become the means of each other's mutual growth. George Darrow inspires passion in both, yet his role is negligible because neither Sophy's nor Anna's sexual awakening is nearly as profound as the awakening to their similarities. In this way Wharton questions traditional roles in heterosexual courtship while more fully developing a theme presented in *The House of Mirth*: the importance of women identifying with others of their own sex.

Wharton knew the pain of sexual awakening firsthand, for her affair with Fullerton spanned almost exactly the years (1907–1910) of his engagement to his cousin, Katherine Fullerton.[7] "I put most of myself into that opus," she wrote her friend and editor, William Brownell.[8] *The Reef* was composed after her affair with Morton Fullerton ended; but, still relying heavily on his advice and perhaps slyly on their history,[9] Wharton wrote him in June 1912:

> I want your opinion on what I have written here, & have asked Anna [her secretary] to make you a duplicate copy of the last chapters. *Vous les rattacherez tant bien que mal* ["You will connect them somehow or other"] to what you've already read: your memory of the general situation will suffice. After this point I can go on alone, but I want your opinion about the chapter in which, between Darrow & Anna, the truth begins to come out. It's not conventional, but I believe it's true.[10]

Fullerton had made her feel as if she now knew "what happy women feel";[11] however, their "indescribable current of communication"[12] was interrupted when she learned of his engagement.[13] Feeling that all one side of her was asleep, Wharton may have been grateful to her lover for rousing her from "a long lethargy, a dull acquiescence in conventional restrictions, a needless self-effacement,"[14] but her heroines complete the story of waking by exposing the pain involved in living *"in the round."*[15] Stories such as "The Letters," "The Day of the Funeral," "Joy in the House," "Diagnosis," "The Pretext," "The Other Two," "The Line of Least Resistance," and "The Lamp of Psyche" revolve around a similar moment of revelation and subsequent disillusionment.

Katherine possessed comparable knowledge of Fullerton's infidelity, and she and Wharton could not fail to note his identical and equally cavalier treatment of them:

> . . . a certain consistency of affection [Wharton admonished] is a fundamental part of friendship. One must know *à quoi s'en tenir* ["where one stands"]. And just as I think we have reached that stage, you revert abruptly to the other relation, & assume that I have noticed no change in you, & that I have not suffered or wondered at it, but have carried on my life in serene insensibility until you chose to enter again suddenly into it.[16]

Wharton felt that Fullerton was avoiding her "on the pretext of illness" and complained: "The one thing I can't bear is the thought that I represent to you *the woman who has to be lied to*."[17]—"Sometimes I feel I *can't* go on like this . . . —being left to feel that I have been like a 'course' served & cleared away!"[18] Clare Colquitt observes that Wharton's letters eerily echo Katherine's (and vice versa), "for both women often expressed their sorrow at Fullerton's failure to answer their love—or their letters—'with equal sincerity.' "[19] Fullerton's involvements with other women may merely have struck Wharton "as more daring versions of her own dilemma and helped give her the courage to break free of the entangling conventions that restrained her,"[20] but he proved to be as untrustworthy as George Darrow. That insight and Wharton's identification with Katherine probably led to the decline of their affair around 1910. The end of the Fullerton–Wharton liaison also marked the end of the cousins' engagement, and Katherine later married Gordon Gerould, an English instructor at Princeton.

As in *The Reef* and in Wharton's fiction in general, the women did not act as rivals, and in fact, in 1922, when *The Glimpses of the Moon* was published, Katherine wrote a favorable review of it for *The New York Times*. The review pleased Wharton, who wrote her editor, Rutger Jewett, that Katherine "is a cousin of my old friend Morton Fullerton, and it was I who sent her first ms. to Mr. Scribner, and called his attention to the literary promise which she already gave. So you see I deserve a good word from her."[21] Similarly, Wharton was pleased when Katherine wrote a sensitive and laudative critical essay on her fiction that Appleton published as a little brochure.[22]

The Reef is a comment on Wharton's own experience: women like Sophy Viner and Anna Leath have more in common than either has with a lover like George Darrow. Although the business of earning a living excludes Sophy from being a lady, in Anna's sense, she in many ways represents the self Anna wants to become. Readers first meet Anna in Book 2, and she is literally frozen between her past and an unknown future: "In the court, halfway between house and drive, a lady stood."[23] "Always a model of lady-like repression" (*Reef*, 87), she longs to experience "all the passions and sensations which formed the stuff of great poetry and memorable action" (*Reef*, 86). If life with her first husband had been like "a walk through a carefully classified museum, where, in moments of doubt, one had only to look at the number and refer to one's catalogue" (*Reef*, 95), life with Darrow promises to penetrate "every sense as the sunlight steeped the landscape" (*Reef*, 111). He is her first love restored to her as her second chance, and she means to take it. However, her previous marriage only protracted her prolonged girlhood, and she wonders how she can learn to say the right words that will make this new life happen.

Both Anna and Darrow believe that he is the "divine" means of her "self-renewal" (*Reef*, 30). His kiss will awaken her to a "world of hidden beauty" (*Reef*, 87) in which she will finally learn to be like other women, "wider awake," "more alert, and surer" (*Reef*, 87) of her wants.[24] Without him, she is "fated to wane into old age repeating the same gestures, echoing the words she had always heard, and perhaps never guessing that, just outside her glazed and curtained consciousness, life rolled away" (*Reef*, 30). Anna imagines being everything to Darrow, except his equal: "She wanted him to feel her power and yet to love her for her ignorance and humility. She felt like a slave, and a goddess, and a girl in her teens" (*Reef*, 125). Darrow muses that he and Anna were made for each other, but actually she was made for him. Despite Anna's wish to make herself "the shadow and echo" of his mood (*Reef*, 125), she shares Charity Royall's fear of being subsumed.

Naturally reticent, Anna worries that the sexual communion she desires will overwhelm and obliterate her sense of self. In this, Anna recalls her creator, who, as Lewis notes, was unsure of herself at the beginning of her affair with Fullerton: "She felt, simultaneously, eager to invite him into a closer kind of intimacy and frightened that, if he responded, she would fail him."[25] Wharton's letters to Fullerton show her experiencing hesitations that are later attributed to Anna:[26] "If I still remained inexpressive, unwilling, 'always drawing away,' as you said, it was because I discovered in myself such possibilities of feeling on that side that I feared, if I let you love me too much, I might lose courage when the time came to go away!"[27]

Anna's romantic illusions are more pronounced and her sensibilities even finer than Wharton's: she cannot bear the thought that Darrow might have met and made love to Sophy on his way to her. She resists seeing and accepting him as he is because she is unprepared to accept her own jealousy, passion, and self-interest. Once found, the "right words" reveal a part of herself that she—like Lily Bart— would prefer to deny. Toward Sophy she feels both revulsion and fascination: "It was humiliating to her pride to recognize kindred impulses in a character which she would have liked to feel completely alien to her" (*Reef*, 319). Such knowledge threatens her with a "certain loss of identity" (*Reef*, 85) by distancing her from all that Givré represents. No matter how much Anna wants Darrow to utter her secret soul, his words prove as inadequate as Mattie Silver's exclamation that the sunset looks just as if it were painted. Instead, reversing and rebelling against plot expectations, Wharton makes Sophy become Anna's initiator into the mysteries of living.

Supposedly worldly, Sophy has been as repressed and starved as Anna. When she first meets Darrow after her dismissal from the disreputable Mrs. Murrett's employ, he realizes that she "had been dying for some one to talk to, some one before whom she could unfold and shake out to the light her poor little shut-away emotions. Years of repression were revealed in her sudden burst of confidence" (*Reef*, 39). In her own way Sophy is as ignorant as Anna: " 'life'—the word was often on her lips" (*Reef*, 61). Her charming unconventionality prompts Darrow to ask the same question that Winterbourne asks about Daisy Miller: "Is she nice or not nice?"[28] Ironically, though, the directness and naturalness that first attract Darrow to Sophy later repel him, for it is not in keeping with his inherited notions of women's behavior: "She might be any one of a dozen definable types, or she might—more disconcertingly to her companion and more perilously to herself—be a shifting and uncrystallized mixture of them all" (*Reef*, 61).

Darrow prefers Anna's predictability, and as a betrothed couple they resemble an older and more privileged version of Lily Bart and Lawrence Selden: "the irresistible word fled with a last wing beat into the golden mist of her illusions" (*Reef*, 90).[29] Darrow also prefers to forget his own morally irresponsible behavior. Willing to admit that he "hadn't spent

a penny" (*Reef*, 167) of emotion, he is still unwilling to acknowledge "the excitement of pursuit" (*Reef*, 70) he experienced and his own motives in making use of Sophy to feel
"less drearily alone" (*Reef*, 56). "More and more aware of his
inability to test the moral atmosphere about him" (*Reef*, 208),
he successfully avoids confronting his own darker nature
and never once examines the double standard he applies to
Sophy when he feels that (like himself) she might have forgotten or trivialized their Paris interlude (*Reef*, 225).

As in most Wharton novels, if Sophy and Anna were combined, they would make the perfect woman, that combination of fire and ice Newland Archer yearns for in *The Age of
Innocence*. Initially, Sophy is fire and Anna is ice, but soon
those categories are inadequate for explaining Anna's selfishness and Sophy's altruism. Darrow succeeds in distinguishing the women only by class. With satisfaction, he reflects that Anna "was the kind of woman with whom one
would like to be seen in public" (*Reef*, 130). In Paris, Sophy
inspired a related feeling, "the primitive complacency of the
man at whose companion other men stare" (*Reef*, 50). This
coupling, which underscores the arbitrariness of classifica-
tions for women such as "nice" and "not nice," becomes even
more pronounced at Givré: "from the point at which he was
placed his eyes could not take in the one face without the
other" (*Reef*, 227). His thinking shows that gender is fate
when neither ideal nor real woman can avoid being owned.
Anna's fear of intimacy in part grows from the knowledge
that the more she reveals, the more she risks losing her self.

The novel's moral dilemma for Darrow is fairly straightforward. As Sophy tells him, "you'd rather I didn't marry
any friend of yours" (*Reef*, 205). For Anna, the problem is not
so simple. Realizing that the process of becoming a lady has
deadened her, she fears that the private self she has been
waiting to share is permanently trapped behind the veil that
"always hung between her and life" (*Reef*, 86). Worse yet, she

suspects that she has no hidden treasure, that her private and public selves are one and the same. For these reasons, Anna envies Sophy her directness, her receptivity, her hunger for experience, and eventually her sexual intimacy with Darrow. Recalling Oscar Wilde's Lady Windermere (1892), she recognizes her own potential for such unthinkable behavior, and it makes her a stranger to herself. In turn, Sophy envies Anna her stability, grace, and discernment. Most of all, Anna's life represents a kind of haven from the business of living. By pairing the heroines, Wharton establishes a dialectic and provides each a model for change. In each other they can see their evolving selves. For this reason they form—according to Anna's definition—the novel's one true marriage, and it threatens not only Darrow's authority as a representative and seemingly well-intentioned male but also his very identity.

As Anna imagines how much Darrow meant to Sophy and how little he perceived or felt, she reads her own future, like Anna Karenina, in the looking glass: "Did such self-possession imply indifference or insincerity? In that problem her mind perpetually revolved; and she dreaded the one answer as much as the other" (*Reef*, 326).[30] Darrow is obviously not going to rescue anyone, and Anna, like Mattie Silver, has the choice of living with her illusion of real life or experiencing it.

Sophy's receptivity and belief "that not missing things matters most" (*Reef*, 104) make her the fitting person to initiate Anna into the "human problem" "without fear and without hypocrisy" (*Reef*, 288). The freedom to make mistakes becomes an increasingly predominant theme in Wharton's later work, such as *The Mother's Recompense* (1925), *The Children* (1928), *Hudson River Bracketed* (1929), *The Gods Arrive* (1932), and *The Buccaneers* (1938). Like all of Wharton's heroines who risk change and censure, Sophy and Anna have sympathetic imaginations.

By gradually experiencing Sophy's point of view,[31] Anna
sheds the veils that separate her from life. The women eventually change positions when Sophy realizes she cannot marry
a man she does not love, and Anna realizes that she must and
will make love to Darrow. The European influence and the
isolation of Givré diffuse the issue of the individual in conflict with societal standards and focus attention on the individual's struggle with self. In the hope of preventing his own
exile, Darrow, who was to have unbandaged his bride's eyes,
does all he can to stay her growing consciousness; and much
of the novel's tension in the last four books centers on scenes
in which either Anna or Sophy tries to get a straight answer
from him. Contradictory impulses compel Anna to pursue the
truth: she wants reassurance, and she wants to live "the stuff
of great poetry and memorable action." Forced to read "the
intricacies of other hearts" (*Reef*, 278) as well as their own,
Anna and Sophy become skilled readers of nuance and in-
terpreters of the unsaid. Their survival and the preservation
of their world depends on their artistry in this area.[32]

Sophy and Anna's mutual understanding illustrates the
potential Lily Bart mistakenly assumed in her relationship
with Bertha Dorset. Sophy is the lone person who does not
"go back" on Anna, and she can be trusted to tell the truth:
"It's my fault for not knowing how to say what I want you to
hear. Your words are different; you know how to choose
them. Mine offend you . . . and the dread of it makes me
blunder. That's why, the other day, I couldn't say anything
. . . couldn't make things clear to you. But now I *must*, even
if you hate it!" (*Reef*, 305).

Sophy's words reveal the primary reason Wharton's heroines resist competition.[33] Competition engages the competi-
tors in a painfully intimate process. Because the self becomes the referent for analyzing the other, the boundaries
between self and other begin to blur, perhaps merge. For
example, Sophy's unrelenting honesty makes her, as Carol
Wershoven suggests, the reef against which Anna and Dar-

row crash.[34] But in a sea where everyone is drowning, a reef offers the hope of a sure footing. Anna grabs at it because Sophy represents all of the principles she has considered violating.

In one last desperate attempt to retain her romantic illusions—"there *was* such a love as she had dreamed" (*Reef*, 302)—Anna transfers them to the younger woman: "It was Sophy Viner only who could save her—Sophy Viner only who could give her back her lost serenity. She would seek the girl out and tell her that she had given Darrow up; that step once taken there would be no retracing it, and she would perforce have to go forward alone" (*Reef*, 360). Wharton herself did not believe in self-sacrifice or (to borrow a phrase from *The Mother's Recompense*) "sterile pain," and Anna's idealization of Sophy and her attempted renunciation are only final stabs at suppressing her burgeoning consciousness. Anna hopes that by self-denial she can return to her old self, but such hopes are futile. There is no going back.[35]

The same is true for Sophy, who now acts like one of the literary heroines Anna admires. Her sacrifice (if giving up a man you do not love qualifies) is her passport. As she tells Darrow, "Then, when I met you again, I suddenly saw that I *had* risked more, but that I'd won more, too—such worlds!" (*Reef*, 259)—worlds forbidden the imprisoned or marginalized women of Anna's class. The tableau of Sophy's sister, Mrs. McTarvie-Birch, her dog, and her masseur is one Sophy has chosen to flee and one that Wharton has purposefully designed to upset the complacency of readers. Sophy's exile is finally a judgment on a society that has no place for women who defy categorization, and with luck it may provide her with an environment "at once freer and finer" (*Reef*, 92).

Sophy's motives match Penelope's in "Friends," and her exile foreshadows Ellen Olenska's departure for Europe in *The Age of Innocence* (1920). She and Ellen Olenska represent all that Wharton remembers the old New York of her youth lacking: beauty, passion, and danger.[36] *The Age of Innocence* spells out what that lack means for men as well as for women by chronicling the slow desiccation of Newland Archer, a cross between George Darrow and Ralph Marvell.[37] Although the story, which repeats many of *The Reef*'s symbols—veils, thresholds, stifling enclosures, and unspoken words—is Archer's; its congruence and integrity are made possible by the artistry of his wife, May, and the woman he thinks he should have married, her cousin Ellen.

Again, the fair and dark women together make a perfect whole: May is as fresh and virginal and definitive as her name, and Ellen is as dramatic and passionate and mysterious as a "hot-house exotic" (*AI*, 197).[38] When Ellen returns home after leaving her morally corrupt husband, old New York does not know how to respond to a woman who might or might not have sexually rewarded the secretary who aided her escape from Count Olenska's house, but her family rallies and decides to champion her cause if she does not demand a divorce. About to marry into the Mingott clan, Archer is elected its spokesperson, and as he defends her point of view, he begins to reassess his own: "he was once more conscious of the curious way in which she reversed his values" (*AI*, 104).

Rebelling against the values of his insular society, Archer distances himself more and more from May. He increasingly sees her as the repository of his discarded opinions, and his boredom with her is a form of self-disgust. He wants to escape the legacy that makes them twins: "The persons of their world lived in an atmosphere of faint implications and pale delicacies, and the fact that he and she understood each other without a word seemed to the young man to bring them nearer than any explanation would have done" (*AT*, 17). After Ellen's intrusion, May becomes the symbol of all that is rigid, oppressive, and stifling.

Assuming that familiarity excludes complexity, Archer never bothers to reassess this judgment.[39] The novel may be told from his point of view, but Wharton subtly illustrates—as in *Ethan Frome*—its limitations. Archer particularly feels the suffocating, "deadly monotony" (*AI*, 293) of his marriage when guilty or thwarted; for example, after forgetting to meet May at her grandmother's, he unwillingly returns home. Ellen has just told him that there is no country where they can "be simply two human beings who love each other, who are the whole of life to each other; and nothing else on earth will matter" (*AI*, 290). Furthermore, she has insisted that "we're only Newland Archer, the husband of Ellen Olenska's cousin, and Ellen Olenska, the cousin of Newland Archer's wife, trying to be happy behind the backs of the people who trust them" (*AI*, 291); and that definition of both herself and Archer in terms of May makes the weight of his marriage bond and the image of May even more oppressive:

> She was so placed that Archer, by merely raising his eyes, could see her bent above her work-frame, her ruffled elbow-sleeves slipping back from her firm round arms, the betrothal sapphire shining on her left hand above her broad gold wedding-ring, and the right hand slowly and laboriously stabbing the canvas. (*AI*, 294–295)

In this sentence, each successive phrase reads like another shovelful of dirt thrown on his coffin; yet it is May, not Archer, who is fixed in place. His choice of historical reading material has determined that she will pass the evening embroidering instead of listening to him read and discuss poetry. In either case, she is reacting to him, and Wharton's use of the passive tense, the verb *bent*, and the qualifier *so* physically anchor her while conveying her helplessness.

May's stabs at the embroidery canvas silently protest Archer's suspected infidelity. Marriage, however, demands that she surrender a part of her identity. She must not berate her husband for failing to meet her, and she must not mention Madame Olenska. Prominent as an actor in Book 1,

May recedes into the background after her wedding, until the farewell dinner; her gradual removal from the plot in part reflects her decreased individuality after marriage. Given a choice, she would rather be riding or rowing, "but since other wives embroidered cushions for their husbands she did not wish to omit this last link in her devotion" (*AI*, 294). May's position in the drawing room, which denies her the active, physical life to which she is suited, chains her as securely as Archer. She is the better sport, though, and her good nature and seeming passivity are all the more galling to him.

Archer thinks that "by merely raising his eyes" he can see his wife, but the slight action is indicative of how little effort he makes throughout the novel to understand or truly perceive her. He has, for example, missed the meaning of each angry stab that demands an answer. He has persistently refused to analyze the invisible claws that clasped May as soon as she accepted his betrothal sapphire and that are now beginning to lock him within their grasp. For him, "it was less trouble to conform with the tradition and treat May exactly as all his friends treated their wives than to try to put into practice the theories with which his untrammeled bachelorhood had dallied" (*AI*, 195). Archer prefers to see her as a type rather than as an individual, and the picture of her at her work-frame is another in a long tradition of women immortalized doing similar handiwork. He commits the identical error with Ellen, perceiving her in turn as "the foreign adventurer," "the wronged wife," "the true love." This failure of both effort and creativity within accepted forms is what differentiates him from Ellen, makes his life predictable, and leaves him at the novel's end little changed from the young dilettante for whom "thinking over a pleasure to come often gave . . . a subtler satisfaction than its realization" (*AI*, 4).

It also explains the inherent egoism in his decision to retain memories of Ellen of which he is the sole author. Ellen functions more as a symbol for his struggling "self" than as a flesh-and-blood person, and his interactions with her are another form of his interactions with May, "hieroglyphic" dialogue composed of "arbitrary signs" (*AI*, 45), pauses, and silences. Archer's misreading of those signs, his "resolute determination to carry to its utmost limit that ritual of ignoring the 'unpleasant' " (*AI*, 26), leads him mistakenly to assume that Ellen was guilty of adultery. That assumption determines the advice he gives her and his future. When Ellen tells Archer that they don't speak the same language, she knows that the topics and the openness of their speech, which includes words such as "adultery" and "mistress," do not disguise the fact that he never really hears her need for the values that he is preparing to cast aside. Wharton's real target is not Archer, though. It is the society that insists on treating its women as children even after marriage has supposedly plunged them into the real business of living.

For there to be an age of innocence, fire cannot be ice and vice versa, yet May and Ellen are more alike than Archer suspects.[40] After all, both are granddaughters of "Catherine the Great" and possess to some extent her sexuality, "strength of will," "hardness of heart, and a kind of haughty effrontery that was somehow justified by the extreme decency and dignity of her private life" (*AI*, 14). The cousins' last "long, good" talk brings them to a closer understanding of each other and of Archer's dilemma. Underlying their mutual desire to protect Archer from himself is the assumption that he could not escape becoming the prisoner of a hackneyed vocabulary. Adultery is adultery, and the individual case does not mitigate that act.

Like Anna and Sophy before them, May and Ellen collude to keep a loved one innocent. Once Archer makes his decision to marry May, Ellen holds him to his choice.[41] May in turn knows from nearly the beginning that the "other woman" is not Mrs. Thorley Rushworth, for she sends Ellen news of the accelerated wedding date before she informs Archer. Ellen is also the first to know of May's pregnancy. Although May lies about its technical verification, she does not necessarily lie about her intuition of it. Likewise, Ellen can be credited with understanding the feelings that prompt May's confidence because she has already switched positions with Archer as a spokesperson for his culture by the time she tells him:

> ". . . if it's not worthwhile to have given up, to have missed things, so that others may be saved from disillusionment and misery—then everything I came home for, everything that made my other life seem by contrast so bare and so poor because no one there took account of them—all these things are a sham or a dream—" (*AI*, 242)

That statement clearly aligns Ellen with May's values and explains why Ellen now seems like her old self to May (*AI*, 315).[42] The symbiotic nature of their relationship fits the pattern of Wharton's paired heroines.

May's life validates Ellen's renunciation, and Ellen's exile supports May's stand for decency and loyalty and domesticity. At the same time, Wharton calls into question just how much of a sacrifice that is. It is hard to imagine Archer and Ellen any more content than Lawrence Selden and Lily Bart would have been with each other; and an earlier draft of the ending of *The Age of Innocence*, in which Archer and Ellen flee, find they are incompatible, and separate, shows Wharton agreeing. All of Archer's training would subvert their union, and over time it would probably grow to resemble his and May's. "Souls Belated," published in 1899, makes much the same point when its heroine discovers that her lover wants to duplicate the stiflingly conventional marriage that she has just fled. Ellen's end, which is a more positive version of Sophy Viner's, seems preferable to either Archer's or May's. She at least has enjoyed good conversation.

Archer's life has little prepared him to meet a grown-up woman, one who has lived and loved independently, and his decision not to see her after his wife's death shows the parameters of his fear. Instead of meeting life, he retreats into his own inner sanctuary. Although the context of his decision makes it appear as a tribute to his life with May, it is primarily motivated by his desire to keep that private space solely his. Inviting a visitor would necessitate a collaborative vision of life, and Archer has never wanted to negotiate that. As a result, his innermost room is nothing more than a tastefully appointed and comfortable prison.

Dallas exposes the waste and pathos of his parents' marrige when he confesses: "She [May] said she knew we were safe with you and always would be, because once, when she asked you to, you'd given up the thing you most wanted" (*AI*, 356). Dallas's indiscretion removes "an iron band" from Archer's heart: "someone had guessed and pitied. . . . And that it should have been his wife moved him indescribably" (*AI*, 356–357). Resembling the protagonist in "The Long Run," who shies from risk and realizes too late what he has missed, Archer rediscovers that his original vision of his life with May proved to be correct: "Evidently she was always going to understand; she was always going to say the right thing" (*AI*, 24). The resurrection of May's image demands a revision of the past and shows how misguided and wrongheaded has been the collusion of husband and children to keep her innocent (*AI*, 348). Like John Marcher in Henry James's "The Beast in the Jungle" (1903), Archer must now contend with all those wasted, silent years in which May (perhaps tragically or heroically or contentedly) occupied her own separate sanctuary. She emerges as the novel's true heroine, for as Ellen told Archer years ago: "The real loneliness is living among all these kind people who only ask one to pretend" (*AI*, 78). In this context May resembles the wives in short stories such as "Joy in the House," "The Letters," "The Quicksand," and "The Lamp of Psyche."

By doing all they can to protect Owen and Archer, Anna and Sophy and Ellen and May condemn themselves to living

with them in "a deaf-and-dumb asylum" (*AI*, 356) in which
the inhabitants—none of whom is artless, naive, or guiltless—
are innocent of completely understanding each other. The fall
may be fortunate, but those who have experienced it rather
chauvinistically dread it happening to those they love. In *The
Age of Innocence*, Wharton draws attention to the absurdity
of the situation while paradoxically seeming to support it, as
if only a lifetime of inarticulation (*AI*, 356) can maintain the
type of innocence necessary to sustain concepts such as
"loyalty" and "fidelity." To apply Nancy K. Miller's observa-
tions about women's fiction, readers "see and hear repeat-
edly a chafing against the 'unsatisfactory reality' " contained
in the maxims about human nature and culture that shape
Wharton's novels, but they do not see a rejection of those
maxims.[43]

All of Wharton's short stories that deal with the marriage
question have qualified endings. In "The Quicksand," for example, a mother tries to convince her future daughter-in-law
not to marry her son, the publisher of a scandal sheet, because he "believes in his work; he adores it—it is a kind of
hideous idol to which he would make human sacrifices!"[44] In
a last effort to save this younger version of herself, the
mother confesses, "He loves you still—I've been honest with
you—but his love wouldn't change him. It is you who would
have to change—to die gradually, as I have died, till there is
only one live point left in me" ("Quicksand," 410). If May's
story were told, it too would be a chronicle of small wakes.
By suggesting its outline, Wharton subtly asks us to see
beyond the appealing image of Newland Archer reaffirming
his past to that of a gentleman who "simply stayed home and
abstained" (*AI*, 126).

The surface text denies May's story by portraying Archer
as a man who has resolved his conflict with "the responsibilities that necessarily precede maturity and individual integrity."[45] This leads Gary Lindberg to argue that "it is difficult
to fault either the understanding or the moral seriousness in-

forming Wharton's portrait of Newland Archer, yet to accept what she says makes one feel somehow smaller."[46] The ending rings false and does so in part because Archer's vision is so myopic. He has spent his life hiding. The fiction he preserves, the renunciation he embraces, and the kind of deaf-and-dumb theatrical he has chosen are all self-protective ways of avoiding the business of living outside the private sanctuary for one. Unlike Ellen and unlike his author, he has not used creatively the freedom his privacy permits. Ellen may also occupy a single sanctuary, but because she has fearlessly met life, it is hard to imagine her missing what eludes Archer, its "flower" (*AI*, 347). Critics who see the ending as confirming "the integrity of his life"[47] are championing a day whose values have proved inadequate for dealing with the individual case. As the case of Dallas Archer and Beaufort's bastard daughter Fanny shows, the world is well rid of many of old New York's values.

Wharton herself seems to agree, but covertly, for these books show the intellectual and emotional limitations of marriage without really challenging the assumption that men and women *must* marry. Although Sophy does not marry, and Ellen lives apart from her husband, they are still ultimately defined in the context of their society by their marital status. Ellen has more respect as Madame Olenska than as the divorced wife of a count; and as a young, pretty, and dependent single young woman, Sophy is particularly vulnerable. Wharton exposes and analyzes the cultural forces that result when women are defined by their mate's status, but she offers no replacement. She never suggests, for example, as did Mary Wilkins and Ellen Glasgow, that women remain single; nor did she, like Mary Austin and Willa Cather, consider women's emotional and/or sexual relationships with each other as an alternative.

Instead, Wharton accepted the status quo and raged against it. Her own life after her divorce from Teddy Wharton resembled Ellen Olenska's, but she did not advocate it for others or approve of the New Woman. In this way Wharton was herself a romantic, who could not abandon the belief that there was a perfect soulmate for most people, even if there was not one for her. This assumption makes her a prisoner of the marriage plot; and although she may revolt against it and see beyond it, she still perpetuates it—at least on the surface of her texts. *The Fruit of the Tree* (1907) particularly illustrates this tension, for Justine Brent has the courage to leave her husband when he no longer believes in her but does not have the heart to destroy the illusion (that eases her return) of his first wife's beneficence. Justine saves Bessy's memory at the cost of her own ideals. The dominant text tells the story of diminished dreams and expectations, but the subtext implies that in a more perfect society women could play a central role in each other's lives.

Despite Wharton's belief that marriage necessarily separates and inhibits relationships between women, friendship supersedes rivalry. *The Reef* and *The Age of Innocence* are illustrations. Unfortunately, the meaning with which marriage or romance is supposed to imbue life is simply absent from any Wharton novel, and it leads to the conclusion that life is at best a compromise lived within a solitary sanctuary. Wharton's paired heroines resist this thinking and act either to save or to reconstruct their worlds. But they do not do enough. All too often their actions preserve a system that victimizes them foremost. If men and women are to share anything but a drawing room, if fire and ice are to coexist, the world must be revisioned. For that to happen, future generations must refuse to spend "an inarticulate lifetime" (*AI*, 356). All consciousness, all communication, all time is "just a perpetual piecing together of broken bits" (*Reef*, 313); and though speaking aloud may shatter the illusion of knowing more about one another's thoughts than one's own, there is the hope that the broken bits can be pieced together to form a serviceable vessel.

CHAPTER SIX

Edith Wharton's Recompense

> *A deep reverence for the family ties, for the sanctities of tradition, the claims of slowly acquired convictions and slowly formed precedents, is revealed in every page of her books.*
>
> —*"GEORGE ELIOT"*

Fourteen years before the publication of *The Mother's Recompense* (1925), Edith Wharton went to great lengths to dissociate *Ethan Frome* (1911) from the local colorist tradition and the "rose-coloured" ranks of Sarah Orne Jewett and Mary Wilkins. Yet the brief explanatory note that also serves as an introduction to the 1925 novel draws attention to her connection with Aguilar, a sentimentalist, by apologizing "to the decorous shade of Grace Aguilar, loved of our grandmothers, for deliberately appropriating and applying to uses so different, the title of one of the most admired of her tales."[1] The description of Aguilar as decorous might be read only as a critical evaluation of her work, but coming from someone who never chose her words lightly, who herself was so conscious of the value of decoration, who desired both to appear decorous and to act with decorum, the adjective is a tribute to the woman and a compliment to another professional.

   The selection of title and subject are a link to Wharton's personal and literary pasts. Although a generation separates their authors, Mrs. Hamilton and Mrs. Clephane exist in a similar sentimental atmosphere. Critics who tend to see Wharton's use of the earlier title as an ironic comment on changes effected not only in decorum but also in the moral complexity of mother-daughter relationships overlook the additional fact that her appropriation commits her to a dialogue with Aguilar.[2] This exchange reverses Wharton's usual pattern of almost belligerently declaring her differences from (and implied superiority to) other women writers. Thinking that the differences with Aguilar speak for themselves perhaps, she is unthreatened and willing to risk comparison between her work and that of another woman writer, whom she would have characterized as belonging to a literary tradition antithetical to hers.[3] Seen together, however, the two novels do not offer as much an index of social change as Wharton probably assumed, for in two significant ways, they are analogous. Both are constrained by the marriage plot and by the social context in which they were written.

   Aguilar's "tale," of more than five hundred pages, could be subtitled "Mother Knows Best." Written as a sequel to *Home Influence*, it fulfills the promise of its title: a pious and dutiful mother is rewarded when her children achieve her own felicity of mind. The most serious threat to the family occurs when one daughter's vanity leads her to suppose herself in love with a man of poor character. Already married, he plans her ruin by encouraging her rebellious and headstrong impulses. His design, though, is thwarted when the image of the girl's mother appears to her as the madonna appeared to Bernadette. Instead of eloping, she flees home. Surrounded at the novel's end by her grandchildren, Mrs. Hamilton can truly say, "There are many sorrows and many cares inseparable from maternal love, but they are forgotten, utterly forgotten, or only remembered to enhance the sweetness of the recompense that ever follows."[4]

Kate Clephane can agree only in part. Pain does help to define and sharpen sweetness, but it brings neither unqualified satisfaction nor forgetfulness. Wharton does not allow her to receive a recompense comparable to Mrs. Hamilton's until she herself has made peace with the past. Called home by the grown daughter she deserted eighteen years earlier, when she left her husband and ran off with another, long-since-forgotten man, Kate slowly realizes that her daughter plans to marry her ex-lover, Chris Fenno. She then torments herself about the advisibility of revealing the past and preventing the marriage. Deciding not to cause "sterile pain" (*MR*, 266) and to let Anne have her own chance, Kate rejects a marriage proposal from an old friend, Fred Landers, and returns to her previous aimless life. Her fate shows how difficult it was for Wharton to mold the standard plot of two women and one man satisfactorily to her own literary and psychological uses.

In her decision to separate herself from contemporary American women writers, Wharton, like Kate, sentenced herself to a self-imposed exile. Yet her claim that other women writers exerted no influence on her work is as accurate as saying that her mother had no effect on her life. In *A Room of One's Own*, Virginia Woolf argues that Jane Austen, the Brontës, and George Eliot could not have written without forerunners such as Aphra Behn, and the same holds true for Wharton. R. W. B. Lewis discusses the novelist herself as one of those forerunners when he describes *The Mother's Recompense* as reflecting "Edith's clarifying sense of herself as a woman and a writer of a certain age, testing out her relationship to those much younger than she."[5] He observes that when Wharton talked about the relationship between generations in the 1920s, she most often "meant *literary* generations—more particularly, her own relation, as a woman in her sixties who had come to literary fruition twenty years before, with the younger writers who were appearing on the postwar scene to varying acclaim."[6] Noting a

similarity between Wharton and Kate Clephane in their expatriation, Lewis speculates that one layer of the novel expresses the author's desire to establish contact with the new
generation of American authors.

The writers Lewis mentions, with whom Wharton felt the
generational literary gap most bridgeable—F. Scott Fitzgerald and Sinclair Lewis—were male. Kate Clephane,
though, comes home to her daughter, and this distinction is
important because, if we accept Lewis's speculation, it indicates Wharton's yearning for a literary daughter rather than
a literary son. Lewis accurately interprets Wharton as a person whose "identity as a human being and a writer could
only be forged, and reforged, by effecting ties in both directions."[7] Unfortunately, she never forged lasting ties with a
younger compatriot woman writer.[8] Reviewers who tended
to discuss Wharton and Woolf together, for example, and
who saw Wharton in comparison as hopelessly old-fashioned
must have increased her sense of isolation from the new generation of women writers. Lewis's discussion of the novel
emphasizes Wharton's ties to the future, but her borrowing
of Aguilar's title is one of those powerful ties backward,
beyond "the age of innocence" she wrote about five years earlier in 1920. Wharton's recycling of Aguilar's title is a first
and significant step in her identification with a women's literary tradition. *Hudson River Bracketed* and *The Gods Arrive* further the journey.

In addition, *The Mother's Recompense* marks a willingness
on the novelist's part to examine fictionally the painful relationship with her own mother, Lucretia Jones. After its
completion, her work suggestively broadens in *Twilight Sleep*
(1927) and *The Children* (1928) to include more obvious examples of poor fathering. Wharton's sensitivity to her fictional mother's dilemma and her exploration of Kate's
growth points to a rethinking of her own mother-daughter
drama. In *The Mother's Recompense*, Wharton creates a

mother who is in many ways the opposite of Lucretia. Kate Clephane, for example, thinks that "reality and durability were attributes of the humdrum, the prosaic, and the dreary" (*MR*, 5). Disliking the prosaic, which Lucretia so represented, Kate recognizes and approves of her daughter's need for an independent artistic life. In a revision of the disastrous "drawing-rooms are always tidy" scene between the author and her own mother, Kate does not make Lucretia's mistake. Instead, she is rewarded by her daughter's pleasure when she instinctively compliments Anne's "rough but vivid oil-sketch of a branch of magnolias" (*MR*, 42).

The Mother's Recompense has as many layered meanings as *A Backward Glance*. It can be read in part as a wishful rewriting of Wharton's history with her mother, in which she creates a mother who is sensitive and appreciative, even a little beholden to and awed by her daughter's character and talents. This reading elevates the daughter, and though mother and daughter must part, the former is rewarded by the latter's magnificence and magnanimity. Underlying this interpretation is the assumption that the mother does not quite deserve the daughter. Only the parent's altruism allows her to reclaim the relationship, and that from the distance of Europe. It is not hard to imagine the part of Wharton that would always remain the unappreciated and rejected child, the child who needed to see Lucretia as not quite deserving if she were to preserve her own sense of self-worth. From this perspective, Kate's dependence on her daughter's judgment of herself as a worthy companion and her intermittent fear of Anne's withdrawal of her approval seem a logical and empowering rewrite of a relationship in which the mother—to borrow D. W. Winnicott's phrase—was not "good enough."[9] It is also not difficult to imagine Wharton creating a mother to replace her own and developing a fantasy in which the daughter reshapes the mother. The puns in Kate's last name (*clef* and fain), for example, underscore the need for another to unlock her. In this reading, which I will develop, Kate Clephane becomes a good mother, a morally and emotionally richer person, through her relationship with her daughter. The Clephanes' example represents the perfect psychological solution for the child who found compensation for the loss of her mother by "making up" in that parent's bedroom. There, through fantasy and play, Wharton created a psychic realm, what Winnicott calls "potential space," in which she achieved a comfortable balance between fusion and separation.[10]

The Mother's Recompense and Wharton's later fiction in general show the author working through her own ambivalence about mother-daughter relationships. In a generational reversal, Kate is the prodigal. Returning to the scene of her unhappy marriage and to the stranger who is her daughter, she proceeds to define herself—in terms that coincide with Nancy Chodorow's and Carol Gilligan's models of female development—by her resemblance to and otherness from Anne.[11] Kate knows that her relationship with Anne depends on her respecting Anne's otherness, but at the same time, her image of herself depends on seeing the sameness.

The women's likenesses are not readily apparent. Rich, powerful, and beloved, Anne possesses all her mother lacks. In comparison, Kate seems immature and assailed by self-doubt. She has lived in a succession of shabby, cramped rooms in third-rate hotels in the company of people who "want to forget" (*MR*, 5) and who live in "a chronic state of mental inaccuracy, excitement and inertia, which made it vaguely exhilarating to lie and definitely fatiguing to be truthful" (*MR*, 27). In such company Kate cannot conceive of unbaring her secret, naming her daughter (*MR*, 34), but in truth she cannot actually name Anne because the child has always been more a concept, a dream, a part of the romance and tragedy of her own narrative than a reality. Even her initial longing for Anne finds imaginative expression through another's story: Anna Karenina's midnight visit to her child's nursery (*MR*, 18).

Kate's habit of seeing herself as a character has resulted in her distancing herself from her feelings. Now "being face to face with her own thoughts was like facing a stranger" (*MR*, 21). Anticipating her reunion with Anne, for example, Kate projects a future drama: "My daughter . . . my daughter Anne. . . . Oh, you don't know my little girl? She *has* changed, hasn't she? Growing up is a way the children have. . . . Yes, it is ageing for a poor mother to trot about such a young giantess. . . . Oh, I'm going gray already, you know —here, on the temples" (*MR*, 15). Her self-absorbed fantasy underscores Kate's own immaturity, for Kate is only grown-up in a wordly sense (knowing what is what), not by the standards of the old New York of her early marriage, where old Mrs. Clephane would have been the first to censor such vanity and implied sexual competition between mother and daughter. When Anne becomes the vehicle for Kate's learning that mothers also must grow up and change, Kate does not again reject the now outdated standards of her youth. Her exile at the novel's end is a replay of the past in its repetition of action but not in its motivation. Whether, in fact, Kate's first leave-taking was impulsive and selfish, the second is deliberate and altruistic. Even if one agrees that the decision to leave is an assertion of her identity, it does not necessarily follow that the identities of woman and mother are mutually exclusive. They might have been if Kate had decided to remain in New York and play grandmother to Anne and Chris's children. But Kate's homecoming forces her to reevaluate her younger self; and when the illusion of herself as the youthful mother of a young Amazon proves woefully inadequate, she must reformulate her definition of "motherhood."

Living for nearly twenty years "with women of her own kind" has ill-prepared Kate for the role of mother. The tele-

gram leading to her recall reads: "Mrs. Clephane dead," simultaneously heralding the death of one Mrs. Clephane and
the second birth of another.[12] The new Kate is a child, innocent of the changes wrought by her daughter's generation
and the war on the old New York of her first youth. Anne
takes her in and protects her: "You must never be tired or
worried about things any more; I won't have it; we won't any
of us have it. Remember, I'm here to look after you now—
and so is Uncle Fred" (*MR*, 57). In Book 2 it is Kate who
needs to sink "down into a very Bethesda-pool of forgetfulness and peace" (*MR*, 57) and be " 'mothered' in that fond
blundering way the young have of mothering their elders"
(*MR*, 59). Wharton's descriptions of Kate in the first stages
of that relationship emphasize her decreasing individuality,
her urge for union with, as opposed to differentiation from,
Anne: "Kate felt as if they were two parts of some delicate
instrument which fitted together as perfectly as if they had
never been disjoined—as if Anne were that other half of her
life, the half she had dreamed of and never lived" (*MR*,
75-76). The image is reminiscent of Lily Bart cradling Nettie Struther's baby in her arms.

Experiencing "the blessed anonymity of motherhood," Kate
understands "how exposed and defenseless her poor unsup-
ported personality had been through all the lonely years"
(*MR*, 81). She is acutely aware of discovering the miracle of
mothering but less aware of the joy of being mothered, as
Anne performs for her many of the traditional motherly ser-
vices: providing security, shelter, safety, and most important, the respectability necessary to relaunch her into society. Kate herself recognizes that "Anne's very insistence on
treating her as the mistress of the house only emphasized
her sense of not being so by right: it was the verbal courtesy
of the Spaniard who puts all his possessions at the disposal of
a casual visitor" (*MR*, 88).

Kate is more than that. We know that before her arrival

Anne was lonely and that she and old Mrs. Clephane often disagreed, but because we see everything through Kate's often limited consciousness, we can only guess to what extent Anne shares Kate's wish:

> To be with Anne, to play the part of Anne's mother—the one part, she now saw, that fate had meant her for—that was what she wanted with all her starved and world-worn soul. To be the background, the atmosphere, of her daughter's life; to depend on Anne, to feel that Anne depended on her; it was the one perfect companionship she had ever known, the only close tie unmarred by dissimulation and distrust. The mere restfulness of it had made her contracted soul expand as if it were sinking into a deep warm bath. (*MR*, 87)

The womb imagery of this passage blurs the distinction between mother and child and emphasizes the innocence and naivete of Kate's wish. By agreeing to Anne's right to take her own chance with Chris and "to buy" her "own experience" (*MR*, 234), Kate does provide the background, the atmosphere, for Anne's life. She is also consenting—at much cost to herself—to be relegated to the background.

The background and atmosphere of Anne's existence has worked its magic and helped her to recognize her need to reassess and readjust her own sense of her identity. Even though Kate has done her best "to organize her life in such a way that it should fit into Anne's without awkward overlapping" (*MR*, 102–103), it is an impossibility. Dissimulation and distrust become a necessary part of life to protect her daughter. As readers, we might well question if Anne and Chris can have a successful marriage, if it were ever possible for Kate to protect Anne, if Kate's silence is another way of not permitting Anne to buy her own experience, and if Kate's self-administered dose of sterile pain is a form of self-flagellation and martyrdom.

Certainly, when Anne wants to marry Chris Fenno, Kate is forced to struggle with the conflicting feelings of mother and woman. She thinks that "life without Anne," "like life before Anne" is now "unthinkable" (*MR*, 105). But she underestimates the power of a love strong enough to make her feel as if "her center of gravity" exists "in a life not hers" (*MR*, 104). Such a love can even make life without Anne thinkable. Motherhood is no longer a pleasant daydream, an illusion. It is a needle in the heart. At the same time, it gives life a new dimension of dignity.

Kate's final renunciation allows her to retain this sense of life's expanded worth, which she has only discerned through her relationship with her daughter. Previously defining herself by her relationships with men, Kate thought that her real self had been born at thirty-nine and that without Chris "she would never have had a self" (*MR*, 18), but she learns that "there was one thing much closer to her now than any conceivable act of Chris's could ever be; and that was her own relation to Anne" (*MR*, 134). Mother and woman are not only no longer mutually exclusive, but now Kate defines herself solely in relation to her gender. This shift in her orientation is reminiscent of Lily Bart and Anna Leath, and in part it explains her refusal to marry Fred. In this context Kate's marriage would seem retrogressive.

The shift means giving up the illusion that Chris left her for another woman, instead of growing tired of her or outgrowing her, and living with the knowledge that "she would never, as long as she lived, be able to think evil of Chris without its hurting her" (*MR*, 164). It means recognizing that what she dislikes in her flamboyant niece Lilla is what she dislikes in herself. It means confronting her own jealousy of her daughter, acquiring a grudging respect for the old Mrs. Clephane, whom Anne in part resembles, facing the fact that she and Fred Landers are nearly the same age, and realizing that there must always be some hurtful truth in

Anne's assertion "You don't know me either, mother!" (*MR*, 191). Inherent in all of these examples of Kate's growing consciousness and maturation is a recognition of lost fictions and a lost definition of self. She has been living as if the past were irrevocable and now finds it is not. This realization makes Kate's last twenty years seem even more seedy to herself in retrospect and leads to the self-abasing and guilt-ridden thought that she was incapable of raising a daughter like Anne: "She was rewarded for having given up her daughter; if she had not, could she ever have known such a moment as this?" (*MR*, 83). Her wish to see Anne living the other half of her life, "to help shape the perfection she had sought and missed" (*MR*, 76), also comes from a sense of her own inadequacy and a desire to redo her own life through Anne's.

The novel's incestuous undercurrent reinforces this sense of Kate and Anne's merger, as when the maid at the Fennos' house thinks that Anne is Kate, the woman who came before and made a scene (*MR*, 198). Kate herself is more repulsed by the idea of her daughter marrying her ex-lover than are any of her confidants, and this discrepancy partly reflects the self-destructiveness inherent in Kate's nearly total identification with Anne. Although the incest motif finds a parallel to some degree in Wharton's own "family romance," the struggle with her mother for possession of her father,[13] the primary focus in *The Mother's Recompense*—as it was in *Ethan Frome*—is on the same-sex bond. The women's identification goes far beyond physical and emotional similarities. At one time Kate feels that "her own sobs were shaking her daughter's body" and that "she no longer knew what she herself was feeling. All her consciousness had passed into Anne" (*MR*, 236). Kate's definition of mothers and daughters explains this sensation: "Mothers and daughters are part of each other's consciousness, in different degrees and in a different way, but still with the mutual sense of something which has always been there" (*MR*, 194). In other words, mothers and daughters are so much of each other that they are unconscious of each other. Kate wanted this kind of relationship with Anne without realizing that it also implies an underlying sense of loss, a decrease in conscious intimacy and in the intensity of living in and breathing each other's atmosphere. This is the hardest of all illusions to surrender. Giving it up means that she must redefine her concept of "mother" as being identical to daughter and must see mothers and daughters more in terms of the model of being same and "other." Kate's acceptance of her difference and separation from Anne brings a feeling of loss, but it also allows her to choose her own identity at the end of the novel; for if her interests were identical to Anne's, then marriage with Fred Landers would almost inevitably be the surest way of securing Anne's peace of mind.

Wharton implies that as a mother Kate cannot escape suffering. This premise, vastly differing from the view of motherhood presented in *Ethan Frome*, also underlies the novella *The Old Maid* (1924) and the short story, "Autre Temps. . . . "[14] In the former, a mother, Charlotte Lovell, protects her daughter from the stain of illegitimacy by having her cousin Delia raise her as her own. Aunt Charlotte lives in the same house as her daughter Tina and must suffer as she sees her daughter confide in and love another first. She must endure the fact that Tina will never truly know her and that what Tina does know about her (she is an old maid) diminishes her in her daughter's eyes. In this story Charlotte receives her recompense when Tina escapes repeating her own folly and is safely married.

Delia may publicly and effortlessly reap all of the commonly accepted joys and tributes of motherhood, but Charlotte too has her joy. Hiding the fact of her actual relationship to Tina adds a poignant and enriching resonance to her life. Every interaction has a nuance known only to herself and to some degree to Delia. Charlotte's secret and heroic altruism is little more than her society expects of women. Yet it also secretly empowers her by allowing her a covert and superior pleasure over those who persist in summing her up as "the old maid." In this way she resembles Mrs. Ansley in "Roman Fever," whose knowledge about her daughter's birth and parentage helps her to maintain a sense of amused tolerance with her best friend and rival, Mrs. Slade. As one of a great army of silent and subversive women, Charlotte represents a lurking threat. If exposed, her and Delia's public masquerade would call into question the ways that their society agrees to construct and define reality.

In "Autres Temps . . . ," a mother, ostracized by society upon her divorce, returns home to protect her daughter in a similar situation and finds, ironically, that times have indeed changed for the younger generation but not for hers. She can take some comfort in the fact that the same is not true for her daughter, even if she will always be the woman whom the ambassador's wife cuts. The mothers in *The Old Maid* and "Autres Temps . . ." refuse to be protected, rescued, or pitied. Even if life is a painful, compromised affair, at least it is one of their own choosing. Kate is not unlike them. The idea that suffering is a component of love and loneliness a component of intimacy echoes *The Old Maid*, just as Kate's return to her former life echoes the ending of "Autres Temps. . . ." Only after Anne, suspicious of her mother's history with Chris, gravely wounds her with the words "a relation . . . can't be improvised in a day," "you must leave me to manage my life in my own way," does Kate claim her daughter by whispering, "Goodnight—my child" (*MR*, 202).

Kate's recognition of the waste in causing sterile pain recalls Ellen Olenska's feeling that it was worthwhile to have missed things "so that others may be saved from disillusionment and misery."[15] This reasoning also further helps to explain Kate's later refusal to marry Uncle Fred: "it seems to me . . . my refusing . . . the one thing that keeps me from being too hopeless, too unhappy. . . . It's what I live by" (*MR*, 341). In this reading, Fred's acceptance of Kate and her past is symbolic of the best of old New York, and as such, Kate can bless him "for giving her the strength to hold out against its pleadings" (*MR*, 342). Kate's new identity, then, is defined by being able to say to herself "that once at least she had stood fast, shutting away in a little space of peace and light the best thing that had ever happened to her" (*MR*, 342). The best thing in this case is not Fred's love but his recognition of and respect for her as an individual. Anne's life distinguishes Kate as a woman who has stood for something. Kate's enlarged vision allows her to see the beneficial, as well as the destructive, side of old New York and to make peace with her husband's point of view and her mother-in-law's standards. Because they have proved such inadequate barricades "against the alarming business of living" (*MR*, 73), she can even think of them a little nostalgically. Marrying Fred would protect Kate from the life to which she returns, but it would also mean giving up a large degree of her own autonomy to live in a society that makes her feel slightly uncomfortable. In this vein, Adeline Tintner argues that Kate's recompense "is the restitution of her own personality which confirms an existence beyond her relation to a husband or a child."[16] What is disturbing, though, about Kate's return to her previous life-style is its resemblance—at least on the surface—to Hester Prynne's return to her New England village and her redonning of the scarlet letter. Like Hester, Kate proudly and defiantly chooses to define herself as an outsider. Her choice highlights how very much she has changed, especially because her growth, like most of Wharton's heroines', is a result of her relationship with another woman, her daughter. Even the man who made her feel first born could not affect her to this degree.

In either reading the ending seems unsatisfactory, as if Kate must indeed sell her soul, her memories, and her future for her daughter (MR, 276). It also shows Wharton rebelling against the three rules of domestic fiction: women must marry if they are not to be parenthesized; husbands by definition hold the balance of power in the family; and a woman must use her influence to acquire power.[17] Rejecting these, Wharton has no satisfactory alternative for disposing of Kate. For this reason Elizabeth Ammons sees the novel as a "harsh book" and one that exposes Wharton's belief that "mothers oughtn't ever to leave their daughters" (*MR*, 235). However, instead of sacrificing Kate "as a person to her theoretical preoccupation with Kate the mother," as Ammons argues, Wharton is trying to give Kate her own plot.[18] Her solution is ironically an endorsement of Aguilar's vision. Like Sophy Viner before her, Kate deserves another chapter several years hence.

Whether or not Wharton was creating a substitute mother in Kate Clephane, the replacement has its own problems. No matter how appealing the idea of unconditional love, it can tacitly exact an oppressive remittance: a mother who feels each pulse of her daughter risks her own identity and threatens to subsume her child's. For mother and daughter to be individuals, they must separate, pursue their own interests, "buy their own experience," no matter how others judge it. Each must think of the other as Wharton thought of Morton Fullerton: "I judged you long ago, & I accepted you as you are."[19] This definition of "love" is embedded in the novel's conclusion. Acceptance does not guarantee approval, and as a working out of this psychological conundrum, perhaps *The Mother's Recompense* must come to an unsatisfactory conclusion.

Anne becomes Anne Clephane Fenno, a person whom we and she cannot yet define and for whom we cannot predict the future. Kate becomes a mother, her definition of that role having changed from one of near total identification with her child to one of controlled and respectful distance. Kate will probably never feel that Chris is the right husband for Anne, but she gives Anne the chance to buy her own experience. Kate cannot refuse her daughter the same chance that she herself more than once has asserted her right to claim, and her acceptance of Anne's right to fashion her own life is itself an affirmation of life, warts and all. It is also a variation from Wharton's usual pattern in that Kate does not protect Anne in the same way that Anna and Sophy protect Owen in *The Reef*. It again suggests that women must help each other to be grown-up, and if Anne, for example, were to ask Kate (as Wharton asked her mother) to explain what happens after marriage, Kate would tell her in sufficient detail.[20] We can only hope that the daughter will not deny her mother the same chance to make her own mistakes and that Anne will respond to her opportunity by becoming more open to her mother's past and present life, following the example of Aunt Enid in response to her daughter Lilla instead of the example of her grandmother, old Mrs. Clephane.

Although Kate has changed and grown as our perception and understanding of her has grown, her return brings the novel full circle. The process of writing a mother-daughter story brings Wharton herself full circle. The writer-daughter is also the mother-creator. The ending to *The Mother's Recompense* shows a mother and daughter who have made a qualified peace, and if Kate in some ways functions as Lucretia Jones, it suggests that Wharton was able to do the same. Lucretia may always remain, for her daughter, prosaic and blindly insensitive, but she was also the least pretty daughter, who had to make do with hand-me-down slippers and who therefore grew up to have an inordinate love of clothes instead of literature. At the same time, a part of Wharton herself may be incorporated in Kate's characterization, the part that longed for a child. In this context Kate's

abdication of her motherly role, her expatriation, her un-
married state, and her independence are all signs of the author's satisfaction with the choices that she bought with her
own experience.

Such insight can bring its own recompense, a sense of
greater freedom from the constraint and restraint of the
past and its internalized voices that manacle the heart. Loos-
ing those chains would give one more latitude to forge ties to
the future without losing the often restrictive but also comforting tether to the past. It would make Wharton's hope
possible: "to keep intact as many links as possible between
yesterday and tomorrow, to lose, in the ardour of new exper-
iment, the least that may be of the long rich heritage of human experience."[21] For Wharton, the stakes in a literary and
a personal past marked an artistic well. The ending to *The
Mother's Recompense* suggests that as she grew older, the
waters tasted less bitter.

Wharton's plea to let one live his or her own life is reiter-
ated three years later in *The Children*, a story of a foster father's love of a fifteen-year-old girl. Martin Boyne, the surrogate father, considers himself "a critical cautious man of
forty-six, whom nobody could possibly associate with the
romantic or the unexpected," but he is captivated by both in
the person of the eldest Wheater child, Judith.[22] She has assumed responsibility for all of the children and stepchildren
of her parents' multiple marriages and has sworn to keep
them together. Boyne admires her efforts, and she soon re-
places his fiancée as "the fixed point on which his need for
permanence could build" (*Children*, 82).

Originally, this novel's ending would have recapitulated
the ending of *Summer*. In Wharton's first version, Boyne
marries Judy, who is now seventeen years old and heart-
broken after the death of her brother Terry. The outline she
sent to Appleton read: "He sees the folly of the marriage, and
yet is so frightened by her loneliness . . . that, having ob-

tained the consent of her parents, Boyne marries her—but as if he were taking a little sister home. . . . The story ends on this note of quiet emotion, sad yet hopeful."[23] This conclusion imprisons Judy in perpetual childhood. As Boyne's little sister she can never fully be his wife. The protection his home offers her and her siblings is at the cost of "the waking consciousness of her beauty and the power it exercised" (*Children*, 347). Both would miss "the flower of life" because this marriage can never be one in which "the power of each sex is balanced by the other"; it can never be what Wharton termed in *French Ways and Their Meaning* "grown-up."[24]

The conclusion on which Wharton decided, however, not only gives Judy her chance to grow up, it also empowers her. When Boyne delicately proposes to Judy, she responds: "Do you really mean you're going to adopt us all, and we're all going to stay with you forever?" (*Children*, 309). Her question marks the termination of Boyne's second boyhood and the beginning of his "long apprenticeship" to "this perpetual obsession, this clinging nearness, this breaking on the rack of every bone, and tearing apart of every fibre" (*Children*, 323). His illusion is as painful to surrender as Kate Clephane's fantasy of her Amazon daughter. More important, Judy's question marks her chance to buy her own experience.

Like the ending to *The Mother's Recompense*, the ending of *The Children* could also be called harsh. Boyne's fiancée, Rose Sellars, is a mature, sensitive, and ethical woman, but he finds her wanting.[25] Because Rose is already defined, because she is more than a blank book waiting to be authored, she bores him. Worse, refusing to be "the shadow and echo of his mood,"[26] she objects to embracing a ready-made family. Boyne's definition of femininity is obviously inadequate, for Rose cannot speak her mind without being metaphorically stripped of her womanhood. She appears either unfeminine or unmotherly. But Wharton does not offer any better model. Judy's mother, for example, is an overaged flapper, and

Judy herself is still largely unformed, untutored, and uncultured.[27] Wharton has some difficulty in imagining a society in which Kate Clephane would flourish, but it is simply impossible for her to envision it being her own. In a Wharton novel, for example, a female equivalent of the American Adam would be doomed, especially since Lewis defines him as "an individual emancipated from history, happily bereft of ancestry, untouched and undefiled by the usual inheritances of family and race; an individual standing alone, self-reliant and self-propelling, ready to confront whatever awaited him with the aid of his own unique and inherent resources."[28] This Adam's Eve is inconceivable to an author who above all valued "taste, reverence, continuity, and intellectual honesty" (*French Ways*, 22).

A woman enters the world, as Wharton knows it, already defiled "by the usual inheritances of family and race." Society dictates that she never stand alone or unprotected and does everything possible to prohibit her becoming "self-reliant and self-propelling." Women exist only in community, only in a social context. Biology denies them the dream of an Emersonian self-reliance. They can neither create utopian communities in the wilderness nor revolutionize the status quo. The outcome of Justine Brent's social evangelism, for example, is at the cost of personal integrity. In this way, Wharton's and Auguilar's purposes are not opposed. Wharton explains that "the woman whose mind is attuned to men's minds has a much larger view of the world, and attaches much less importance to trifles, because men, being usually brought by circumstances into closer contact with reality, insensibly communicate their breadth of view to women" (*French Ways*, 119). She attributed this breadth of view to French women and saw it denied to her own compatriots. In response, her characters, like Charlotte Lovell, are sleeping giants who outwardly conform while inwardly they rebel.

Even her heroines such as Sophy Viner, who most defy

categorization, have no really viable alternative to marriage. Wharton could not summarily dismiss the importance of an institution that she believed necessary for the continuation of the family and, by extension, of the culture (*French Ways,* 128). Belonging to a European tradition, Ellen Olenska perhaps best utilizes her "own unique and inherent resources," but she does so at the cost of expatriation.[29] Although Ellen and Justine most resemble the self-reliant, independent women of Mary Wilkins and Willa Cather, they are seen through a social filter that reduces their images. Wharton agreed that what William Dean Howells said of the American theater was true for "the whole American attitude toward life": "what the American public wants is *a tragedy with a happy ending*" (*French Ways,* 65). Believing that "every serious picture of life contains a thesis" and that only method separates "the literary artist from the professed moralist,"[30] she was not willing to give the public the happy ending: " 'The sheltered life, ' whether of the individual or of the nation, must either have a violent and tragic awakening—or never wake up at all" (*French Ways,* 66). By tipping her hat to the status quo and by qualifying the potential happiness of her single heroines, Wharton hoped to wake her readers to rebellion but not to anarchy.

Only if we compare Ellen Olenska's position with May Archer's do we see its advantages. This is as far as Wharton overtly revolts, and it leaves her with only a few more options than Aguilar. The values by which Kate has chosen to structure her life are not so very dissimilar from those of her literary sister, Mrs. Hamilton. Both have received their recompense or their reward through the lives of their children; and if Mrs. Clephane and Mrs. Hamilton ever shared tea together, Mrs. Clephane would agree—perhaps for different reasons—that the many sorrows and many cares that are inseparable from maternal love are "only remembered to enhance the sweetness of the recompense that ever follows" (*MR,* 498).

It is true that in a Wharton novel Mrs. Hamilton's way-
ward daughter might have run off with a disreputable man
and then be sent to Europe to live the rest of her life in seclu-
sion; or, as an old woman, she might unsuccessfully attempt
to stop a younger version of herself from making the same
mistake. In either case, however, the underlying and assumed values are the same; and that is why, in *A Room of
One's Own*, Virginia Woolf observed the revolutionary nature of Mary Carmichael's line, "Chloe liked Olivia" (86), for
until a woman could pen that line and accept its myriad social, political, and sexual ramifications, there was little alternative to the marriage plot.[31]

CHAPTER SEVEN

The Self-Made Man, a Grown-Up Woman, and the Female Artist

The years had not been exactly what she had dreamed; but if they had taken away certain illusions they had left richer realities in their stead.

— *"THE LETTERS"*

The two novels in which Edith Wharton most directly attempted to examine the development of an artist, *Hudson River Bracketed* (1929) and *The Gods Arrive* (1932) are considered among her worst. Critics fault their loose, uncontrolled structure[1] and agree—to quote an early reviewer—that "despite the title, the gods have not yet arrived."[2] Since Wharton's last book, *The Buccaneers*, shows her heroine, Nan St. George, struggling to define herself independently of marriage, perhaps they were not needed. Nonetheless, most readers concur that Vance Weston never makes a satisfactory artistic or personal statement, though few credit his problem to gender.

Wharton's adoption of a male persona served three purposes: it legitimized a narrative that she saw as traditionally belonging to the other sex, it allowed her to maintain the distance she felt so necessary between subject and author, and it subversively politicizes the novel's final sentimental scene.

When Vance Weston submissively kneels before the pregnant Halo Tarrant, "man-making words"—to quote David Leverenz—have indeed "yielded to mother-made temperaments."[3]

This conclusion marks a decided shift in Wharton's presentation of the artist. Deploring what she considered the current trend in fiction writing, the barely disguised autobiographical novel, Wharton never wanted to be heard shrieking her tale.[4] Early stories such as "Mrs. Manstey 's View" or "The Pelican" do have female artists, but they are disguised; for example, Mrs. Manstey is "at heart" an artist, "sensible of many changes of color unnoticed by the average eye."[5] Wharton treats her better than "The Pelican" 's Mrs. Amyot. Drawing lecture audiences more for their charitable contribution to her son's education than for the content of her talks, Mrs. Amyot continues to speak long after her son has reached a prosperous maturity, and her ceaseless vacuities reflect the new author's anxiety about writing and saying nothing.

Margaret Aubyn, the one woman of genuis she creates, misses being loved "by just such a hair-breadth deflection from the line of beauty as had determined the curve" of her lips, and the 1900 novella in which she figures, *The Touchstone*, focuses on Glennard, the more-than-ordinary man who could not imagine her mouth's individual charm.[6] The psychological, social, and historical reasons for Wharton's ambivalence toward herself as a woman writer have already been discussed,[7] but this story in particular shows what she called "the feminine me" opposed to (what I would call) "the writing me." Only through the legacy of her letters does Glennard come close to loving the dead author. How he would cope with the reality of her is not even open to debate—he could not.

Despite her gifts, Margaret Aubyn's role fits the pattern established in "Friends" (also written in 1900) and later

developed in *The Reef*, for she becomes the means of unban-
daging Mrs. Glennard's eyes. After reading the writer's love
letters to her husband, Glennard's wife sees him as wanting.
Their estrangement leads to his moral development and to a
more realistic and honest renewal of their marriage. As
Glennard's wife explains to him, "Don't you see that you've
never before been what she thought you, and that now, so
wonderfully, she's made you into the man she loved?" (*TT*,
82). Although Margaret Aubyn's own life and work become
the means of rehabilitation, the touchstone, for the Glenn-
ards' marriage, her greatest work of art ironically is a weak
man.

Unlike *The Touchstone*, *Hudson River Bracketed* and *The
Gods Arrive* do not directly concern relations between wom-
en, but they do illustrate how Wharton was defining and at-
tempting to reconcile woman and author at the end of her
career. In superficial and obvious ways, Vance Weston is
Wharton's alter ego, and his story is hers: he sees his first
novel much as Wharton grew to see *The Valley of Decision*
(1902)—"an emanation"—and like her, he never writes another historical novel.[8] He shares her love of the pure sound
of words, and they sing to him as they do to her "like birds in
an enchanted forest."[9] He values the same speech she learned
in her parents' house, "good English words, rich and expres-
sive, with hardly a concession to the local vernacular, or the
passing epidemics of slang";[10] and for both author and character, writing is a means of self-discovery and self-healing, a
way of dispelling "the awful sense of loneliness" (*HRB*, 30).[11]

His similarities with Wharton, though, are primarily ideo-
logical. As Vance becomes an increasingly successful novelist, for example, his tours of the literary salons of New York,
Paris, and London allow her to parody pet peeves, such as
the Bloomsbury group, the "slice-of-life" writers (*HRB*, 194),
the "me" novelist, James Joyce, and the "Pulsifer" Prize.[12]
As a result, we never see him in the round. Vance's theoreti-

cal function obscures the more interesting story of his artistic development, and too often he seems a part of the scene his author is parodying.

The main problem with the novels is tone. Both Lewis and Wolff observe a certain defensiveness and hurt, if not anger,[13] at being critically underrated or disregarded.[14] It occurs because Wharton saw the story of a great artist as only possible for "a man of genius," and in fact she originally toyed with that subtitle. But when a woman writes in a man's character, to quote Sarah Orne Jewett's warning to Willa Cather, "it must always be . . . something of a masquerade."[15] If "Vance" were "Vanessa," the link between the artist's work and life would be more convincing.[16]

The similarities between Vance and his author obscure the narrative and barely mask her awareness of his failings. It is not without at least unconscious intent that Vance seems to be a parody of a male writer who has little distinction. Further complicating the novelist's relationship to her material is the part of her that saw and liked herself as the self-made man or as a woman with a masculine mind. Wharton, for example, wrote to Robert Grant: "I conceive my subjects like a man—that is, rather more architectonically & dramatically than most women—& then execute them like a woman; or rather, I sacrifice, to my desire for construction & breadth, the small incidental effects that women have always excelled in, the episodical characterisation, I mean."[17] The quotation shows Wharton's ambivalence about men's "larger view of the world" and their "closer contact with reality."[18] Her definition of intelligence as a masculine trait partially inclines her to identify with Vance; however, she also and almost scornfully finds him incomplete without Halo Spear, a woman whose name especially incorporates both male and female sexual images. The faults of *Hudson River Bracketed* and *The Gods Arrive* illustrate that the voice of authorship is not universal or genderless.

Wharton herself wants to femininize Vance. His realization that "the fellows that write those [superficial] books are all Motherless!" (*HRB*, 336) does not at first extend to himself, but the narrative reveals his awakening to this fact and remedying it with his reunion with Halo. The novel's dominant spiritual image comes from *Faust*, "the mysterious Mothers, moving in subterranean depths among the primal forms of life" (*HRB*, 336), and is meant to be read as a rejection of a patriarchal God. The Mothers are also the source of creative power, and Vance needs to feel "the arms of Life, the ancient mother, reaching out to him, winding about him, crushing him fast again to her great careless bosom" (*HRB*, 31) if he is to feel "the artisan's full control of his implements."[19]

Wharton repeats the image of the ancient mother at the novel's end, when Vance and Halo embrace. The couple's elemental connection is like an invisible umbilical cord that links mother and child but also leaves what he calls "the god in him" free to walk around (*HRB*, 6–7). A marriage of selves must preserve the "irreducible core of selfness," the "hidden cave" in which one hoards his or her "secretest treasures" (*HRB*, 272), for that inviolate private space is vital for the development of a self that can function in a relationship without being subsumed. Vance values "the true artist's faculty of self-isolation,"[20] and this shows a change in Wharton's thinking from her early short story, "The Fullness of Life," in which the soul, sitting in the self's innermost room, mournfully awaits a footstep that never comes.

Halo goes through a similar transformation. Her altruism in the service of genius masks an abdication of responsibility to herself, and it transforms her from a self-confident, independent woman into a self-doubting recluse. The desire to be like the air her lover breathes (*GA*, 31) as well as the lathe on which he shapes his fictions nearly destroys her. Halo no longer cares "to make her life comely for its own sake; she thought of it only in relation to her love for Vance" (*GA*, 104). Nothing matters to her "except that she should go on serving and inspiring this child of genius with whom a whim of the gods had entrusted her" (*GA*, 105). Only by separating from Vance can Halo recover a sense of her lost identity and find the woman who was herself.[21] At first she spends the days tending her garden at Oubli, and later she creates a home for herself and her expected baby at the Willows. Although the garden metaphor ties her to nature's cycles by foreshadowing her pregnancy and participation in the "endless function" (*GA*, 311), it also underlies her own need to tend her self, "to be Halo Spear again—that's all" (*GA*, 368). In actuality, Halo's altruism has been a form of selfishness, prompted by her desire to be Vance's guide, his sounding board, his muse, and it resembles the ruinous altruism that Mary Wilkins's Amelia Lamkin practiced in the service of her family.[22]

If Wharton had told her own story, there would have been no male equivalent of Halo, as she envied the British author Mrs. Humphrey Ward for being surrounded by a supportive and appreciative family. Wharton's unrelenting treatment of Halo in part results from her lifelong dislike of seeing wasted self-sacrifice, but it also results from her contempt for women who feed and perpetuate the myth of "the man of genius," a man not bound by conventions or morality. A similar path was denied to any but the most socially radical woman writer, such as George Sand, whom Wharton admired but did not consider imitating. Vance's return to Halo and hearth show that Wharton not only saw the necessity of these ties for the regulation, maintenance, and continuance of life but that she also grew to recognize the limitations of defining mind and body, men and women, as unfusable, binary opposites.[23] In fact, the female principle, as embodied in the final vision of Halo, takes precedence.

By the end of *The Gods Arrive*, Vance has learned the

truth of his grandmother's last words, "Maybe we haven't
made enough of pain—been too afraid of it" (*GA*, 409). He is
now prepared to accept the feminine in himself. His willingness also reflects his author's wish to make herself whole, to
wed the male and female in herself, for abstractly Vance
and Halo represent the two parts of their creator's nature:
the intellectual male half, who wrote fictions, and the nur-
turing female half, who tended gardens.[24]

In 1929 the self that wrote novels and the self that created
gardens dramatically merged. During the winter the gardens at St. Claire were devastated by cold weather and
winds. The destruction equally devastated the author, for as
her close friend, Margaret Chanler, writes in *Autumn in the
Valley*, they were "a symbol of the real Edith."[25] She imme-
diately initiated their rebuilding and replanting while working on *Hudson River Bracketed* at a desk set up in the Pavil-
lon Colombe Garden in St. Brice-sous Fôret.[26] This merger of
writer and gardener finds its fictional equivalent in the union of Vance, who as a writer tends and culls "the secret
garden" of his imagination, and Halo, who nurses her seed-
lings at Oubli.

The last image in *The Gods Arrive* is of Halo, pregnant
and standing before the light with her arms lifted "in the
ancient attitude of prayer" (*GA*, 439). Vance's arms encircle
her and promise that their reunion will be fruitful both personally and artistically. Their embrace is a recognition and
acceptance of the interdependence of masculinity and femininity.

The self-embrace it marks is also necessary for the creation of "Literature," the novel's working title. The Vance
and Halo characters were originally named Dick and Rose—
again, gender-rich names. Both were writers, although Dick
was "the man of genius" in the novel's subtitle. Wharton
planned, as Nancy R. Leach writes, "to consider the personal
problems in the life of a creative artist."[27] Her characters,

however, also illustrate her own dilemma as a woman writer forced to choose between a critically legitimized male tradition and a more emotive, "sentimental," female one. Wharton's notations clearly align Rose's writing with the latter: she "has the hyper-sensitivity, the over-exquisitiveness of perception, the too-prompt 'emoting' which are apt to be found with a certain kind of distinguished talent."[28] In contrast, Dick has "the cool command of all his aesthetic reactions which belongs to is genius. She spends in feeling (aesthetically and emotionally) what he finds full *outlet* for in expression."[29]

Rose resembles Margaret Aubyn in the sense that she ultimately creates Dick, for when he dies unexpectedly, she collaborates with a friend to write his biography. The form of her art creates a wider audience for his, and ironically she has the final word on his genius. In this way the two are interdependent. Although Wharton clearly aligned herself with Dick's tradition, the ending reveals a move toward approximation, and perhaps—since Dick dies in several outlines of the story—more. His death could be read psychologically as an expression of anger at the tradition he represents and symbolically as the triumph and endurance of Rose's.[30]

One symbol may be as good as another, to paraphrase Vance (*HRB*, 449), but the image of the Mothers has particular importance.[31] It shows Wharton acknowledging all of those women who made an art of "hem-stitching" and "pumpkin pie making" and mothering.[32] Vance desires to do with words what Halo will do in the flesh, bring a human soul to life, to give birth (*GA*, 172).[33] By coupling Vance's and Halo's activities Wharton is recalling Grandma Scrimser's belief that "man is always creating God; that wherever a great thought is born, or a noble act performed, there God is created. *That* is the real Eucharist, the real remaking of Divinity. If you knew God, you knew that: you knew you had in your soul the power to make Him" (*HRB*, 455). At the beginning of her career, Wharton did not so nearly equate those activities with the making of literature, and the change reflects her impulse to reconcile and more clearly align herself with her own gender.[34] This change, increasingly foreshadowed in the novels proceeding *Hudson River Bracketed* and *The Gods Arrive*, also shows her elevating—rather than suppressing or denying—what she described in *A Backward Glance* as "the feminine *me* in the little girl's vague soul" (*ABG*, 2).

The "seed of a new vitality" (*GA*, 429) that Halo carries is a wish for a future in which there can be a true and equal marriage among the many selves that form an individual's composite identity. It is a wish that disparate selves can "become a nucleus, their contradictory cravings" meeting "in a common purpose," so that "their being together and belonging to each other" can aquire "a natural meaning" (*GA*, 323). At the end of the novel Vance's repetition of St. Augustine's words, "I am the Food of the full-grown. Become a man and thou shalt feed on Me" (*GA*, 418), although emphasizing that the vision is for the mature, the "full-grown," the grown-up,[35] also underscores how true manhood can be achieved only through an incorporation of the feminine.

The Buccaneers details a similar course of growing up but for an artistically inclined young woman, Nan St. George. Nan's ingenuous honesty and respect for the past make her a daughter of both continents. Unlike Daisy Miller, she values other women and relies on their support and mentorship. They begin the process of her becoming "full-grown," and the experience of marriage completes it.

Nan is only one of a charming group of new American girls whose backgrounds have been found wanting by the Mrs. Parmores of old New York. Under the tutelage of an undauntable and androgynously named English governess, Miss Testvalley (originally Testavaglia), they leave the new world to take the old by storm, and not a one dies of the British equivalent of Roman fever. Cultured, clear-sighted, and self-supporting, Laura Testvalley possesses all of the traits of a grown-up woman and as such is a fit mentor for her American charges.[36] The girls themselves are gentler versions of the great Wharton invader, Undine Spragg, whose advance from Apex City to New York to the St. Faubourg leaves, like Attila the Hun's, a wake of wounded civilizations. But unlike Undine, these girls want the approval and embrace of their adopted country. "Divinely dull" Virginia St. George's lovely blankness most recalls Undine; too often she has to trust "the length of her eyelashes and the lustre of her lips" to plead for her.[37]

Different in the tradition of Justine Brent, Sophy Viner, and Ellen Olenska, her sister, Nan, is the true offspring of Laura Testvalley. The two share a mature love of poetry, especially the sensual verse of Dante Gabriel Rossetti, as well as equal disregard for frivolity and convention. History speaks of them, sounding "like the long murmur of the past breaking on the shores of a sleeping world" (*Buccaneers*, 134); Nan wants to understand England's soul and see "houses that are so ancient and so lovely that the people who live there have them in their bones" (*Buccaneers*, 163). As her friend, Conchita Closson, now Lady Dick, says, she is "unfashionable among the unfashionable" (*Buccaneers*, 244), who spend their time playing practical jokes and flirting. Even when Nan becomes the Duchess of Tintagel, her young heart, "beset with vague dreams and ambitions" (*Buccaneers*, 245), still seek an echo from and a haven with her old governess. Valuing taste, reverence, continuity, and intellectual honesty, she is Wharton's answer to the New Woman.

Her sister and the Elmsworth girls are more conventional. Having come to England in search of romance, they are aided by Miss March, who many years ago won and subsequently lost the heart of Lord Brightlingsea (after the wedding gown had been ordered). She has since made a career of

discreetly introducing rich Americans to British society, but
her history makes her feel an "affinity with this new band of
marauders, social aliens though they were . . . come out to
look over the ground, and do their own capturing" (*Buccaneers* 103). Weary of smiling and nodding when her usurper
and friend Lady Brightlingsea (pronounced "Brittlesey") insists that the Virginia reel is a dance the wild Indians taught
to the Americans (*Buccaneers*, 279) and "of hearing her
compatriots discussed and criticized and having to explain
them" (*Buccaneers*, 281), Miss March realizes that by melting
so modestly into the background she has almost disappeared.
Wharton permits her a triumphant but ladylike laugh at the
English aristocracy, whose financial and emotional compromises make them appear more vulgar than their naive
American friends.[38]

As the champion of these transatlantic daughters, Miss
March validates and asserts her own identity and shows that
the benefits of female solidarity are cross-generational.[39] She
and her charges represent an updated version of Louisa May
Alcott's little women, the Marches. When Conchita's engagement to the younger son of British nobility secures her the
sole invitation to an exclusive assembly, for example, Virginia generously rearranges Conchita's rose garland in a more
becoming way. Miss Testvalley observes that "had there
been any malice in Virginia she might have spoilt her
friend's dress instead of improving it" (*Buccaneers*, 74). Rather, the friends "circle gaily" around her, "applauding, criti-
cizing, twitching as critically at her ruffles and ribbons as
though these were to form a part of their own adornment"
(*Buccaneers*, 72), and when the older girls do attend the assembly under the pretext of being Lord Richard's sisters, the
narrator notes that "each of the three girls was set off by the
charms of the others. They were so complimentary in their
graces, each seemed to have been so especially created by
Providence, and adorned by coiffeur and dressmaker, to

make part of that matchless trio, that their entrance was a sight long remembered" (*Buccaneers*, 84). Wharton's meaning seems straightforward: women should not, in Lily Bart's words, "go back" on each other.

The girls' partnership allows them to make the marriages that will complete their educations. In the novel's most dramatic scene, Lizzy Elmsworth shows the power of this maxim. Her dark beauty and "active wit" and Virginia St. George's "profile" have almost equally captivated Lord Seadown, and as Hector Robinson observes, "he needed the combined stimulus of both to rouse his slow imagination" (*Buccaneers*, 193). At any moment the balance could tip in favor of one friend or the other. Mabel Elmsworth sees that "those two inseparable friends were gradually becoming estranged" (*Buccaneers*, 193) and enlists Robinson's help. As she explains to him, "what I say is it's time he chose between them, if he's ever going to. It's very hard on Lizzy, and it's not fair that he should make two friends quarrel. After all, we're all alone in a strange country, and I daresay our ways are not like yours, and may lead you to make mistakes about us" (*Buccaneers*, 195).

The already strained atmosphere is intensified when Seadown's recent lover, Lady Churt, arrives intending to assert her hold over him. In the scene that ensues, Lady Churt insults Virginia, prompting her friend (and supposed rival) to fling herself into the fray: "Virginia! What are you waiting for? Don't you see that Lord Seadown has no right to speak till you do? Why don't you tell him at once that he has your permission to announce your engagement?" (*Buccaneers*, 207). Her impassioned words catalyze Seadown, who acknowledges the engagement and takes possession of Virginia's hand while "with her other hand" his betrothed draws her ally close (*Buccaneers*, 208). Lizzy's spirit wins Hector Robinson's admiration ("Gad, she looks like an avenging goddess—I can almost hear the arrow whizzing past! What a party-leader she'd make") and saves her from being thrown away on Lord Seadown, a "poor nonentity" (*Buccaneers*, 208). Instead, she marries Hector, making the most happy and egalitarian of all the girls' marriages. Lizzy resembles "the Frenchwoman [who] rules French life . . . under a triple crown, as a business woman, as a mother, and above all as an artist" (*French Ways*, 111).

After the glorious victories of courtship, marriage seems anticlimatic; and the girls, who, together "arm-in-arm," were "like a branch hung with blossoms" separately wither (*Buccaneers*, 34). Wharton's vision of female support and friendship is shadowed by the seeming necessity of marriage, which constricts horizons, limits endless possibilities, and locks husband and wife in separate cells. The friends now communicate like prisoners, tapping out coded messages, as when Conchita's request to Nan for £500 reveals her love of a man other than Lord Richard.

After marrying England's greatest catch, the Duke of Tintagel, Nan discovers that, like the American women Wharton describes in *French Ways and Their Meaning*, she had more freedom of movement and expression when single. Her marriage fails for reasons precisely opposite to those that make Lizzy's marriage succeed. Tintagel chooses Nan for "her childish innocence, her indifference to money and honours" (*Buccaneers*, 227). He denies her any active part in the management of his estate and wants "to shield her from every contact with life" (*Buccaneers*, 227). Continuing to mature after her marriage, however, Nan turns out to be exactly what Miss Testvalley suspected, "a woman who didn't want to be shielded" (*Buccaneers*, 227). Not responding to the voices of tradition, which are embodied in his first name, Ushant discovers that his mother was right, "women are not quite as simple as clocks" (*Buccaneers*, 245).

The Dowager's insight does not mean that she feels any particular sympathy for the new Duchess. The women are natural adversaries because the Dowager wants her daughter-in-law to conform like a soldier and produce heirs, and Nan feels that she is being asked to cut the cloak of her identity to fit a different-size model. Finding it difficult to order her life by traditions in which she sees no meaning, she feels alienated from herself:

> To begin with, what had caused Annabel St. George to turn into Annabel Tintagel? That was the central problem! Yet how could she solve it, when she could no longer question that elusive Annabel St. George, who was still so near to her, yet as remote and unapproachable as a plaintive ghost?
>
> Yes—a ghost. That was it. Annabel St. George was dead, and Annabel Tintagel did not know how to question the dead, and would therefore never be able to find out why and how that mysterious change had come about. (*Buccaneers*, 241–242)

The Dowager Duchess must have had to make a similar transformation, but she had the example of centuries of "inherited obligations" (*Buccaneers*, 266) "precedents, institutions and traditions to sustain her" (*Buccaneers*, 246) and now feels little sympathy for Annabel—except in one crucial and related area—and that sympathy shows Wharton's indictment of marriage as an institution that denies women the right to self-determination and development.

Wedlock, the great leveler, makes all women master the same agonizing and humiliating lessons. After suffering a miscarriage, for example, Nan refuses to have sexual relations with Ushant. Already she has told him, "I'd rather be dead than see a child of mine taught to grow up as—as you have!" (*Buccaneers*, 255). Intimidated, he respects her wishes, but after leaving an envelope containing £500 on her dressing table for a "private charity," he expects her to accept his attentions. Seeing the exchange of money for sex within marriage as commonplace, Ushant is thrown off balance when he goes to seek Annabel's "gratitude" and is informed that she hadn't understood he was driving a bargain with her (*Buccaneers*, 328). The Dowager hears her son's story with conflicted emotion. One part of her listens as a mother, overwhelmed by her son's generosity and horrified at his treatment from a mere chit of a girl. The other part of her responds as a woman: "The Duchess's hard little eyes filled with sudden tears. Her mind was torn between wrath at her daughter-in-law's incredible exactions, and the thought of what such generosity on her own husband's part might have meant to her, with those eight girls to provide for" (*Buccaneers*, 327). The woman in her, simultaneously resentful and envious, thinks that this was "one of the strangest hours of her life, and not the least strange part of it was the light reflected back on her own past, and on the wary nights when she had not dared to lock her door" (*Buccaneers*, 329). Time and time again "the memory of her own past thrust[s] itself between her and her wrath against her daughter-in-law" (*Buccaneers*, 329), and on this ground, mother and daughter-in-law meet.

On this ground all of the women in the novel meet, including Nan and her own mother, Mrs. St. George. Nan's husband and Mrs. St. George's husband, whether separated by the Atlantic Ocean, history, background, or sensibility, are similar in their notions about the relationship between money and sex: "Mrs. St. George did not own many jewels, but it suddenly occurred to her that each one marked the date of a similar episode. Either a woman, or a business deal—something she had to be indulgent about" (*Buccaneers*, 32). Mrs. St. George, though, is still attracted to her husband. She sees him reflected in other women's eyes and is proud of the figure he cuts, but she knows that "he was a costly possession, but (unlike the diamonds, she suspected) he had been paid for—oh how dearly!—and she had a right to wear him with her head high" (*Buccaneers*, 33). All too often the women in Wharton's fiction are like Lily Bart, "a moment's ornament," or like Nan, "a rare piece" for a husband's collection (*Buccaneers*, 227),[40] but here a woman voices thoughts commonly attributed to the male perspective. The shift more strongly and blatantly reiterates Wharton's belief—first made in *The Age of Innocence*—that "the custom of the country" exploits, victimizes, and demeans both sexes.[41]

The St. George and Elmsworth girls owe their success to a recognition of their importance to each other, but the marriages they make, with the exception of Lizzy's, seem small recompense. As matrons, their adventures are too likely to resemble Conchita Marable's, and this aspect of *The Buccaneers* makes it seem as bleak as *The House of Mirth*. Virginia and Conchita have made Undine Spragg's mistake of defining themselves in relationship to their husband's status, and Nan repeats Newland Archer's by assuming that setting reflects character. Ellen Olenska was not as different and exotic as her unconventional room,[42] and the Duke is not as romantic as the ruins of Tintagel.

Both patterns, repeated time and time again in Wharton's fiction, have disastrous consequences for women and sometimes for the men they marry. Wharton shows us no way out of this dilemma: women must marry or they make do with dinginess, like Gerty Farrish in *The House of Mirth*. *The Fruit of the Tree* (1907) in particular outlines the difficulties of sustaining a relationship, for there is always the chance of misreading either oneself or another. Although Justine Brent and John Amherst are reunited, like Vance and Halo, at the novel's conclusion, their new relationship is cemented with silence about his first wife's true nature and actual behavior. The only person who benefits is Bessy's daughter Cicely, who has both the memory of her less-than-perfect mother and the presence of her much-loved stepmother. Once independent and self-supporting, Justine is now "an angel in the house."

Marriage is at best a compromise that severely suppresses or limits the self. At worst, it recalls the punchline of a joke that Wharton recorded in a 1913 notebook:

> "Did you know that John and Susan committed suicide on Tuesday?"
> "What? No?—How?"
> "They got married."[43]

Because it can never fulfill one's expectations, life has meaning, as it does for the Dowager Duchess of Tintagel, through personal denial and duty.

The Buccaneers partially breaks this pattern because its projected ending grants Nan a chance at happiness, whereby she can perhaps once again talk face to face with herself and tear down "the walls which had built themselves up about the new Duchess" (*Buccaneers*, 262). But that chance can at first exist only outside of marriage, and unfortunately, her lover's name, Guy Thwarte, does not sound altogether promising. In addition, as outlined in the synopsis, Nan buys her happiness at the expense of her beloved Miss Testvalley, whose help to the lovers prevents her from finding a haven with Guy's father, Sir Helmsley Thwarte. Wolff notes that the projected ending seems "hardly credible"[44] because Nan would not be likely to harm the one person with whom she felt most herself. It does, however, repeat the pattern of the stronger, more independent, and less conventional woman making a sacrifice for friend, child, mother, or sister. Had *The Buccaneers* been completed, we might now have a better idea of how Ellen Olenska spent those unrecorded twenty years.

If we accept, as most critics do, that Nan and Guy are meant to achieve the one happy marriage in all of Wharton's fiction, then they owe their success to Nan's refusal to be self-sacrificing. That decision leads to her becoming grown-up. In *French Ways and Their Meaning*, Wharton defined "grown-up" as being involved with the business of living (*French Ways* 119–120). Nan is initiated into the business of living through her bad marriage, and in this way she resembles the nineteenth-century heroine whose first unsatisfactory husband dies, leaving her free to marry a more suitable mate. Nan's flight from her marriage could have provided an alternative ending—for example, Conchita's South American relatives might have offered her shelter and occupation—but the final solution, whether resulting from death or divorce, is another marriage. In this way the ending of *The Buccaneers* parallels "Souls Belated." Wharton knew how a woman could be grown-up—leaving a marriage could achieve that—but then she did not realistically know what to do with her. Wharton saw herself as an exception, able to approximate her roles as woman and artist and to maintain strong same-sex friendships. As a result, her artist-heroines are women such as Lily Bart, Anna Leath, Sophy Viner, Ellen Olenska, and Nan St. George, whose identities are their sole canvases.

Very seldom do men and women in Wharton's fiction find the right word to say to each other or see the "beyondness" of things from the same angle of vision (*Buccaneers*, 137), and for this reason women's relationships with other women are crucial. Wharton's work can be seen as voicing this belief with increasing volume and resonance. *The Buccaneers* illustrates that women's friendships can give an added richness and sense of safety to life, but the soul—if it is to experience "the fullness of life"—must learn self-sufficiency. Women's partnerships are not an alternative to male-female relationships, but Wharton's vision of the world makes us ask why not.

It seems particularly poignant that Wharton would overtly state the importance of women's relationships in her final novel, *The Buccaneers*, for those last years also brought the deaths of close women friends, in particular, her housekeeper, Gross. In Wharton's later years she was drawn more and more to the young, especially to Royall and Elisina Tyler's son, William. Her reaching out to youth poignantly reflects her longing to be part of "the long rich heritage of human experience."[45] That desire makes Wharton the opposite of her bewildered heroine, Nan Tintagel, "isolated in her new world, no longer able to reach back to her past, and not having yet learned how to communicate with the present" (*Buccaneers*, 262), for her novels bridge past and present worlds.

Wharton and Her Contemporaries, Cather, Austin, and Glasgow

> *"Do you wonder that we novel-
> ists find such an inexhaustible
> field in Woman?"*
>
> —*"WRITING A WAR STORY"*

Despite Edith Wharton's own identi-
fication with Nathaniel Hawthorne and Henry James, she
began her career by telling a story so often used by women
writers and so central to feminist critical theory: the Deme-
ter-Persephone myth. Her version of the myth, *Bunner Sisters* (1900), is bleak. The fall into a post-Freudian world
brings death. The sisters are Ann Eliza and Evelina, and
they live a life of comfortable if circumscribed domesticity
until their world is invaded by the ominous presence of a potential suitor, Mr. Ramy. Mr. Ramy first proposes to the
elder sister, Ann Eliza, but her refusal persuades him to
honor the younger. Ann Eliza's altruism is Evelina's curse,
for Mr. Ramy is a drug addict who steals their money, beats
his wife, and deserts her when she is giving birth. After the
death of her child, Evelina returns to her sister to die. Her
conversion to Catholicism, however, assures that the sisters'
estrangement, which began with Evelina's marriage, will

continue beyond this life. Ann Eliza watches her sister's slow death from tuberculosis and feels that "once more she found herself shut out of Evelina's heart, an exile from her closest affections."[1] Mr. Ramy's intrusion has destroyed the Bunner sisters' world just as effectively as Pluto's destroyed the "female world of love and ritual" that Demeter and her daughter inhabited, for Ann Eliza dies a "stranger in her [sister's] arms" (*Bunner*, 308).

Eleven years later Wharton revised this story by transforming it into a short verse play called "Pomegranate Seed." It restates the point she made in *Bunner Sisters* while illuminating the social and literary context in which she and her female contemporaries worked. Writing after the gender crisis at the turn of the century, Wharton saw no alternative but to return a willing Persephone to Hades. Before Persephone can make that choice, though, she must again visit her mother. Their reunion is crucial for her development. Not until she both battles and accepts Demeter can she don a unique (but related) mantle of identity.

Wharton's Demeter defines herself only in relation to her daughter. When Hecate, for example, arrives with the news that Persephone lives, "yet never sees the sun," Demeter responds, "Blind am I in her blindness."[2] Seeing her immortal grief as greater than "the cry that mortal mothers make" when they lose a child, for "happier they, that make an end at last" ("PS," 286), she transforms the entire earth into a grave for Persephone, till nothing marked the place where she had stood / But her dropped flowers—a garland on her grave" ("PS," 285). Persephone's abandoned garland could also grace the grave of her mother's old self because Demeter's new identity is determined by her undaughtered condition. The world weeps as she destroys her artistry and its canvas. Her ruthlessly Olympian gesture causes all creation to share and suffer the magnificent magnitude of her own mourning.

As the protectress of the social order and marriage, Demeter should want to promote, not prevent, her daughter's participation in the business of living, but instead she resembles Wharton's own mother in her attempts to deny Persephone that knowledge. Persephone is not her mother's daughter in the sense that she feels and tries to ease the suffering souls, now dead, who still know "the lust of some old anguish" ("PS," 289). Her experience of the other side, her consciousness of life's complete cycle, has resulted in her giving suck to a grief that her mother is incapable of knowing. The two are separated as surely as the Victorians were from their postwar young. The Persephone who is momentarily restored to her mother can never be the same young woman who walked among the almonds. Her rent veil is the price of initiation, and this time it both separates her from and makes her superior to her parent; as in *The Mother's Recompense*, daughter and mother change positions.

The verse play ends with mother and daughter forever divided, forever attuned to different voices. Demeter hears "the secret whisper of the wheat"; and Persephone, the voices of her dead ("PS," 291). The possessive pronoun shows that Persephone has claimed the dead and their eternally living sorrows for her own, and in this egocentric way she is perhaps most her mother's daughter. Demeter may appear less sympathetic because the sounds that whisper in her ears are inanimate. As a reader of Pater, Wharton knew that Demeter and Persephone, considered a dual goddess, were worshipped as one,[3] and as in all of her novels, the two women are halves of a whole, forming the entirety of nature. They resemble the cross-generational pairing of Sophy Viner and Anna Leath in *The Reef* or of Miss March and the American girls in *The Buccaneers*.

Pluto does not figure as a character in "The Pomegranate Seed," but it is to him also that Persephone returns. His physical absence is even more glaring than George Frederic

Jones's from his daughter's autobiography, but his sexual presence cannot be ignored, for Persephone's sojourn with him has made her grown-up. In her case, rape has been the equivalent of Nan St. George's bad marriage.

The myth's resolution illustrates the dilemma of women writing on the cusp that divided a pre- and post-Freudian world. Sarah Orne Jewett would have had no difficulty reuniting sisters or mother and daughter, who would have then started home, gathering herbs along the way in anticipation of a shared pot of tea. Mary Wilkins might have had them set up housekeeping again, only to find that they were now incompatible and would be much happier tending separate gardens. Wharton did not see herself as having these choices. If Persephone returned home, she was a failure like Evelina or lacking in the way that Charlotte Lovell is lacking in *The Old Maid*; and if she chose to live with another woman, she was degenerate. Wharton knew that Persephone almost had to return to her husband, and considering her own view of marriage, his place of residence is not surprising. Without a husband she could be an object of pity and condescension or a Riviera drifter, but through her husband's agency a woman had her best chance of leaving the Montessori infant school and graduating into the business of living. This social reality is the determination of her plots.

As Ellen Olenska tells Newland Archer, there is no country that is not bounded by social restrictions, and that belief perhaps most differentiates Wharton from her contemporaries, Cather (1873–1947), Austin (1868–1932), and Glasgow (1873–1941). In different ways, each learned—to quote Wharton—that "the creative mind thrives best on a reduced diet."[4] All had complex relationships with their mothers and felt ambivalent about marriage. Glasgow could never bring herself to marry, and Austin left her husband. Willa Cather voiced a collective fear when she begged Elizabeth Sargeant to tell her whether "she might have committed the unforgivable female literary sin of overwriting" or being too emotional in *O, Pioneers!*[5] But even though these women experienced professional and personal difficulties similar to Wharton's, they were able to create characters who saw alternatives, who found or created the other country that Newland Archer could only imagine.

At one time in her career each writer must have asked herself the question that Paula Becker poses to Clara Westhoff in the Adrienne Rich poem: "Which of us, Clara, hasn't had to take that leap / out beyond our being women / to save our work? or is it to save ourselves?"[6] The question perhaps had most import for Cather, who as a lesbian writer felt it necessary to adopt a male persona either to mask her own identity or to universalize her experience. Like Wharton, she made a point of separating herself from other women writers, and her work contains a curious tension between author and subject that recalls Wharton's problems with tone in *Hudson River Bracketed* and *The Gods Arrive*. What exactly is her relation to *My Antonia*'s narrator, Jim Burden, or to female characters such as Antonia, toothless and aged before her time; Marie, passionate and murdered; or Marion Forrester, sexually exploited and exploitive and ultimately triumphant?

Cather's tone is most consistent when she tells the story of a female artist from her point of view—something Wharton never did. However, that point of view is similar to Vance Weston's. In *The Song of the Lark* Thea Kronberg discovers what Weston calls "The Mothers," the connection between womanhood and creativity. For Thea the connection is even more direct because the art of operatic singing involves her whole body.

Although Wharton and Cather agree about the power of femininity, they differ about its inherited restrictions and obligations. As the characterization of Lena in *My Antonia* illustrates, Cather is less accepting of the inescapable measure of the double standard. The relationship between Carl and Alexandra in *O, Pioneers!* shows that Cather is also less bound by traditional views on courtship, marriage, and gender roles, though her version of the Demeter–Persephone myth in that novel ends even more violently than Wharton's. Alexandra Bergson and Marie Shabata may resemble that mother and daughter as they work cozily together side by side in the story's winter section, but Marie's sexual fall ensures her death and the death of her lover.

Underlying Cather's fiction is a belief in the individual's ability to transcend the grasp of time and place; for example, in *A Lost Lady*, Marion Forrester refuses to comply with the narrator's conventional definitions of "woman"; Godfrey St. Peter in *The Professor's House* sets himself adrift from the moorings of home, family, and culture; and in *Death Comes to the Archbishop*, Bishop Latour's spiritual flights are not solely grounded in the dogma of his church. Cather associates the desert with something "soft and wild and free, something that . . . softly picked the lock, slid the bolts, and released the prisoned spirit of man into the wind, into the blue and gold, into the morning, into the morning!"[7] Wharton envisions no similar space. At best the soul accepts its single cell and—to quote Emily Dickinson—"selects her own society" (1862).

Like Cather, Mary Austin created what Gaston Bachelard called more "felicitous spaces."[8] Her relationship to the land and her openness to non-European cultural traditions in part explain the greater range of alternatives she envisioned for her heroines. For example, in the story "The Man Who Was Loved by Women" she successfully—and humorously—weaves all of the colored strands that Wharton saw as clashing: egalitarian marriage, female community, and individual empowerment. These alternatives, however, are often incompatible with eastern values and the dominant culture. Stories such as "Frustrate" and "The Portrait" show Austin encountering the same hurdles that Wharton did, for the female artist figures in them are easily recognizable as Margaret Aubyn's sisters. Austin's overt feminism and politicism, which distinguishes her from Wharton and Cather, contributed to her conscious efforts to develop a tradition that incorporated folk and Native American culture, plus something that Mary Hallock Foote described as "pure woman."[9]

Austin shared with Wharton and Cather an admiration for Henry James, and in 1920 she wrote a novel, *26 Jayne Street*, set in his original territory, the upper-class world of old New York. Its heroine, Neith Schuyler, admires and learns to love a leading political radical, Adam Freer, because she assumes that he has "the ability to act on the intrinsic merits of a situation, independently of its emotions."[10] In his relationships with women, though, Adam is autocratic, chauvinistic, and conventional, and Neith soon learns that her happiness is at the expense of another woman's, Rose Matlock, Adam's companion, lover, and political collaborator, his wife in all but name, objects when he discards her; and Neith agrees— the breaking of a contract should be negotiated. Neith has only respect and admiration for Rose, and the novel ends with her dissolving her engagement to Adam.

In *The Reef* and *The Age of Innocence* Wharton approaches this conclusion, and in a key way her thinking resembles Austin's: because there is no democracy between men and women, women must begin to take responsibility for saying no. The consequences of doing this are more severe in a Wharton novel, as the fate of Lily Bart or any of her exiled heroines illustrates. Wharton sees society as essentially fixed, Austin envisions its evolution. The change is not without pain for Austin, even as its advantages are more clearcut. In *A Woman of Genius* (1912), for example, Austin's Olivia Lattimore learns the same lesson that Lily Bart (1905) and later Susan Lenox (1917) learned: respectability inhibits female development. The knowledge costs her the love of her life, but it does not deny her the friendship and comfort of a companionate marriage. It is questionable whether either Anna Leath or May Archer experience even this quiet joy.

Ellen Glasgow shared Austin's feminism and Wharton's vision. Her ironic analysis of southern morals and manners and her scathing studies of the destructive double standard inherent in the cult of her region's womanhood align her with Wharton. Margaret Fleming of "The Difference" is very familiar to Wharton readers. The serenity of her twenty-year marriage is destroyed when she learns of her husband's affair with a young artist. Margaret tests the depth of her love and finds the strength to step aside, only to discover that her sacrifice is neither needed nor desired. Resembling Austin's Neith Schuyler, she is—as her husband tells her—disappointed and angry that he is not in love with his mistress. The tear in her veil reveals a commonplace and vulgar world.

Like Wharton, Glasgow was accused of creating weak men and treating them harshly; but unlike Wharton, she was able to create a strong, self-willed, and iron-veined woman in *Barren Ground* (1925). After being seduced and abandoned, Dorinda Oakley dedicates her life to reclaiming the soil and finds, as did Alexandra Bergson and Olivia Lattimore, some solace in a companionate marriage. She finally triumphs and is revenged, but, like Newland Archer, she misses "the flower of life." Glasgow could have been describing her fiction as a whole when she wrote to Van Wyck Brooks that the two overlapping themes of *The Sheltered Life* were "we cannot put up a shelter against life and we kill what we love too much."[11] Wharton would certainly agree. These two women had similar ideas about their art, for as Glasgow wrote to Allen Tate: "I am not writing of Southern nature, but of human nature. By the Sheltered Life, I meant the whole civilization man has built to protect himself from reality. . . . I was not concerned with the code of Virginia, but with the conventions of the world we call civilized. . . . I was dealing with the fate of the civilized mind in a world where even the civilizations we make are uncivilized."[12] In Glasgow's fiction, as in Wharton's, the individual does not escape, redefine, or recreate the existing world. Rather, he or she struggles within the confines and the context of civilization. What most distinguishes these authors of manners is Glasgow's emphasis on psychological truth and Wharton's emphasis on social realism, a point illustrated by the titles of their respective autobiographies, *The Woman Within* and *A Backward Glance.*

In *The Woman Within* (1954) Glasgow wrote: "A sensitive mind would always remain an exile on earth, and regarding life itself I had preserved no illusions."[13] Her contemporaries could also make that claim, for in their own ways Wharton, Cather, Austin, and Glasgow had to remove "the veil of literature" that Wharton describes as hanging between George Eliot's eyes and Life.[14] Each had to confront and mold to their own purposes, as did Eliot, "the familiar marionettes of fiction."[15] Once that veil was removed, it revealed an era of overwhelming historical, economic, and sociological changes. During their lifetimes these women witnessed their country's shift from an agrarian to an industry-based economy. Their homes acquired refrigeration, electricity, and telephones. They saw the nation's population migrate from country to city and the face of America develop Irish, Slavic, Semitic, and multiracial features. They saw the intercontinental railroad and the first airplane, the rise of millionaires and labor unions, and the continued struggle for suffrage, racial equality, and economic parity. All born before a decade had marked the end of the Civil War, they lived through the Spanish-American War and World War I.

Austin's *A Woman of Genuis*, Glasgow's *The Descendant*, and Cather's *The Professor's House* are responses to these upheavals (as is the work of Hamlin Garland, Stephen

Crane, Theodore Dreiser, Henry Adams, Sherwood Anderson, and Sinclair Lewis). A social historian and a novelist of manners, Wharton in particular chronicles cultural transitions as they clash with, thwart, and redirect individual aspirations. She was equally aware of the poverty of the past and its grandeur worth preserving. In this regard her work resembles that of her female contemporaries.

Wharton perhaps most differs from the women writers mentioned in her unresolved conflict about marriage's necessity and its impossibility. Her heroines are denied the solace of a helpmate's support and sympathy. Clearly able to see the sources of the problems she analyzed, she had greater difficulty in envisioning a viable alternative, such as Cather and Austin's companionate marriage or Glasgow's "strength that enables one to stand alone."[16] Rather, her skill lies in the quality of her analysis, the questions it poses, and the reasoning it undermines. Wharton in particular was personally and artistically tied to the two-women-one-man plot, which in her mind could be resolved only by an either-or choice.

In her fiction, male and female worlds seldom intersect, but women strain to bridge the gulf. When they succeed, they experience a double loss: they are still left awaiting the footstep that never comes, and they lose the person with whom they are in truth most intimate, another woman. Although Wharton looks at the two-women-one-man plot from the perspectives of competition and cooperation, the result is the same. In "Roman Fever," for example, Mrs. Slade and Mrs. Ansley are vital to each other's definitions of self. Both have defined their lives through their girlhood rivalry for Mrs. Ansley's husband; and though Mrs. Ansley obviously won the man, Mrs. Slade had his child. Mrs. Ansley envies her friend that brilliant and beautiful daughter without knowing her parentage. The best friends secretly feel sorry for each other, but that sympathy is only a disguised form of competitiveness. In this way their identities are collaborative and interdependent. When Mrs. Slade reveals the truth, both women lose the relationship that has been the foundation of their separate worlds. Wharton treats her characters ironically, yet Mrs. Slade and Mrs. Ansley have been more important to each other's sense of well-being than any of her married couples. They also have the opportunity to establish a new and perhaps more meaningful relationship.

From the other perspective, *The Reef* and *The Age of Innocence* shows pairs of women who were more intimate with each other than they were or will ever be with their mates. Unlike her contemporaries, Wharton does not allow her heroines to have a husband and a best woman friend. *The Buccaneers* comes closest to achieving this goal, but that too appears to be at the friend's expense, for Wharton never lost sight of the conflicting and often antithetical demands of love and friendship. She believed that all human ties were subject to the society in which they were formed, and any new tie realigned an old one. Yet her work shows a persistent effort to make all relationships between men and women and women and women more honest and more inclusive, as she more closely approximated the poles in her own life that were characterized by her relationship with her mother and her friendship with Sara Norton.

The strength of Wharton's fiction comes from what Herbert Marcuse defines as "the hidden categorical imperative of art," the impetus to make the fictitious or the ideal real.[17] This impetus can be traced in Wharton's efforts to present a model of female cooperation, which runs like an underground railroad throughout her work. Her exposure of the false simplicity of female stereotypes and her portrayal of the complexity and individuality of her heroines in an equally complicated world earned Wharton the response that a friend wrote to *The Times* after her obituary appeared: "The excellent obituary notices in *The Times* of August 14 [1937] rightly mentioned the many distinguished men who were

proud to be called Edith Wharton's friends. But at least one
undistinguished woman, slightly younger than Edith, would
like to bear testimony to her generous, sympathetic, and understanding kindness to herself and to many others of the
same sex and calibre."

In "A Further Glance," Wharton speculated about the future reception of her work:

> It is such bits of vanished life that I should like to
> gather up now, & make into a little memorial like the
> boxes adorned with exotic shells that sailors used to
> fabricate in the long leisure between voyages. That the
> shells will be very small, & the box when made a mere
> joke of a thing, (unless one puts one's ear to the shells—
> & how many will?) is what I should like to forestall my
> critics by mentioning that I have already foreseen—.[18]

Wharton was wrong. The shells she gathered more than
whisper in an eager ear. They still echo an ocean's roar.

NOTES

INTRODUCTION
The Alliance between Artist and Woman (pp. 1–11)

1. Percy Lubbock, *Portrait of Edith Wharton* (New York: D. Appleton-Century, 1947), 11.
2. William R. Tyler, "Personal Memories of Edith Wharton," *Proceedings of the Massachusetts Historical Society* 85 (1973): 94.
3. Lubbock, *Portrait of Edith Wharton*, 11.
4. Edith Wharton, *Ethan Frome* (New York: Charles Scribner's Sons, 1911; 1939), 11.
5. See Judith Saunders, "Becoming the Mask: Edith Wharton's Ingenues," *Massachusetts Studies in English* 8 (1982): 33–39. Saunders discusses the absences in Wharton's heroines but does not link them to their author.
6. Henry Dwight Sedgwick, "The Novels of Mrs. Wharton," *Atlantic*, 6 Aug. 1906, 219.
7. Q. D. Leavis, "Henry James's Heiress: The Importance of Edith Wharton," *Scrutiny* 7 (1938–39): 261–276.
8. David Leverenz, *Manhood and the American Renaissance* (Ithaca, N.Y.: Cornell University Press, 1989), 34.
9. Quoted from Robert Herrick in an unsigned article, "Edith Wharton: Two Conflicting Estimates of Her Art," *Current Opinion*, 15 Apr. 1915, 272.
10. Millicent Bell, *Edith Wharton and Henry James: The Story of Their Friendship* (New York: George Braziller, 1965).
11. R. W. B. Lewis, *Edith Wharton: A Biography* (New York: Harper and Row, 1975; Fromm International Publishing, 1985). Also see Cynthia Griffin Wolff, *A Feast of Words: The Triumph of Edith Wharton* (New York: Oxford University Press, 1977) and Blake Nevius, *Edith Wharton: A Study of Her Fiction* (Los Angeles and Berkeley: University of California Press, 1953).
12. See Margaret McDowell, "Viewing the Custom of Her Country:

Edith Wharton's Feminism," *Contemporary Literature* 15 (1974): 521–538; Elizabeth Ammons, *Edith's Wharton's Argument with America* (Athens: University of Georgia Press, 1980); Annette Clair Schreiber Zilversmit, "Mothers and Daughters: The Heroines of Edith Wharton's Novels," *DAI* 41 (1981): 5104A; Carol Wershoven, *The Female Intruder in the Novels of Edith Wharton* (Rutherford, N.J.: Fairleigh Dickinson University Press, 1982); and Wendy Gimbel, *Edith Wharton: Orphancy and Survival*, Landmark Dissertations in Women's Studies Series, ed. Annette Baxter (New York: Praeger, 1984).

13. Shari Benstock, *Women of the Left Bank: Paris, 1900–1940* (Austin: University of Texas, 1986), 64.

14. Janet Malcolm, "The Woman Who Hated Women," *The New York Times Book Review*, 16 Nov. 1986, 11.

15. Edith Wharton, *A Backward Glance* (New York: D. Appleton-Century, 1934), 212 (hereafter cited as *ABG*).

16. Edith Wharton, *The House of Mirth* (New York: Charles Scribner's Sons, 1905; 1933; reprint 1975), 57.

17. Edith Wharton, "Permanent Values in Fiction," *The Saturday Review of Literature*, 10 (7 Apr. 1934): 603. The handwritten draft of the sentence quoted shows far less disapproval and reads: "The novel, in short, in its most serious form is a sort of anthology of the author's ideas." It can be found in the Wharton Archives, the Beinecke Rare Book and Manuscript Library, Yale University, New Haven, Connecticut.

18. *The Valley of Decision* (1902) and *A Son at the Front* (1923) are not included in this study because they do not contain the plot outlined in "Friends." Although *The Glimpses of the Moon* (1922) provides another example of this plot, and *Twilight Sleep* (1927) can be read in the context of Wharton's relationship with her mother, Lucretia Jones, I have chosen not to discuss them because they are two of Wharton's least successful novels. For my purposes, texts such as *The Fruit of the Tree, The Children,* or *The Mother's Recompense* can be used as illustrations more effectively.

19. Edith Wharton, "Friends," *The Collected Short Stories of Edith Wharton*, ed. R. W. B. Lewis (New York: Charles Scribner's Sons, 1968), 200.

20. Edith Wharton, "Friends," 214.

21. Edith Wharton, *French Ways and Their Meaning* (New York: D. Appleton and Co., 1919; 1930), 102.

22. Edith Wharton, *French Ways*, 102.

23. For the source of the term "buried fable," see Gary H. Lindberg, *Edith Wharton and the Novel of Manners* (Charlottesville: University Press of Virginia, 1975), 45.

24. Leverenz, *Manhood*, 67.
25. Edith Wharton, "The Fullness of Life," in *The Collected Short Stories of Edith Wharton*, vol. 1, ed. R. W. B. Lewis (New York: Charles Scribner's Sons, 1968), 14.

CHAPTER ONE

The Continuing Contest in A Backward Glance *(pp. 13–28)*

1. See R. W. B. Lewis, *Edith Wharton: A Biography* (New York: Harper & Row, 1975; Fromm International Publishing, 1985), 86. Also see Edith Wharton, letter to Edward Burlingame, July 10, 1898, in *The Letters of Edith Wharton*, ed. by R. W. B. Lewis and Nancy Lewis (New York: Charles Scribner's Sons, 1988), 36.
2. See Cynthia Griffin Wolff, *A Feast of Words: The Triumph of Edith Wharton* (New York: Oxford University Press, 1977), 33. Wolff observes that the first part of *A Backward Glance* is devoted to a discussion of the mother's ancestral line.
3. See Bell Gale Chevigny, "Daughters Writing: Toward a Theory of Women's Biography," in *Between Women: Biographers, Novelists, Critics, Teachers, and Artists Write About Their Work on Women*, ed. Carol Ascher, Louise De Salvo, and Sara Ruddick (Boston: Beacon Press, 1984), 356–379. Chevigny observes that identifying with another's life can make one want to rationalize certain disturbing facts.
4. See Edith Wharton, "Life and I," Wharton Archives, the Beinecke Rare Book and Manuscript Library, Yale University, New Haven, Connecticut, 35 (hereafter cited as "Life"). In this first and more frank draft of her autobiography, Wharton writes that her mother's refusal to tell her about sex "did more than anything else to falsify & misdirect my whole life." Also see Lewis, *Edith Wharton*, 23–26, 30, 51, 53–54, 67 esp.
5. See Wolff, *A Feast of Words*, 9–54 esp.
6. Edith Wharton, *A Backward Glance* (New York: D. Appleton-Century, 1934), viii (hereafter cited as *ABG*).
7. Georges Gusdorf, "Conditions and Limits of Autobiography," in *Autobiography: Essays Theoretical and Critical*, ed. James Olney (Princeton, N.J.: Princeton University Press, 1980), 36.
8. Susan Stanford Friedman, "Women's Autobiographical Selves, Theory and Practice," in *The Private Self: Theory and Practice of Women's Autobiographical Writings*, ed. Shari Benstock (Chapel Hill and London: The University of North Carolina Press, 1988), 34–40 esp. Friedman contends that the assertion of a unique identity is a predominant pattern in the works of

male autobiographers. See also, in the same volume, Shari Benstock's essay, "Authorizing the Autobiographical," 7–33. Benstock suggests that female autobiographers are less successful than their male counterparts at keeping the ego intact (p. 12).

9. Mary Mason, "Autobiographies of Women Writers," in *Autobiography: Essays Theoretical and Critical*, ed. James Olney (Princeton, N.J.: Princeton University Press, 1980), 210. Also see Friedman, "Women's Autobiographical Selves," 38. Friedman explains that the cultural mirror projects "an image of WOMAN, a category that is supposed to define the living woman's identity" (p. 38).

10. Lewis, *Edith Wharton*, 207.

11. Jessica Benjamin, *The Bonds of Love: Psychoanalysis, Feminism, and the Problem of Domination* (New York: Pantheon Books, 1988), 95.

12. For the source of this concept of "mother," see Dorothy Dinnerstein, *The Mermaid and the Minotaur: Sexual Arrangements and the Human Malaise* (New York: Harper and Row, 1976), 111, 112.

13. See Carol Gilligan, *In a Different Voice: Psychological Theory and Women's Development* (Cambridge, Mass.: Harvard University Press, 1982), 46, 172 esp. She describes female development as a process in which the child forms her identity by seeing herself as similar and dissimilar to her mother. Also see Nancy Chodorow, *The Reproduction of Mothering: Psychoanalysis and the Sociology of Gender* (Berkeley and Los Angeles: University of California Press, 1978), 126–127, 169. As object relations theorists, Chodorow and Gilligan argue that identity is established by a sense of relatedness to and difference from another. Because mother and daughter share the same gender, the process of differentiation can be more difficult than for a son (Chodorow, 166–167).

14. See Elizabeth Ammons, *Edith Wharton's Argument With America* (Athens: University of Georgia Press, 1980), 56–96. She discusses the myth of Prince Charming in Wharton's fiction.

15. In "Life and I" Wharton apologizes for her "vanity" by calling it an "aesthetic desire" "*to make the picture prettier*" (p. 1). This explanation makes her recede into that picture because her importance is only as a part of the pleasing whole. The revision of this scene in *A Backward Glance* shows Wharton dominating the picture.

16. Benjamin, *The Bonds of Love*, 76.

17. Sigmund Freud, "Family Romances," in *The Standard Edition of the Complete Psychological Works of Sigmund Freud*, vol. 9

(1906-1908), trans. and ed. James Strachey in collaboration with Anna Freud, assisted by Alix Strachey and Alan Tyson (London: The Hogarth Press and the Institute of Psycho-analysis, 1973), 238.

18. Benjamin, *The Bonds of Love*, 221.
19. Wharton's attitude toward Emelyn was both compassionate and dismissive. Wharton saved a letter, now in the Beinecke Library, that Emelyn had written her after reading *A Backward Glance*. Emelyn wrote: "I loved your mother dearly. She was very good to me. I can't write about your book. I care and feel too much to write" (Jan. 14, 1935). How Wharton responded to this praise of her mother can only be conjectured. She felt that Emelyn was always complaining about her poverty and her health, and yet she was very generous to her financially. The author was particularly exasperated that "a brilliantly educated woman, a remarkable linguist & a really learned mind" never tried to earn a living and develop herself; nevertheless, the two were friends for more than fifty years (letter to Mary Cadwalader Jones, dated Jan. 30, 1924).
20. Edith Wharton, "A Little Girl's New York," *Harper's Magazine*, March 1938, 357.
21. Benjamin, *The Bonds of Love*, 83.
22. For a detailed analysis of Wharton's "making up" and her use of *The Alhambra*, see Judith Fryer, "Edith Wharton's 'Tact of Omission': Harmony and Proportion in *A Backward Glance*," *Biography* 6 (2) (1983): 148-169.
23. See Edith Wharton, "The Portrait," in *The Greater Inclination* (New York: Charles Scribner and Sons, 1899), 229-254. The story is the last in the volume, and its position creates the effect of "closing a chapter." It indicates that Wharton may have begun rethinking her relationship with her father. The heroine of "The Portrait" is a young woman who idolizes her unsavory father. When his portrait is unveiled, so are her eyes. Its idealized image only highlights the father's falseness, and the daughter, no longer able to deny the truth, dies. If Wharton's own veil were wearing thin, it would explain in part her difficulty in compiling the volume and the emotional problems that ensued after its completion. Even more dramatically, a rejection of her father would necessitate a painful reevaluation of the "prosaic " mother.
24. Adrienne Rich, *Of Woman Born: Motherhood as Experience and Institution* (New York: Norton, 1976), 236.
25. For information on Ebenezer Stevens, see *A Backward Glance*, 11-14.
26. See Sandra M. Gilbert and Susan Gubar, *The Madwoman in the*

Attic: The Woman Writer and the Ninteteenth-Century Literary Imagination (New Haven and London: Yale University Press, 1979), 54–57. Their reading of "Snow White" has many parallels with Wharton's relationship with her mother; for example, they note that motherhood transforms the queen into a monster in the king's absence (p. 37). Wharton's portrayal of herself incorporates the role of the queen, "artist," and the stepdaughter, "angel in the house." Lucretia represents the part of herself she would like to kill (Snow White) and the part she would like to have (queen) (p. 41).

27. Lewis, *Edith Wharton*, 181.
28. Lewis, *Edith Wharton*, 430.
29. For her last novel, *The Buccaneers*, Wharton was still scrupulously checking details about life in Saratoga sixty years before by sending a typewritten questionnaire to a friend. See the notebook numbered III, 1928, "Notes & Subjects, *The Gods Arrive, The Buccaneers*," in the Wharton Archives, the Beinecke Rare Book and Manuscript Library, Yale University, New Haven, Connecticut.
30. See Elaine Showalter, *A Literature of Their Own: British Women Novelists from Brontë to Lessing* (Princeton, N.J.: Princeton University Press, 1977), 61.
31. The expression is taken from Rachel Brownstein, *Becoming a Heroine: Reading about Women in Novels* (New York: Viking, 1982). Brownstein discusses how a female reader's identification with fictional heroines allows her to admire her own image and prompts her to interpret her own life through their plots. She argues that the marriage plots of many eighteenth- and nineteenth-century novels have been influential in shaping the female imagination.
32. See Edith Wharton, *The Buccaneers* (New York: D. Appleton-Century, 1938), 50–51. When the governess asks Mrs. St. George what stage her daughter Annabel has reached in her studies, she answers with the inspiration born of panic, "I have always left these things to the girls' teachers" (p. 51).
33. Edith Wharton, *The Mother's Recompense* (New York: D. Appleton, 1925).
34. See Percy Lubbock, *Portrait of Edith Wharton* (New York: D. Appleton-Century, 1947), 71–72. For background information on Lubbock's relationship with Wharton, see Lewis, *Edith Wharton*, 515–516.
35. Showalter, *A Literature of Their Own*, 29.
36. Showalter, *A Literature of Their Own*, 29.
37. See Viola Hopkins Winner, ed., "Introduction," in Edith Whar-

ton's *Fast and Loose*, (Charlottesville: University Press of Virginia, 1977), xxi. Winner states that from Broughton, Wharton "derived hints for the character of Georgie as capricious, self-willed, and flirtatious" and that she also adopted Mrs. Boughton's shorthand method of setting the scene with a series of visual details set forth like stage directions.

38. Ellen Glasgow, *The Woman Within* (New York: Harcourt, Brace, and World, 1954), 56.
39. Gusdorf, "Conditions and Limits of Autobiography," 46.
40. Edith Wharton, "The Fullness of Life," in *The Collected Short Stories of Edith Wharton*, vol. 1, ed. R. W. B. Lewis (New York: Charles Scribner's Sons, 1968), 14.
41. Lewis, *Edith Wharton*, 413.
42. Roy Pascal, *Design and Truth in Autobiography* (Cambridge, Mass.: Harvard University Press, 1960; New York: Garland Publishers, 1985).
43. Edith Wharton, "The Criticism of Fiction," *The Times Literary Supplement* 14 May 1924, 230.

CHAPTER TWO
A Safe Forum: Edith Wharton's Correspondence with Sara Norton (pp. 29–47)

1. Edith Wharton, letter to Sara Norton, June 3, 1901, the Beinecke Rare Book and Manuscript Library, Yale University, New Haven, Connecticut. All subsequently quoted letters are in the Wharton collection at the Beinecke Library and will be noted solely by date.
2. See Walter J. Ong, *Orality and Literacy; The Technologizing of the Word* (New York: Methuen, 1982), and Judith Gardiner, "The (Us)es of (I)dentity: A Response to Abel on (E)merging Identities," *Signs* 6 (Spring 1981): 438. Ong argues the importance of writing for the formation of more abstract, analytical, and interiorized thinking, and Gardner observes that threats to identity are lessened when one is in relationship with "an absent other who can be recreated in imagination and memory" (p. 438).
3. Carroll Smith-Rosenberg, "The Female World of Love and Ritual: Relations between Women in Nineteenth-Century America," *Signs* 1 (1975): 1–29.
4. October 19, 1908.
5. R. W. B. Lewis, *Edith Wharton: A Biography* (New York:

Harper and Row, 1975; Fromm International Publishing, 1985), 183.

6. Percy Lubbock, *Portrait of Edith Wharton* (New York: D. Appleton-Century, 1947), 28.

7. Lubbock, *Portrait of Edith Wharton*, 28.

8. Janet Malcolm, "The Woman Who Hated Women," *The New York Times Book Review*, 16 Nov. 1986, 11. Malcolm describes Wharton as a misogynist. Percy Lubbock's portrait, which is a series of her friends' recollections strung together with his commentary, reinforces this view. For a discussion of Lubbock's bias, see William R. Tyler, "Personal Memories of Edith Wharton," *Proceedings of the Massachusetts Historical Society* 85 (1973): 91–104; and Lewis, *Edith Wharton*, 515–516. Tyler presents his own portrait of Wharton, whom he remembers as a loving and supportive friend, and Lewis discusses the disintegration of Lubbock and Wharton's friendship following Lubbock's marriage to Sybil Cutting. Although most critics now recognize the waspish tone of Lubbock's book, the image of Wharton personally preferring the company of men to that of women has yet to be adjusted.

9. Lubbock, *Portrait of Edith Wharton*, 28.

10. Nancy Sahli, "Smashing: Women's Relationships before the Fall," *Chrysalis* 8 (1979): 17–27.

11. Sahli, "Smashing," 18.

12. Lewis, *Edith Wharton*, 27. See also Edith Wharton, "Life and I," the Beinecke Rare Book and Manuscript Library, New Haven, Connecticut, 34–35.

13. See Carroll Smith-Rosenberg, "The New Woman as Androgyne: Social Disorder and Gender Crisis, 1870–1936," in Smith-Rosenberg, *Disorderly Conduct: Visions of Gender in Victorian America* (New York: Alfred A. Knopf, 1985), 245–296.

14. Virginia Woolf outlines the problems of the "extraordinary" woman and her debt to all "ordinary" women in her essay, "Women and Fiction," in *Collected Essays* (New York: Harcourt, Brace, and World, 1967), 142.

15. Edith Wharton, *A Backward Glance* (New York: D. Appleton-Century, 1934), 293–294 (hereafter cited as *ABG*). Wharton's insistence on her difference from Jewett and Wilkins almost begs one to see her debt, especially in the case of Wilkins, whose treatment of the New England poor is akin to Wharton's. In fact, Wharton's novel *The Fruit of the Tree* (1907) in part deals with the plight of factory workers, a topic that was of concern to Wilkins in her novel *The Portion of Labor* (1901).

16. Edith Wharton, *The House of Mirth* (New York: Charles Scribner's Sons, 1905; 1933; reprint 1975), 5.

17. Lubbock, *Portrait of Edith Wharton*, 28.
18. For a discussion of James and Wharton's personal and literary friendship, see Millicent Bell, *Edith Wharton and Henry James: The Story of Their Friendship* (New York: George Braziller, 1965).
19. Edith Wharton, "The Fullness of Life," in *The Collected Short Stories of Edith Wharton*, vol. 1, ed. R. W. B. Lewis (New York: Charles Scribner's Sons, 1968), 14.
20. In *A Backward Glance*, Wharton gives Berry credit for teaching her whatever she knew about "the writing of clear concise English" (p. 108); see also pp. 114-117. For a different view of their relationship, see Lubbock, *Portrait of Edith Wharton*, 42-45. Millicent Bell discusses Wharton and James's suppressed rivalry for the recognition of the critics and the paying public. For insight into Wharton's personal and literary relationship with Fullerton, see Claire Colquitt, "Unpacking Her Treasures: Edith Wharton's 'Mysterious Correspondence' with Morton Fullerton," *Library Chronicle of the University of Texas* 31 (1985): 73-107; and Alan Gribben, " 'The Heart Is Insatiable': A Selection from Edith Wharton's Letters to Morton Fullerton," *Library Chronicle of the University of Texas* 31 (1985): 7-18.
21. Charles Eliot Norton, *Letters of Charles Eliot Norton*, ed. Sara Norton and M. A. DeWolfe Howe (Boston: Houghton Mifflin, 1913), 491. Charles Eliot Norton had a wide circle of friends that included Darwin, Dickens, Gaskell, Arnold, Ruskin, Dante Rossetti, Emerson, and Leslie Stephen.
22. March 23, 1903, and Sept. 1, 1902, respectively.
23. June 5, 1903. Also published in *The Letters of Edith Wharton*, ed. R. W. B. Lewis and Nancy Lewis (New York: Charles Scribner's Sons, 1988), 84-85.
24. Nov. 22, 1901.
25. Sat., 1901.
26. For a discussion of the woman artist in Wharton's fiction, see Elizabeth Ammons, "Cool Diana and the Blood-Red Muse: Edith Wharton on Innocence and Art," in *American Novelists Revisited*, ed. Fritz Fleischman (Boston: Hall, 1982), 217-223 esp.
27. See Cynthia Griffin Wolff, *A Feast of Words: The Triumph of Edith Wharton* (New York: Oxford University Press, 1977).
28. Lewis, *Edith Wharton*, 100-101.
29. June 3, 1901.
30. July 7, 1908. Also published in *The Letters of Edith Wharton*, 159-160.
31. July 9, 1916.
32. June 12, 1908.

33. Jan. 24, 1902.
34. Jan. 11, 1902.
35. Dec. 4, 1905.
36. Apr. 12, 1908. Also published in *The Letters of Edith Wharton*, 139–140.
37. Feb. 13, 1902. Also published in *The Letters of Edith Wharton*, 56–57.
38. Feb. 24, 1902. Also published in *The Letters of Edith Wharton*, 59.
39. Sept. 1, 1902.
40. The James letter is dated Aug. 17, 1902.
41. Sara Norton privately printed *New Nursery Rhymes on Old Lines by an American* (Boston, 1916). The family donated a copy in 1927 to the Houghton Library, Harvard University, Cambridge, Massachusetts. The book was originally sold for the benefit of the American Volunteer Motor-Ambulance Corps.
42. Sept. 30, 1905.
43. Aug. 7, 1906.
44. Jan. 10, 1906.
45. Nov. 1, 1912.
46. Jan. 26, 1911/1912 folder.
47. Nov. 26, 1914.
48. Aug. 23, 1907.
49. The poem is dated Nov. 18, 1904, and was published in *Scribner's*, Feb. 1902, 180.

CHAPTER THREE

The Context of Women's Relationships (pp. 48–66)

1. Joan Lidoff, "Another Sleeping Beauty: Narcissism in *The House of Mirth*," *American Quarterly* 32 (1980): 535.
2. Janet Malcolm, *The New York Times Book Review*, 16 Nov. 1986, 11.
3. Wharton is frequently compared with the naturalist writer Theodore Dreiser. See Alan Price, "Lily Bart and Carrie Meeber: Cultural Sisters," *American Literary Realism* 13 (1980): 238–245. Also see Blake Nevius, *Edith Wharton: A Study of Her Fiction* (Berkeley and Los Angeles: University of California Press, 1953), 58–59. Nevius states: "The quality in the novel [*The House of Mirth*] that seizes and holds the reader, and that accounts more than any other for its persistent vitality, is the same which we find in the novels of Dreiser. In the spectacles of a lonely struggle with the hostile forces of environment, there is a particular kind of fasination which is not at all diminished by the certainty of defeat."

4. David Graham Phillips, *Susan Lenox: Her Fall and Rise* (New York: D. Appleton, 1917; Upper Saddle River, N.J.: The Gregg Press, 1968), 104. Wharton calls *Susan Lenox* "a neglected masterpiece" in her autobiography, *A Backward Glance*, (New York: D. Appleton-Century, 1934), 235 (hereafter cited as *ABG*). Phillips is perhaps better known as the journalist whose 1902 *Cosmopolitan* article, "Treason in the Senate," inspired an incensed Theodore Roosevelt to coin the term "muckraker." Roosevelt, however, showed more restraint than the man who believed that his sister was the model for the character of Margaret Severance in *The Fashionable Adventures of Joshua Craig*. That unflattering portrait of an upper-class American woman cost Phillips his life, just days before the publication of *Susan Lenox*, when the avenging brother fired six bullets into his body (*Susan Lenox*, i–ii).

5. Edith Wharton, *The House of Mirth* (New York: Charles Scribner's Sons, 1905; 1933; reprint 1975), 85 (hereafter cited as *HM*).

6. Numerous critics have made this point. See Elizabeth Ammons, *Edith Wharton's Argument with America* (Athens: University of Georgia Press, 1980), 26–37; and Cynthia Griffin Wolff, *A Feast of Words: The Triumph of Edith Wharton* (New York: Oxford University Press, 1977), 117. Also see Nevius, *Edith Wharton: A Study of Her Fiction*, 55–58; Robert Shulman, "Divided Selves and the Market Society," *Perspectives on Contemporary Literature* 11 (1985): 10–19; Wai-Chee Dimock, "Debasing Exchange: Edith Wharton's *The House of Mirth*," *PMLA* 100 (Oct. 1985): 783–792; Irving Howe, "A Reading of *The House of Mirth*," in *Edith Wharton*, ed. Irving Howe (Englewood Cliffs, N.J.: Prentice-Hall, 1962), 119–129; Alfred Kazin, "Edith Wharton," in *Edith Wharton*, ed. Irving Howe, 89-94; Cathy N. Davidson, "Kept Women in the House of Mirth," *Markham Review* 9 (1979): 10–13; Judith Fetterley, " 'The Temptation to Be a Beautiful Object': Double Standard and Double Bind in *The House of Mirth*," *Studies in American Fiction* 5 (1977): 199–211; Judith Saunders, "A New Look at the Oldest Profession in Wharton's *New Year's Day*," *Studies in Short Fiction* 17 (1980); 121–126. Saunders draws a parallel between the heroine of *New Year's Day* and Lily Bart.

7. The wording of the following passage suggests that someday Selden may learn the truth:

> he remembered long afterward how the red play of the flame sharpened the depression of her nostrils, and intensified the blackness of the shadows which struck up from her cheekbones to her eyes. She knelt there for a few moments in si-

lence; a silence which he dared not break. When she rose he
fancied that he saw her draw something from her dress and
drop it into the fire; but he hardly noticed the gesture *at the
time* [italics added]. (*HM*, 310)

8. Wharton's next novel, *The Fruit of the Tree* (1907), grew from
   similar political and sociological concerns with class. The
   heroine, Justine Brent, is a self-supporting nurse deeply committed to easing the problems of the working class by imple-
   menting humane working and living conditions in the town in
   which her husband, John Amherst, manages the mill.
9. See Elaine Showalter, "The Death of a Lady (Novelist): Edith
   Wharton's *House of Mirth*," *Representations* 9 (1985): 134.
   Showalter notes that "Lily is stranded between two worlds of
   experience: the intense female friendships and mother-daughter bonds characteristic of nineteenth-century American wom-
   en's culture, which Carroll Smith-Rosenberg has called 'the
   female world of love and ritual,' and the dissolution of single-
   sex relationships in the interest of more intimate friendships
   between men and women that was part of the gender crisis at
   the turn of the century." Showalter's analysis of Lily also serves
   to describe the author's predicament of being professionally
   stranded between two literary traditions, one male and the
   other female. Wanting to be critically recognized as a writer,
   not as a woman writer, she felt it necessary to distinguish herself from Sarah Orne Jewett and Mary Wilkins and to align
   herself with Theodore Dreiser, Henry James, and later Sinclair
   Lewis.
10. For the organization of old New York society in *The House of
    Mirth*, *The Custom of the Country*, and *The Age of Innocence*, see
    Mary Ellis Gibson, "Edith Wharton and the Ethnography of
    Old New York," *Studies in American Fiction* 13 (1) (Spring
    1985): 57–69, 60 esp.
11. Jennifer Radden, "Defining Self-Deception," *Dialogue* 23 (1)
    (March 1984): 103–120.
12. Adrienne Rich, "Women and Honor: Some Notes on Lying," in
    On Lies, Secrets, and Silence (New York: W. W. Norton, 1979),
    186, 188.
13. Showalter, "The Death of a Lady (Novelist)," 136.
14. Margaret McDowell, "Viewing the Custom of Her Country:
    Edith Wharton's Feminism," *Contemporary Literature* 15
    (1974): 521–538. McDowell observes that Wharton often initially
    sets up stereotypical assumptions about women's behavior and
    then undercuts those assumptions.
15. Showalter ("The Death of a Lady [Novelist]") sees Bertha as

Lily's "nemesis" (p. 139), and Ammons describes the relationships between women in this novel as "frequently hostile" (p. 39). Also see Janet Malcolm, *The New York Times Book Review*, 16 Nov. 1987. She characterizes Bertha as "the personification of female treachery and malevolence" (p. 11).

16. Later Lily smiles "to think of recapturing him [Gryce] from Evie Van Osburgh" (*HM*, 92). She enjoys the sexual competition for the advantage it gives her over the women with whom she cannot compete materially. This theme, with slight variations, is the basis of several of Wharton's short stories, including "Her Son," "Roman Fever," "Pomegranate Seed," and "Bewitched."

17. See Carolyn Karcher, "Male Vision and Female Revision in James's *The Wings of the Dove* and Wharton's *The House of Mirth*," *Women's Studies* 10 (1984): 241. Karcher states that in *The House of Mirth* "Wharton seems to be suggesting that the availability of satisfying and remunerative careers is a prerequisite for ending women's dependency" and that the image of Gerty holding Lily "points toward the creation of a feminine support network that promises to facilitate women's achievement of independence" (p. 241).

18. Mrs. Bart raised her daughter with much the same motivation and purpose as Miss Havisham raised Estella in *Great Expectations*: "Only one thought consoled her [Mrs. Bart], and that was the contemplation of Lily's beauty. She studied it with a kind of passion, as though it were some weapon she had slowly fashioned for her vengeance" (*HM*, 34). Lily envies the "lucky girls who grow up in the shelter of a mother's love. . . . it takes a mother's unerring vigilance and foresight to land her daughters safely in the arms of wealth and suitability" (*HM*, 91). See Gibson, "Edith Wharton and the Ethnography of Old New York," 60. Gibson describes Lily as "an orphan to old traditions," who is "unable to accommodate to the new promiscuity." Also see Wendy Gimbel, *Edith Wharton: Orphancy and Survival*, Landmark Dissertations in Women's Studies Series, ed., Annette Baxter (New York: Praeger, 1984).

19. Showalter, "The Death of a Lady (Novelist)," 145.

20. Ammons, *Edith Wharton's Argument with America*, 42–43.

21. See Willa Cather, *A Lost Lady* (New York: Alfred A. Knopf, 1923; Vintage, 1972); and Ellen Glasgow, *The Sheltered Life* (Garden City, N.Y.: Doubleday, 1932; London: Virago, 1981). *The Sheltered Life* is thematically similar to *The House of Mirth* but ends more violently. Like Lily Bart, Eva Birdsong lives in a society that is primarily maintained by women's silence and the feigning of ignorance. Eva too is an objet d'art, the flesh-and-

blood embodiment of the myth of southern womanhood, and the price she pays for homage and chivalry is as dear as Lily's: "As late as the spring of 1906, she was still regarded less as a woman than as a memorable occasion" (*Sheltered Life*, 7). When Eva is ultimately unable to lie to herself or to maintain a willful blindness to her husband's affairs, she fatally shoots him. Her act is seen as a moment of madness brought on by postoperative depression, but it can be interpreted as an act of sanity and read as a warning. Also see Marianne Hirsch, "Spiritual Bildung: The Beautiful Soul as Paradigm," in *The Voyage in: Fictions of Female Development*, ed. Elizabeth Abel, Marianne Hirsch, and Elizabeth Langland (Hanover, N.H.: University Press of New England, 1983). Hirsch makes the point that inward journeys that heroines such as Lily make often end in death, but they do not have to be interpreted as personal failures.

22. See Elizabeth Ammons, "The Business of Marriage in Edith Wharton's *The Custom of the Country*," *Criticism* 16 (1974); 326–338.

23. Edith Wharton, *The Custom of the Country* (New York: Charles Scribner's Sons, 1913; reprint n.d.), 430 (hereafter cited as *CC*).

24. R. W. B. Lewis, *Edith Wharton: A Biography* (New York: Harper and Row, 1975; Fromm International Publishing, 1985), 349–350.

25. Edith Wharton, "A Little Girl's New York," *Harper Magazine*, March 1938, 357.

26. Carroll Smith-Rosenberg, "The New Woman as Androgyne: Social Disorder and Gender Crisis, 1870–1936," in *Disorderly Conduct: Visions of Gender in Victorian America* (New York: Alfred A. Knopf, 1985) 245–296.

27. See Carol Wershoven, *The Female Intruder in the Novels of Edith Wharton* (Rutherford, N.J.: Fairleigh Dickinson University Press, 1982), 59. Wershoven sees Indiana and Undine's relationship as having nothing to do with friendship because it is an alliance that works for their mutual benefit.

28. Phillips, *Susan Lenox*, 188.

CHAPTER FOUR

The Buried Fables in
Ethan Frome *and* Summer *(pp. 67–84)*

1. Letter to Sara Norton, dated Sept. 1, 1902, Wharton Archives, the Beinecke Rare Book and Manuscript Library, Yale University, New Haven, Connecticut.

2. Edith Wharton, *A Backward Glance* (New York: D. Appleton-Century, 1934), 293 (hereafter cited as *ABG*).

3. For discussions of this theme, see Barbara White, "Edith Wharton's *Summer* and 'Woman's Fiction,' " *Essays in Literature* 11 (1984): 223–235. Also see Nancy Walker, " 'Seduced and Abandoned': Convention and Reality in Edith Wharton's *Summer*," *Studies in American Literature* 11 (1983): 107–114; Geoffrey Walton, *Edith Wharton: A Critical Interpretation* (Rutherford, N.J.: Fairleigh Dickinson University Press, 1970; revised 1982), 94; Blake Nevius, *Edith Wharton: A Study of Her Fiction* (Berkeley and Los Angeles: University of California Press, 1953), 173.

4. The term "buried fable" and its definition are borrowed from Gary H. Lindberg, *Edith Wharton and the Novel of Manners* (Charlottesville: University Press of Virginia, 1975), 45.

5. See Nevius, *Edith Wharton: A Study of Her Fiction*, 123. Also see Orlene Murad, "Edith Wharton and Ethan Frome," *Modern Language Studies* 13 (3) (Summer 1983): 94.

6. Carroll Smith-Rosenberg, *Disorderly Conduct: Visions of Gender in Victorian America* (New York: Alfred A. Knopf, 1985), 265.

7. Joanna Russ, "What Can a Heroine Do? Or Why Women Can't Write," in *Images of Women in Fiction: Feminist Perspectives*, ed. Susan Koppelman (Bowling Green, Ohio: Bowling Green University Popular Press, 1972; reprint 1973), 3–20.

8. See Margaret B. McDowell, "Viewing the Custom of Her Country: Edith Wharton's Feminism," *Contemporary Literature* 15 (1974): 530.

9. Edith Wharton, *Ethan Frome* (New York: Charles Scribner's Sons, 1911; 1939), 14 (hereafter cited as *EF*).

10. *ABG*, 200; also see 199–205. For further information on Wharton's ideas about the treatment of character, see Edith Wharton, *The Writing of Fiction* (New York: Charles Scribner's Sons, 1925; reprint, New York: Octagon Books, 1977), 26–29, 72–73, 86–87 esp. (hereafter cited as *WF*).

11. See Cynthia Griffin Wolff, *A Feast of Words: The Triumph of Edith Wharton* (New York: Oxford University Press, 1977), 170–172 esp.

12. See Edith Wharton, "Permanent Values in Fiction," *Saturday Review of Literature*, 7 Apr. 1934, 603.

13. See Joseph X. Brennan, "*Ethan Frome*: Structure and Metaphor," *Modern Fiction Studies* 12 (Winter 1961–1962): 347–356. He notes the narrator's identification with Ethan and concludes: "It seems to me, therefore, that it would be much more reasonable to judge the novel in terms of the special character

of the narrator's mind . . . rather than in terms of psychological realism" (p. 356). Wolff (*A Feast of Words*) starts her discussion of the novel from this point, according to R. B. Hovey in
his essay "*Ethan Frome*: A Controversy about Modernizing It,"
American Literary Realism 19 (1) (Fall 1986): 4–20.

14. Edith Wharton, *The Decoration of Houses* (New York: Charles
    Scribner's Sons, 1897), 9.

15. For a reading of the economic and emotional deprivation suf-
    fered by the women Zeena represents, see Elizabeth Ammons,
    Edith Wharton's Argument with America (Athens: The Univer-
    sity of Georgia Press, 1980), 68–73. Unfortunately, the narra-
    tor's story dictates that Ethan's romantic vision of Mattie has
    an attendant image of Zeena as the wicked witch. Ammons
    states that the final vision of Mattie is Ethan's romantic vision
    "brought to its sterile conclusion" (p. 76). See also David Eg-
    genschwiler, "The Ordered Disorder of *Ethan Frome*," *Studies
    in the Novel* 9 (1977): 237–246. Eggenschwiler argues that
    Frome's fancies vascillate between "romantic adventure and
    domestic stability" (p. 240).

16. See "Edith Wharton Letters Selected, Transcribed, and Edited
    by Alan Gribben," *The Library Chronicle of the University of
    Texas* 31 (1985): 24. From a letter that Wharton wrote to Mor-
    ton Fullerton, dated Friday, June 5, (1908), Gribben deduces
    that the source of this scene was a minor road accident in
    France. R. W. B. Lewis, *Edith Wharton: A Biography* (New
    York: Harper and Row, 1975; Fromm International Publish-
    ing, 1985), traces the antecedent to a disastrous sled ride in
    Lenox in 1904 that left one girl dead and another lame (p. 308).
    For alternatives to my reading, see Peter L. Hays, "First and
    Last in *Ethan Frome*," *Notes on Modern American Literature* 1
    (1) (Winter 1976): Item 15, no. 10259. He views Ethan as a care-
    taker, who positions himself first on the sled to protect Mattie
    by absorbing the full impact of the crash. Also see Carol Wer-
    shoven, *The Female Intruder in the Novels of Edith Wharton*
    (Rutherford, N.J.: Fairleigh Dickinson University Press, 1982),
    21–22. Wershoven describes Mattie as courageous and energet-
    ic.

17. Brennan ("*Ethan Frome*: Structure and Metaphor") categorizes
    the imagery symbolically associated with Mattie as having to
    do with birds, lovely and delicate objects, nature, and the color
    red. In contrast, Zeena is linked with her cat, a predator, and
    things unnatural.

18. See Cynthia Griffin Wolff, "Edith Wharton and the 'Visionary'
    Imagination," *Frontiers: Journal of Women's Studies* 2 (3)

(1977): 28. Wolff notes that throughout Wharton's life the term "visionary" applied "both to simple daydreaming and to the more rigorous act of preparing to write fiction" and that as she grew older and matured as an artist, she developed a more "flexible and comfortable understanding of the 'visionary' " (p. 25). The ultimate moral of *Ethan Frome* is, as Wolff writes, the "clear and controlled distinction between 'vision' and 'reality' " (p. 28).

19. Edith Wharton, "The Criticism of Fiction," *Times Literary Supplement*, 14 May 1914, 230 (hereafter cited as "CF").

20. The point is noted by Wolff, *A Feast of Words*, 163-164 and Ammons, *Edith Wharton's Argument with America*, 76.

21. Edith Wharton, "Life and I," Wharton Archives, the Beinecke Rare Book and Manuscript Library, Yale University, New Haven, Connecticut, 3 (hereafter cited as "Life").

22. For a discussion of winter imagery as it relates to the narrator's identification with Ethan, see Wolff, *"A Feast of Words,"* 170-172 esp.

23. I am indebted to Eggenschwilen, "The Ordered Disorder of *Ethan Frome*," for this image (p. 241). He sees Ethan and Mattie lying side by side in "chaste twin beds of the graveyard."

24. Edith Wharton, "Pomegranate Seed," *Scribner's Magazine*, Mar. 1912, 284-291.

25. See Lewis, *Edith Wharton*, 396.

26. Lewis, *Edith Wharton*, 397.

27. Edith Wharton, *Summer* (New York: Appleton, 1917; New York: Charles Scribner's Sons, 1972), 15 (hereafter cited as *Summer*).

28. Lewis, *Edith Wharton*, 397.

29. Lewis, *Edith Wharton*, 397.

30. Wolff, *A Feast of Words*, 301.

31. Wolff, *A Feast of Words*, 304.

32. Wolff, *A Feast of Words*, 305.

33. Wolff, *A Feast of Words*, 303.

34. Ammons, *Edith Wharton's Argument with America*, 131.

35. Critics who see the ending as a form of perpetual imprisonment and daughterhood include Elizabeth Ammons, *Edith Wharton's Argument with America*, 133, 136-137, 141; Geoffrey Walton, *Edith Wharton: A Critical Interpretation*, 91, 97-98; Blake Nevius, *Edith Wharton: A Study of Her Fiction*, 168-171; Judith Fryer, *Felicitous Space: The Imaginative Structures of Edith Wharton and Willa Cather* (Chapel Hill and London: University of North Carolina Press, 1986), 199; and John W. Crowley, "The Unmastered Streak: Feminist Themes in Edith

Wharton's *Summer*," *American Literary Realism* 15 (1) (1982): 86–96. For more positive readings, see Wolff, *A Feast of Words*, 290; Marilyn French, "Introduction," in *Summer* (New York: Berkeley Books, 1981) xlviii; and White, "Edith Wharton's *Summer* and 'Women's Fiction,' " 233. Also see Carol Wershoven, "The Divided Conflict of Edith Wharton's *Summer*," *Colby Library Quarterly* 21 (1) (1985): 5–10. Wershoven argues that Royall and Charity grow in tandem.

36. See Margaret B. McDowell, *Edith Wharton*, (Boston: G. K. Hall, 1976), 70. She sees Charity's mother's death as yet another abandonment.

37. Lewis, *Edith Wharton*, 397.

38. See Wolff, *A Feast of Words*, 290.

39. Wolff, *A Feast of Words*, recognizes the allure of retrogression in her discussion of *Ethan Frome* and states that there is "a sensuous attraction in the notion of annihilation—of comforting nothingness" (pp. 174–175).

40. Janet Flanner, "Dearest Edith," *New Yorker*, 2 March 1929, 26; also in her *An American in Paris* (New York: Simon and Schuster, 1940), 185.

CHAPTER FIVE

Female Partnerships in the Business of Living (pp. 85–104)

1. For discussions of the marriage plot, see Mary P. Ryan, *The Empire of the Mother: American Writing about Domesticity 1830–1860* (New York and London: Harrington Park Press, 1985), 120–124.

2. For an earlier and cruder version of this pattern of approach and avoidance, see Edith Wharton, "Life and I," Wharton Archives, the Beinecke Rare Book and Manuscript Library, Yale University, New Haven, Connecticut, 51 (hereafter cited as "Life"). On a trip to Germany with her parents, Wharton confesses that she was "rather bored, & tired" and decided to distract herself by flirting with another young woman's unacknowledged fiancé because it appealed to her sense of humor. She stresses that this one incident with a man, who was engaged to "a dull & rather solemn" ("Life," 51) heiress who bored him, marks the single flirtation of her life. Wharton's choice to see the man as unattainable makes her feel more comfortable with making his fiancée miserable. For an analysis of this incident, see Annette Clair Schreiber Zilversmit, "Mothers and Daughters: The Heroines in the Novels of Edith Wharton," (Ph.D. diss., New York University, 1980). Zilversmit empha-

sizes the female rivalry in this anecdote and sees it underlying most of Wharton's work. Women choose men who are attached as a way of fleeing adult sexuality and independence (p. 23). I see the choice as necessary, rather than retrogressive, and identify it as one Wharton found vital for her own artistic development.

3. Edith Wharton, *A Backward Glance* (New York: D. Appleton-Century, 1934), 115. For more information on Wharton's relationship with Berry, see R. W. B. Lewis, *Edith Wharton: A Biography* (New York: Harper and Row, 1975; New York: Fromm International Publishing, 1985), 48–49, 238, 344.

4. Downplayed in *The Reef*, mother-daughter competition underlies the plots of *The Children, Ethan Frome, The Mother's Recompense*, "Les Metteurs en scène," and especially several of the ghost stories, such as "Bewitched" and "Pomegranate Seed," in which the dead refuse to relinquish their lovers to a replacement. However, after Lily Bart, Wharton's heroines deliberately prefer not to make other women feel miserable for their own amusement.

5. Elizabeth Ammons, *Edith Wharton's Argument with America* (Athens: The University of Georgia Press, 1980), 91.

6. Ammons (*Edith Wharton's Argument with America*) notes that it is as if writing *Ethan Frome* freed Wharton to write *The Reef*, but she finds it hard to see how writing the former cleared the way for the latter (p. 78). If writing *Ethan Frome* helped its author to resolve some of her conflicted feelings about her mother, though, it could have allowed Wharton to investigate less competitive and destructive relationships between women.

7. See Lewis, *Edith Wharton*, for detailed information on the Fullerton-Wharton relationship (pp. 203–328). Katherine was Fullerton's cousin but was raised as his sister. They became engaged when the true relationship was revealed (see esp. pp. 200–203, 211–212, 248–250, 285–287).

8. Letter to William Brownell, Aug. 29, 1918, Wharton Archives, Amherst College, as quoted by Cynthia Griffin Wolff, in *A Feast of Words: The Triumph of Edith Wharton* (New York: Oxford University Press, 1977), 218.

9. See Jean Gooder, "Unlocking Edith Wharton: An Introduction to *The Reef*," *The Cambridge Quarterly* 15 (1) (1986): 49. Gooder observes that in the midst of writing *The Reef* Wharton made "a dash" to visit George Sand's estates as if "Sand provided some necessary touchstone" (p. 45).

10. Clare Colquitt, "Unpacking Her Treasures: Edith Wharton's

'Mysterious Correspondence' with Morton Fullerton," *Library Chronicle of the University of Texas* 31 (1985): 100. The letter is dated June 10 (1912).

11. Lewis, *Edith Wharton*, 208.

12. Lewis, *Edith Wharton*, 207.

13. Colquitt, "Unpacking Her Treasures," quotes from a June 8, 1908, letter that Wharton wrote to Fullerton, in which she asked, "Is there any possibility of [Katherine] coming our way before she goes to Europe?" (p. 96). Also see Wolff, *A Feast of Words*, 145–151 and esp. 198–202.

14. Edith Wharton, letter to Morton Fullerton, Aug. 26, 1908 (letter 6), as quoted by Alan Gribben in " 'The Heart Is Insatiable': A Selection from Edith Wharton's Letters to Morton Fullerton," *Library Chronicle of the University of Texas* 31 (1985): 18. Also published in R. W. B. Lewis and Nancy Lewis, eds., *The Letters of Edith Wharton*, (New York: Charles Scribners Sons, 1988), 161.

15. Letter of [1910] as quoted in Colquitt, "Unpacking Her Treasures," 76. Colquitt uses brackets to indicate letters dated in the Zeitlen and Ver Brugge Booksellers catalog accompanying the collection of Wharton's letters to Fullerton housed in the Harry Ranson Humanities Research Center at the University of Texas at Austin. Also published in Lewis and Lewis, eds., *The Letters of Edith Wharton*, 216.

16. See "Edith Wharton's Letters Selected, Transcribed, and Annotated by Alan Gribben," *The Library Chronicle of the University of Texas* 31 (1985): 46. Gribben explains that this letter is especially difficult to date but notes that it accords in tone with those Wharton wrote in the latter half of 1910. Also published in Lewis and Lewis, eds., *The Letters of Edith Wharton*, 207.

17. Gribben, " 'The Heart Is Insatiable,' " 16. For the Tuesday [Winter 1910] letter from which this quotation is taken, see Lewis and Lewis, eds., *The Letters of Edith Wharton*, 196–197.

18. Lewis and Lewis, eds., *The Letters of Edith Wharton*, 145. The letter is dated Tuesday [May 17, 1908].

19. Colquitt, "Unpacking Her Treasures," 90–91. The quotation Colquitt cites is from a letter of [1909].

20. Gribben, " 'The Heart Is Insatiable,' " 16.

21. Lewis, *Edith Wharton*, 445.

22. In *Edith Wharton, A Critical Study* (New York: D. Appleton, n.d.), Katherine Fullerton Gerould defends Wharton against these common charges: she is James's "prize" pupil (p. 6); she has lost touch with the lives of ordinary people; she is unemotional; and she does not deal with a broader American theme. Wharton "is an author passionately preoccupied with her coun-

try," Katherine asserts, who "disdains equally the popularly sentimental and the fashionably subversive" (9–10). She especially praises Wharton's technical achievement and sees it as a reason for her work's popularity. Katherine argues that "inhibitions are as necessary to real drama as passions" (p. 8).

23. Edith Wharton, *The Reef* (New York: Charles Scribner's Sons, 1912; 1965), 8 (hereafter cited as *Reef*).

24. Ammons (*Edith Wharton's Argument with America*) compares Wharton's treatment of Anna in *The Reef* to Sleeping Beauty and her characterization of Sophy to Cinderella (p. 29).

25. Lewis, *Edith Wharton*, 206.

26. At times Wharton seems to be borrowing from the journal she kept during her affair with Fullerton; for example, compare Anna's thinking, "Don't I feel things as other women do?" (*Reef*, 342) with Wharton's journal entry, "I have never in my life known what it is to be happy (as a woman knows happiness) even for a single hour—" (Lewis, *Edith Wharton*, 207).

27. Letter of 26 Aug., as quoted in Colquitt, "Unpacking Her Treasures," 84. Wharton did not include the year, but from internal evidence Colquitt determines that it was written in 1908. Also published in Lewis and Lewis, eds., *The Letters of Edith Wharton*, 161.

28. This question similarly concerns Newland Archer in *The Age of Innocence* (New York: D. Appleton-Century, 1920; New York: Charles Scribner's Sons, 1970), 44, 83 (hereafter cited as *AI*). He bemoans the fact that a "nice" woman like May cannot claim the kind of freedom that would allow her individuality to emerge, but an Ellen Olenska, no matter how wronged, is somehow always to blame (p. 97).

29. Sophy is also associated with Lily Bart because Darrow's "man-to-man" talk with her is reminiscent of Rosedale's with Lily (*Reef*, 71).

30. Other echoes of Tolstoy's heroine include the following: "She wondered what she had to hold or satisfy him. He loved her now; she had no doubt of that; but how could she hope to keep him? They were so nearly of an age that already she felt herself his senior. As yet the difference was not visible; outwardly at least they were matched; but ill-health or unhappiness would soon do away with this equality" (329); "She knew how he disliked these idle returns on the irrevocable, and her fear of doing or saying what he disliked was tinged by a new instinct of subserviency against which her pride revolted. She thought to herself: 'He will see the change, and grow indifferent to me as he did to *her*'" (346–347).

31. See Gary H. Lindberg, *Edith Wharton and the Novel of Man-*

ners (Charlottesville: University Press of Virginia, 1975). Lindberg makes this point about Wharton's fiction in general, stating that "the moral crises . . . so often emerge from such changes in perception that the essence of a character's moral development seems to involve shifts in his ways of seeing" (p. 57). Nevius, *Edith Wharton: A Study of Her Fiction* (Berkeley and Los Angeles: University of California Press, 1953), makes the same point more specifically about Archer and Ellen in *The Age of Innocence* (p. 187).

32. See Judith Gardiner, "The (Us)es of (I)dentity: A Response to Abel on '(E)merging Identities," *Signs* 6 (Spring 1981): 438. Gardiner suggests that in the *Bildungsroman* or the novel of female development the artist is represented by a pair of women. That pattern coincides with Wharton's perpetual pairing of heroines.

33. Wharton's heroines also resist competition because it is associated with the aggressive and masculine pubic sphere, characterized by Wall Street. For the historical context, see Barbara Welter, "The Cult of True Womanhood: 1820–1860," *American Quarterly* 18 (Summer 1966): 151–174. Also see Valerie Miner and Helen E. Longino, eds., *Competition: A Feminist Taboo?* (New York: The Feminist Press, 1988), 248–258.

34. Carol Wershoven, *The Female Intruder in the Novels of Edith Wharton* (Rutherford, N.J.: Fairleigh Dickinson University Press, 1982), 98. Also see Elizabeth Ammons, *Edith Wharton's Heroines: Studies in Aspiration and Compliance* (Urbana-Champaign: University of Illinois, 1974), 50. She describes "the reef" as the double standard that beaches Anna's dreams.

35. Critics are divided on how to read the ambiguous ending. See James Gargano, "Edith Wharton's *The Reef*: The Genteel Woman's Quest for Knowledge," *Novel* 10 (1) (Fall 1976): 40–48. Gargano envisions Anna's repudiating Darrow and Sophy and reads the final scene as exposing "the tawdriness and banality of the 'romantic lie' which promotes the idea of personal indulgence against the interests of the human order" (p. 47). Gooder ("Unlocking Edith Wharton") also thinks that Anna gives up Darrow because they have struck the dangerous realities of feelings from the unmapped regions of experience" (p. 52). For alternative readings, see Blake Nevius, *Edith Wharton: A Study of Her Fiction*. Nevius imagines Sophy's future "foreshadowed in the vulgar outlines of her sister's career" (p. 135) while Anna and Darrow retreat to the status quo. See also Geoffrey Walton, *Edith Wharton: A Critical Study* (Rutherford, N.J.: Fairleigh Dickinson University Press, 1970; updated 1982). Walton in-

terprets the contrast between Sophy and her sister as heavily underlining all of the novel's implied criticism of Anna; it diminishes her tragedy. He sees only qualified happiness for Anna and Darrow in the open ending. Carol Wershoven (*The Female Intruder*) agrees that any marriage between them will be disappointing for "Anna will bring the eternal surveillance of a jealous and disillusioned woman" (p. 107), but she also sees the final scene demonstrating Sophy's strength to transcend her environment.

36. See Edith Wharton, "A Little Girl's New York," *Harper's Monthly Magazine*, March 1938, 357.

37. For a discussion of Wharton's attitude toward her male characters, see Julie Olin-Ammentorp, "Edith Wharton's Challenge to Feminist Criticism," *Studies in American Fiction* 16 (Autumn 1988): 237–244.

38. Wharton's description is reminiscent of her description of herself and Sara Norton as "wretched exotics produced in a European glass-house." Letter to Sara Norton June 5, 1903, Yale University, the Beinecke Rare Book and Manuscript Library, New Haven, Connecticut.

39. Wolff (*A Feast of Words*) notes May's often overlooked complexity (p. 323), as does Lindberg, *Edith Wharton and the Novel of Manners*, 135–136.

40. For a differing interpretation, see Ammons, *(Edith Wharton's Argument with America)* who describes Ellen as an artist at heart "whose creative medium is her own life" (p. 145) and May as another of Wharton's child-women (p. 147). She views their relationship, based on rivalry, as hostile (p. 151).

41. Wershoven, *The Female Intruder*, 85.

42. Judith Fryer, *Felicitous Space: The Imaginative Structures of Edith Wharton and Willa Cather* (Chapel Hill: University of North Carolina Press, 1986). Fryer observes that May is what Wharton might have become if she had remained in old New York (p. 127), and Geoffrey Walton (*Edith Wharton: A Critical Study*) notes that in the combined characterizations of Anna Leath, Rose Sellars in *The Children*, and Ellen Olenska, Wharton idealizes and partly criticizes her own nature (pp. 145–146).

43. Nancy K. Miller, *Subject to Change: Reading Feminist Writing* (New York: Columbia University Press, 1988), 44.

44. Edith Wharton, "The Quicksand," in *The Collected Short Stories of Edith Wharton*, vol. 1, ed. R. W. B. Lewis (New York: Charles Scribner's Sons, 1968), 410 (hereafter cited as "Quicksand"). Also see "The Dilettante," in the same volume, in which

a man's betrothed decides not to marry him after visiting his mistress.

45. Wolff, *A Feast of Words*, 328.
46. Lindberg, *Edith Wharton and the Novel of Manners*, 137.
47. Wolff, *A Feast of Words*, 325.

CHAPTER SIX

Edith Wharton's Recompense (pp. 105–25)

1. Edith Wharton, *The Mother's Recompense* (New York: D. Appleton, 1925) (hereafter cited as MR). For a discussion of Edith Wharton's relationship to the sentimental tradition, see Amy Kaplan, *The Social Construction of American Realism* (Chicago: University of Chicago Press, 1988), 65–88.
2. For background information on Aguilar and a discussion of *The Mother's Recompense*, see Adeline R. Tintner, "Mothers, Daughters, and Incest in the Late Novels of Edith Wharton," in *The Lost Tradition: Mothers and Daughters in Literature*, ed. Cathy N. Davidson and E. M. Broner (New York: Frederick Ungar, 1980), 147–156. Both Aguilar's and Wharton's novels are mostly told from the mothers' points of view, and for this reason Tintner sees Wharton as "a liberal—if rebellious—descendant of Grace Aguilar" (p. 155).
3. Edith Wharton's well-balanced, Latinate sentences, comprising unsentimental, bleak stories, like *The House of Mirth* and the enormously successful *Ethan Frome*, made her writing seem more "masculine" than "feminine"; and though her subject matter—adultery, incest, suicide, mercy killing—was often sensational, she wrote with restraint. This trait caused misunderstandings in her personal life, but it earned her critical admiration and is probably tied to the notion (which she herself shared) of her having a masculine mind. *The Mother's Recompense* does not fit or reinforce this image, and for this reason, Margaret McDowell and Marilyn Jones Lyde see it as inferior to previous work. See Margaret B. McDowell, *Edith Wharton* (Boston: Twayne, 1976), 40–41, 142–143; and Marilyn Jones Lyde, *Edith Wharton: Convention and Morality in the Work of a Novelist* (Norman: University of Oklahoma Press, 1959), 160–161. For a slight note of dissension, see Blake Nevius, *Edith Wharton: A Critical Study* (Berkeley and Los Angeles: University of California Press, 1953), 202. Nevius commends Wharton's fiction for a "willingness to test the clichés of her fellow novelists in the double light of her obdurate rationalism

and what we suppose to be her bitter private experience"
(p. 202).

4. Grace Aguilar, *The Mother's Recompense* (New York: D. Appleton, 1850), 498.

5. R. W. B. Lewis, *Edith Wharton; A Biography* (New York: Harper and Row, 1975; Fromm International Publishing, 1985), 464.

6. Lewis, *Edith Wharton*, 465.

7. Lewis, *Edith Wharton*, 465.

8. Wharton had great affection for several French women writers, Anna de Noailles and Philomène de Lévis-Mirepoix, for example, but as yet there are no studies of mutual influence. For information on Wharton's relationship with Anna de Noailles, see Lewis, *Edith Wharton*, 162, 169, 193, 196, 444 esp. For references to Philomène de Lévis-Mirepoix, see R. W. B. Lewis and Nancy Lewis, eds., *The Letters of Edith Wharton* (New York: Charles Scribner's Sons, 1988), 10, 418, 434–435, 450–452, 454, 461, 475, 495, 516, 517n, 537, 590, 591n; and Lewis, *Edith Wharton*, 438–439. For information on Anna de Noailles, see Shari Benstock, *Women of the Left Bank* (Austin: University of Texas, 1986), 68–70.

Wharton probably did inspire two American writers, Jean Stafford (1915–1979), another ironically comedic observer of manners, and Zona Gale (1874–1938), the author of *Miss Lulu Bett* (1920). See Louis Auchincloss, "Edith Wharton and Her Letters," *Hofstra Review* 2 (3) (Winter 1967): 1–7. He recounts that Stafford was interested in writing a biography of Wharton, but when she heard the (discredited) rumor that the novelist's real father might have been her brothers' English tutor, she exclaimed, "I'll do the tutor instead" (p. 2). Gale began intermittently corresponding with Wharton after Wharton's editor at Appleton sent her a letter from Gale, praising *The Glimpses of the Moon*. Wharton replied by naming *Miss Lulu Bett* and *Main Street* "the two significant books in recent American fiction." A copy of the letter is in the Beinecke Rare Book and Manuscript Library, Yale University, New Haven, Connecticut.

9. D. W. Winnicott, *Human Nature* (New York: Schocken, 1988), 101.

10. D. W. Winnicott, *Playing and Reality* (London: Tavistock Publications, 1971), 1–25, 112–118. Also see Ruth Perry, "Introduction," in *Mothering the Mind: Twelve Studies of Writers and Their Silent Partners*, ed. Ruth Perry and Martine Watson Brownley (New York: Holmes and Meier, 1984), 3–24. Perry

points out that mother figures play many key roles: "intercept-
ing the world, conferring unconditional approval, regulating
the environment, supplying missing psychic elements, and mir-
roring certain aspects of the self of the artist" (pp. 5–6).

11. Nancy Chodorow, "Family Structure and Feminine Personality," in *Women, Culture, and Society*, ed. Michelle Rosaldo and
Louise Lamphere (Stanford, Calif.: Stanford University Press,
1974), 43–66, 51–54 esp.; and Carol Gilligan, *In a Different
Voice: Psychological Theory and Women's Development* (Cambridge, Mass.: Harvard University Press, 1982), 46, 172. For a
review of literature about motherhood and daughterhood, see
Marianne Hirsch, "Mothers and Daughters," *Signs* 7 (Winter
1981): 200–222. In *Hudson River Bracketed* (1929) and *The
Gods Arrive* (1932), Vance Weston and his lover, Halo Spear,
learn to define their relationship in terms of Chodorow's paradigm.

12. See Cynthia Griffin Wolff, *A Feast of Words* (New York: Oxford University Press, 1977), 362.

13. Wolff (*A Feast of Words*) states that " 'incest' was absorbed into
Wharton's fictional vocabulary as a significant mode of representation" (p. 380). She suggests that Wharton's unresolved
feelings for her father might have affected all subsequent sexual, as well as cross-generational, relationships (p. 379). See
also Tintner, "Mothers, Daughters, and Incest," who sees the
struggle between mothers and daughters in Wharton's late
novels as the struggle for the father (p. 155). In "Family Romances" (1908), Freud states that daydreaming—like Wharton's
making up—serves to correct actual life and that it has two
principal aims, erotic and ambitious. These aims correspond to
Wharton's need, as discussed in Chapter 1, for adoration and
domination. See Sigmund Freud, "Family Romances," in *The
Standard Edition of the Complete Psychological Works of Sigmund Freud*, vol. 9 (1906–1908), trans. and ed. by James Strachey in collaboration with Anna Freud, assisted by Alix Strachey and Alan Tyson (London: The Hogarth Press and the
Institute of Psycho-analysis, 1973), 238.

14. Edith Wharton, *The Old Maid* (New York: D. Appleton, 1924)
and Edith Wharton, "Autres Temps . . . ," in *The Collected
Stories of Edith Wharton*, vol. 2 ed. R. W. B. Lewis (New York:
Charles Scribner's Sons, 1968), 257–281.

15. Edith Wharton, *The Age of Innocence* (New York: D. Appleton,
1920; New York: Charles Scribner's Sons, 1970), 242.

16. Tintner, "Mothers, Daughters, and Incest," 152.

17. Mary P. Ryan, *The Empire of the Mother: American Writing*

about Domesticity 1830-1860 (New York and London: Harrington Park Press, 1985), 120.

18. Elizabeth Ammons, *Edith Wharton's Argument with America* (Athens: The University of Georgia Press, 1980), 163.

19. R. W. B. Lewis, "Edith Wharton in Love: 'My Life Was Better Before I Knew You,' " *The New York Times Book Review*, 1 May 1988, 30.

20. See Edith Wharton, "Life and I," Wharton Archives, the Beinecke Rare Book and Manuscript Library, Yale University, New Haven, Connecticut, 34. She writes:

> A few days before my marriage, I was seized with such a dread of the whole dark mystery, that I summoned up courage to appeal to my mother, & begged her, with a heart beating to suffocation, to tell me "what being married was like." Her handsome face at once took on the look of icy disapproval which I most dreaded. "I never heard such a ridiculous question!" she said impatiently; & I felt at once how vulgar she thought me.

21. Edith Wharton, *A Motor-Flight Through France* (New York: Scribner's Sons, 1908), 11.

22. Edith Wharton, *The Children* (New York: D. Appleton, 1928), 3 (hereafter cited as *Children*).

23. See Wolff, *A Feast of Words*, 381.

24. Edith Wharton, *French Ways and Their Meaning* (New York: D. Appleton, 1919; 1930), 113 and 100, respectively (hereafter cited as *French Ways*). The phrase "the flower of life" is taken from Edith Wharton's *The Age of Innocence* (New York: D. Appleton-Century, 1920; New York: Charles Scribner's Sons, 1970), 347.

25. See Geoffrey Walton, *Edith Wharton: A Critical Study* (Rutherford, N.J.: Fairleigh Dickinson University Press, 1970; revised 1982). Walton observes that, in Rose Sellars, Edith Wharton created a character like herself, and he sees an element of self-criticism in her (p. 165).

26. For the source of this phrase, see Edith Wharton, *The Reef* (New York: Charles Scribner's Sons, 1912; 1965), 125.

27. See Ann Abigail Hamblen, "The Jamesian Note in Edith Wharton's *The Children*," *University Review* 31 (1965): 209–211. She observes similarities between Judith and James's Maisie and Nanda Brookenham (p. 210).

28. R. W. B. Lewis, *The American Adam: Innocence, Tragedy and Tradition in the Nineteenth Century* (Chicago: University of Chicago Press, 1955), 5.

29. See Elizabeth Ammons, "Cool Diana and the Blood-Red Muse: Edith Wharton on Innocence and Art," in *American Novelists Revisited: Essays in Feminist Criticism*, ed. Fritz Fleischman (Boston: Hall, 1982), 209–224. She makes the comparison between Ellen Olenska and her author and argues that as a woman writer Wharton had to be an expatriate.

30. Edith Wharton, "Fiction and Criticism," Wharton Archives, the Beinecke Rare Book and Manuscript Library, Yale University, New Haven, Connecticut, 4.

31. Virginia Woolf, *A Room of One's Own* (New York and London: Harcourt Brace Jovanovich, n.d.), p. 86.

CHAPTER SEVEN

The Self-Made Man, a Grown-up Woman, and the Female Artist (pp. 126–44)

1. Blake Nevius, *Edith Wharton: A Study of Her Fiction* (Berkeley and Los Angeles: University of California Press, 1953), 226, 235; and Cynthia Griffin Wolff, *A Feast of Words: The Triumph of Edith Wharton* (New York: Oxford University Press, 1977), 392.

2. Elmer Davis, "History of an Artist," *The Saturday Review of Literature*, 1 Oct. 1932, 145.

3. David Leverenz, *Manhood and the American Renaissance* (Ithaca, N.Y.: Cornell University Press, 1989), 67.

4. See R. W. B. Lewis, *Edith Wharton: A Biography* (New York: Harper and Row, 1975; Fromm International Publishing, 1985), 86. Lewis quotes from a letter to Burlingame at Scribner's in which Wharton wrote that "The Fullness of Life" is "one long shriek." He speculates that it was not included among her collected stories because its description of a mismated pair was too embarrassingly true to life.

5. Edith Wharton, "Mrs. Manstey's View," in *The Collected Short Stories of Edith Wharton*, vol. 1, ed. R. W. B. Lewis (New York: Charles Scribner's Sons, 1968), 5 (hereafter cited as "MV"). For a reading of the story as a self-portrait, see Wolff, *A Feast of Words*, 65–67.

6. Edith Wharton, *The Touchstone* (New York: Charles Scribner's Sons, 1900) in *Madame de Treymes and Others: Four Novelettes* (New York: Charles Scribner's Sons, 1970), 11 (hereafter cited as *TT*).

7. The sexual unattractiveness of Wharton's women writers in

stories such as "The Temperate Zone," expose again her ambivalence about the wedding of her gender and profession. Also note the woman writer in "Copy," who wants to effect a bargain with a former and now famous lover to prevent their letters to each other from being posthumously published. As in *The Touchstone*, the emphasis is on woman, not writer. The quality and integrity of an artist's work was the subject of many of Wharton's short stories, such as "The Verdict," "The Potboiler," "That Good May Come," "The Recovery," "The Portrait," "The Muse's Tragedy," "Full Circle," and "The Daunt Diana," but in these stories the artist figures are male. See Edith Wharton, *The Collected Short Stories of Edith Wharton*, ed. R. W. B. Lewis (New York: Charles Scribner's Sons, 1968).

8. See Lewis, *Edith Wharton*, 493; and Nevius, *Edith Wharton: A Study of Her Fiction*, 224. Wharton gives her opinion of her first novel in *A Backward Glance* (New York: D. Appleton-Century, 1934): " 'The Valley of Decision' was not, in my sense of the term, a novel at all, but only a romantic chronicle . . . and I doubted whether I should ever have enough constructive power to achieve anything beyond isolated character studies, or the stringing together of picturesque episodes" (p. 205).

9. Edith Wharton, "Life and I," Wharton Archives, the Beinecke Rare Book and Manuscript Library, Yale University, New Haven, Connecticut, 8.

10. Edith Wharton, *Hudson River Bracketed* (New York: D. Appleton, 1929), 15 (hereafter cited as *HRB*).

11. For a fuller analysis of the relationship between Wharton's writing and emotional and physical health, see Wolff, *A Feast of Words*, 75–91 esp. Also see Lewis, *Edith Wharton*, 76; Nevius, *Edith Wharton: A Study of Her Fiction*, 223; and Edith Wharton, *A Backward Glance*, 48–51, 70, 211 esp. Nevius notes that the Willows' library is modeled after the library of Wharton's father, George Frederic Jones. Wharton describes her father's library in *A Backward Glance*, 65–72.

12. For an excellent discussion of the similarities between Weston and Wharton, see Margaret B. McDowell, "*Hudson River Bracketed* and *The Gods Arrive*," in *Edith Wharton*, ed. Harold Bloom (New York: Chelsea House, 1986), 53–56 esp. McDowell notes that Wharton would have disliked the stream-of-consciousness technique because its association with the Naturalist movement and its underlying determinism reduces free will. Also see Wolff, *A Feast of Words*, who speculates that a novel such as *Ulysses* threatened Wharton because its technique,

which breaks down the barriers between life and fiction, leads
"back to the practices that distorted her own first work"
(p. 395). Wharton's need for personal and professional control
would have made the technique unsuitable.

13. Wolff, *A Feast of Words*, 393.
14. Lewis, *Edith Wharton*, 492.
15. See Sharon O'Brien, *Willa Cather: The Emerging Voice* (New
    York: Oxford University Press, 1987), 336.
16. See Wolff, *A Feast of Words*, 349. Wolff states that Wharton
    "fails to explain why Vance Weston wants so desperately to
    write; she fails as well to demonstrate a convincing link be-
    tween his life and his work" (p. 349). Also see Nevius, *Edith
    Wharton: A Study of Her Fiction*, who thinks that in *The Gods
    Arrive* it is impossible to define Wharton's attitude toward
    Weston. Only in the final scene, he argues, is the theme of "in-
    dividual responsibility" emphasized to give a retrospective sem-
    blance of unity to the work as a whole (p. 231).
17. Letter from Edith Wharton to Robert Grant, Nov. 19, 1907, as
    quoted in *The Letters of Edith Wharton*, ed. R. W. B. Lewis and
    Nancy Lewis (New York: Charles Scribner's Sons, 1988), 124.
18. Edith Wharton, *French Ways and Their Meaning* (New York:
    D. Appleton, 1919; 1930), 119 (hereafted cited as *French Ways*).
19. Edith Wharton, *A Backward Glance*, 209. The full quotation
    reads: "It was not until I wrote 'Ethan Frome' that I suddenly
    felt the artisan's full control of his implements."
20. Edith Wharton, *The Gods Arrive* (New York: D. Appleton, 1932;
    New York: Charles Scribner's Sons, 1969), 282 (hereafter cited
    as *GA*).
21. See Carol Wershoven, *The Female Intruder in the Novels of
    Edith Wharton* (Rutherford, N.J.: Fairleigh Dickinson Univer-
    sity Press, 1982), 143. Wershoven notes that Halo has to regain
    her own selfhood.
22. Mary Wilkins Freeman, "The Selfishness of Amelia Lamkin,"
    in *Short Fiction of Sarah Orne Jewett and Mary Wilkins Free-
    man*, ed. Barbara Solomon (New York and Scarborough, On-
    tario: New American Library, 1979), 466–484.
23. For the historical context of Wharton's thinking about gender,
    see Carroll Smith-Rosenberg, *Disorderly Conduct: Visions of
    Gender in Victorian America* (New York: Alfred A. Knopf,
    1985), 261. The title of *The Gods Arrive*, taken from Emerson's
    poem "Give All to Love" (1846), supports this interpretation.
    The last two lines read: "When half-gods go, / The gods arrive."
24. See R. W. B. Lewis, "A Writer of Short Stories," in *Edith
    Wharton*, ed. Harold Bloom (New York: Chelsea House, 1986),
    23. It was originally published as the "Introduction" to *The Col-*

lected Short Stories of Edith Wharton, edited by Lewis (New York: Charles Scribner's Sons, 1968), xxi. Lewis gives examples of those two halves when he recounts that Wharton was much amused by the masculine form of the salutation "Cher ami" "and willing to admit its propriety." At the same time, he observes that Wharton was a "great woman" and that her strength as an artist was her "distinctively feminine sensibility" (p. 23).

25. Margaret Chanler, *Autumn in the Valley* (Boston: Little, Brown, 1936), 114-115. Lewis (*Edith Wharton*) describes the gardens as a projection of herself (p. 487).

26. Lewis, *Edith Wharton*, 490.

27. Nancy R. Leach, "Edith Wharton's Unfinished Novel," *American Literature* 25 (Nov. 1953): 347. The manuscript of "Literature" is in the Wharton Archives, the Beinecke Rare Book and Manuscript Library, Yale University, New Haven, Connecticut.

28. Leach, "Edith Wharton's Unfinished Novel," 347.

29. Leach, "Edith Wharton's Unfinished Novel," 347.

30. The way Wharton attempts to reconcile these two traditions is reminiscent of another short story by Mary Wilkins, "The Poetess." In Wilkins's story, the poetess, Betsey, writes obituary verse and with it ministers to her community until the minister, himself a published poet, deprecates her work. When Betsey hears that her work is inferior, she burns it all and wastes away, a martyr to art. On her deathbed Betsey asks the minister to write her own obituary poem and by doing so to continue her—a woman's—literary tradition. In this manner the minister's genre (the kind magazines print) is subverted. Wharton is not as radical as Wilkins, but her projected ending to "Literature" suggests that she was contemplating similar issues. See Mary Wilkins Freeman, "The Poetess," in *The Short Fiction of Sarah Orne Jewett and Mary Wilkins Freeman*, 374-387.

31. See Elizabeth Ammons, *Edith Wharton's Argument with America* (Athens: The University of Georgia Press, 1980), 160, 191-196 esp.

32. Edith Wharton, letter to Sara Norton, Sat., 1901, Wharton Archives, the Beinecke Rare Book and Manuscript Library, Yale University, New Haven, Connecticut. In *A Backward Glance*, however, Wharton could equate domestic and literary arts when speaking of her family's cooks: "Ah, what artists they were!" (58-59). See Marie Theresa Logue, "Edith Wharton and the Domestic Ideal," Ph.D. diss., Rutgers University, 1984, 61-65, 383-388 esp. Logue argues that the image of the mothers locates the source of creativity in the domestic ideal.

33. The chapter specifically on her writing in *A Backward Glance*

is titled "The Secret Garden" (pp. 197–212). Wharton says, "I shall try to depict the growth and unfolding of the plants in my secret garden, from the seed to the shrub-top—for I have no intention of magnifying my vegetation into trees!" (p. 198). She describes Vance's writing as she does her own in *A Backward Glance*: "his book was a secret garden into which he shut himself away from her [Halo] as he might have done into a clandestine love-affair" (*GA*, 339).

34. For alternative readings, see Geoffrey Walton, *Edith Wharton: A Critical Study* (Rutherford, N.J.: Fairleigh Dickinson University Press, 1972; revised 1982). He finds it noteworthy that "Halo has the last word and that Vance is a supplicant as well as a child" (p. 182), but he also finds it confusing because one is left with "considerable uncertainty as to how seriously to take it all and how clear Edith Wharton herself was about the issues raised" (p. 182). Also see Ammons, *Edith Wharton's Argument with America*, who argues that Halo is symbolic of Wharton's belief in "inherent female superiority" (p. 195).

35. Edith Wharton, *French Ways and Their Meaning*, 110. The words also echo the minister's at Charity Royall's mother's funeral: "*yet in my flesh shall I see God*" (*Summer*, 186).

36. Laura Testvalley recalls another Wharton governess whose plain exterior belies her interior opulence. In her youth she had an illegitimate child. See Edith Wharton, "The Governess," the Wharton Archives, the Beinecke Rare Book and Manuscript Library, Yale University, New Haven, Connecticut.

37. Edith Wharton, *The Buccaneers* (New York: D. Appleton-Century, 1938), 146 (hereafter cited as *Buccaneers*).

38. Walton (*Edith Wharton: A Critical Study*) observes that she endorses the "American values of sincerity, honesty, and free-speaking, despite any incidental brashness or predatoriness, over aristocratic corruption and sophistication" (p. 198).

39. See Margaret B. McDowell, *Edith Wharton* (New York: Twayne, 1976), 138. She calls Laura the link between the older conservative generation in America and England and the younger, more liberal girls. Also see Carol Wershoven, "Edith Wharton's Final Vision: *The Buccaneers, American Literary Realism* 15 (1982): 209–220.

40. "A Moment's Ornament" was the working title of *The House of Mirth*, and in *The Gods Arrive* a would-be critic, Chris Churley, uses the phrase to describe himself (p. 248). Another title for *The House of Mirth* was "The Year of the Rose" (Lewis, *Edith Wharton*, 155).

41. In a less satisfying way, the scene suggests that Wharton might

have been having a self-mocking laugh at herself, feeling a need for retaliation or some residual bitterness in remembering the less savory details of her relationship with Morton Fullerton. See Lewis, *Edith Wharton*, 263–264 esp.; and Wolff, *A Feast of Words*, 195–198 esp., about her involvement in the purchase of blackmail letters for Fullerton.
42. Gary H. Lindberg, *Edith Wharton and the Novel of Manners* (Charlottesville: University Press of Virginia, 1975), 103.
43. Notebook of 1913 in the Wharton Archives, the Beinecke Rare Book and Manuscript Library, Yale University, New Haven, Connecticut.
44. Wolff, *A Feast of Words*, note 441.
45. Lewis, *Edith Wharton*, 169.

CONCLUSION
Wharton and Her Contemporaries, Cather, Austin, and Glasgow (pp. 145–56)

1. Edith Wharton, *Bunner Sisters*, in *Madame de Treymes and Others: Four Novelettes* (New York: Charles Scribner's Sons, 1970), 307 (hereafter cited as *Bunner*).
2. Edith Wharton, "Pomegranate Seed," *Scribner's Magazine* 51, March 1912, 284 (hereafter cited as "PS").
3. See Walter Pater, "The Myth of Demeter and Persephone," in *Greek Studies* (New York: Macmillan, 1894), 81, 102. This essay was first published in *Fortnightly Review*, January and February, 1876.
4. Edith Wharton, "A Little Girl's New York," *Harper's Magazine*, March 1938, 357.
5. Sharon O'Brien, *Willa Cather: The Emerging Voice* (New York: Oxford University Press, 1987), 446.
6. Adrienne Rich, "Paula Becker to Clara Westhoff," in *The Dream of a Common Language* (New York: W. W. Norton, 1978), 43.
7. Willa Cather, *Death Comes to the Archbishop* (New York: Alfred A. Knopf, 1927; reprint Vintage, 1973), 276.
8. Gaston Bachelard, *The Poetics of Space*, trans. Maria Jolas (Boston: Beacon Press, 1969).
9. Melody Graulich, "Introduction," *Western Trails: A Collection of Short Stories by Mary Austin* (Reno and Las Vegas: University of Nevada Press, 1988), 26. Graulich describes Austin as a "writer, ecologist, feminist, philosopher, poet, and folklorist" and observes that by rejecting repressive religions, anti-intel-

lectualism, and rigid gender roles, she sought new patterns for organizing her life (p. 4).

10. Mary Austin, *26 Jayne Street* (Boston and New York: Houghton Mifflin, 1920), 303.

11. Ellen Glasgow, *Letters of Ellen Glasgow*, ed. Blair Rouse (New York: Harcourt, Brace and World, 1958), 262.

12. Glasgow, *Letters of Ellen Glasgow*, 124.

13. Ellen Glasgow, *The Woman Within* (New York: Harcourt, Brace, 1954), 271.

14. Edith Wharton, review of *George Eliot*, by Leslie Stephen, *Bookman* 15 (May 1902): 249.

15. Wharton, review of *George Eliot*, 249.

16. Ellen Glasgow, "The Difference," in *The Shadowy Third and Other Stories* (New York: Doubleday, Page, 1923), 236.

17. Herbert Marcuse, *The Aesthetic Dimension: Toward a Critique of Marxist Aesthetics*, trans. and rev. Erica Sherover (Boston: Beacon Press, 1978), 57.

18. Edith Wharton, "A Further Glance," the Beinecke Rare Book and Manuscript Library, Yale University, New Haven, Connecticut, 3. "A Further Glance" was later published as "A Little Girl's New York." The passage in the latter reads:

> It is these fragments that I should like to assemble and make into a little memorial like the boxes formed of exotic shells which sailors used to fabricate between voyages. And I must forestall my critics by adding that I already foresee how small will be the shells I shall collect, how ordinary their varieties, and the box, when it is made, what a mere joke of a thing—unless one should put one's ear to the shells; but how many will? (p. 356)

BIBLIOGRAPHY

PRIMARY SOURCES

Ammons, Elizabeth. "The Business of Marriage in Edith Wharton's *The Custom of the Country.*" *Criticism* 16 (1974): 326–338.

————. "Cool Diana and the Blood-Red Muse: Edith Wharton on Innocence and Art." In *American Novelists Revisited: Essays in Feminist Criticism,* edited by Fritz Fleischman, 209–224. Boston: Hall, 1982.

————. *Edith Wharton's Argument with America.* Athens: The University of Georgia Press, 1980.

————. "Edith Wharton's *Ethan Frome* and the Question of Meaning." *Studies in American Fiction* 7 (1979): 127–140.

Aguilar, Grace. *The Mother's Recompense.* New York: D. Appleton, 1850.

Anderson, Hilton. "Edith Wharton as Fictional Heroine." *South Atlantic Quarterly* 69 (1970): [118]–123.

Auchincloss, Louis. *Edith Wharton: A Woman in Her Time.* New York: Viking Press, 1971.

Beaty, Robin. "Lilies That Fester: Sentimentality in *The House of Mirth.*" *College Literature* 14 (Fall 1987): 263–275.

Bell, Millicent. *Edith Wharton and Henry James: The Story of Their Friendship.* New York: George Braziller, 1965.

Bendixen, Alfred, ed. "A Guide to Wharton Criticism, 1974–1983." *Edith Wharton Newsletter* 2, no. 2 (Fall 1985): 1–8.

————. "Recent Wharton Studies: A Bibliographic Essay." *Edith Wharton Newsletter* 3, no. 2 (Fall 1986): 5, 8–9.

Blackall, Jean Frantz. "The Sledding Accident in *Ethan Frome.*" *Studies in Short Fiction* 21, no. 2 (1984): 145–146.

Bloom, Harold, ed. *Edith Wharton.* New York: Chelsea, 1986.

Boydston, Jeanne. " 'Grave Endearing Traditions': Edith Wharton and the Domestic Novel," In *Faith of a (Woman) Writer*, edited by Alice Kessler-Harris and William McBrien, 31-40. Westport, Conn.: Greenwood Press, 1988.

Brennen, Joseph X. "*Ethan Frome*: Structure and Metaphor." *Modern Fiction Studies* 12 (1961): 347-356.

Collins, Alexandra. "The *Noyade* of Marriage in Edith Wharton's *The Custom of the Country*." *English Studies in Canada* 9, no. 2 (1983): 197-212.

Colquitt, Claire. "Unpacking Her Treasures: Edith Wharton's 'Mysterious Correspondence' with Morton Fullerton." *Library Chronicle of the University of Texas* 31 (1985): 73-107.

Crowley, John. "The Unmastered Streak: Feminist Themes in Edith Wharton's *Summer*." *American Literary Realism* 15, no. 1 (1982): 86-96.

Davidson, Cathy N. "Kept Women in *The House of Mirth*." *Markham Review* 9 (1979): 10-13.

Dimock, Wai-Chee. "Debasing Exchange: Edith Wharton's *The House of Mirth*." *PMLA* 100, no. 5 (Oct. 1985): 783-792.

Dupree, Ellen Phillips. "Wharton, Lewis, and the Nobel Prize Address." *American Literature* 56, no. 2 (1984): 262-270.

Eggenschwiler, David. "The Ordered Disorder of *Ethan Frome*." *Studies in the Novel* 9 (1977): 237-246.

Fetterley, Judith. " 'The Temptation to Be a Beautiful Object': Double Standard and Double Bind in *The House of Mirth*." *Studies in American Fiction* 5 (1977): 199-211.

Fishbein, Leslie. "Prostitution, Morality, and Paradox: Moral Relativism in Edith Wharton's *Old New York: New Year's Day (The 'Seventies)*." *Studies in Short Fiction* 24, no. 4 (Fall 1987): 399-406.

Flanner, Janet. "Dearest Edith." *New Yorker*, 2 March 1929, 26-28.

French, Marilyn. "Muzzled Women." *College Literature* 14, no. 3 (Fall 1987): 219-229.

Fryer, Judith. "Edith Wharton's 'Tact of Omission': Harmony and Proportion in *A Backward Glance*." *Biography* 6, no. 2 (1983): 148-169.

————. *Felicitous Space: The Imaginative Structures of Edith Wharton and Willa Cather*. Chapel Hill: University of North Carolina Press, 1986.

————. "Purity and Power in *The Age of Innocence*." *American Literary Realism* 17 (1984): 153-168.

Gargano, James W. "Edith Wharton's *The Reef*: The Genteel Woman's Quest for Knowledge." *Novel* 10 (1976): 40-48.

Gibson, Mary Ellis. "Edith Wharton and the Ethnography of Old New York." *Studies in American Fiction* 13, no. 1 (Spring 1985): 57-69.

Gimbel, Wendy. *Edith Wharton: Orphancy and Survival.* Landmark Dissertations in Women's Studies Series. Ed., Annette Baxter. New York: Praeger, 1984.

Godfrey, David A. " 'The Full and Elaborate Vocabulary of Evasion': The Language of Cowardice in Edith Wharton's Old New York." *Midwest Quarterly: A Journal of Contemporary Thought* 30 (Autumn 1988): 27-44.

Gooder, Jean. "Unlocking Edith Wharton: An Introduction to the Reef." *The Cambridge Quarterly* 15, no. 1 (1986): 33-52.

Gribben, Alan. " 'The Heart Is Insatiable': A Selection from Edith Wharton's Letters to Morton Fullerton." *Library Chronicle of the University of Texas* 31 (1985): 7-18.

Gubar, Susan, "The 'Blank Page' and Female Creativity." In *Writing and Sexual Difference*, edited by Elizabeth Abel, 73-94. Chicago: University of Chicago Press, 1982.

Hamblen, Abigail Ann. "Edith Wharton in New England." *New England Quarterly* 38 (1965): 239-244.

———. "The Jamesian Note in Edith Wharton's *The Children*." *University Review* (Kansas City) 31 (1965): 209-211.

Hays, Peter L. "Edith Wharton and F. Scott Fitzgerald." *Edith Wharton Newsletter* 3, no. 1, (Spring 1986): 2-3.

———. "First and Last in *Ethan Frome*." *Notes on Modern American Literature* 1, no. 1 (Winter 1976): Item 15, no. 10259.

Hovey, R. B. "Ethan Frome: A Controversy about Modernizing It." *American Literary Realism* 19, no. 1 (Fall 1986): 4-20.

Howe, Irving. *Edith Wharton: A Collection of Critical Essays.* Englewood Cliffs, N.J.: Prentice Hall, 1962.

Iyengar, K. R. Srinivasa. "A Note on 'Ethan Frome.' " *Literary Criterion* 5, no. 3 (1962): 168-178.

Jessup, Josephine Lurie. *The Faith of Our Feminists: A Study in the Novels of Edith Wharton, Ellen Glasgow, and Willa Cather.* New York: Richard R. Smith, 1950.

Joslin-Jeske, Katherine. "What Lubbock Didn't Say." *Edith Wharton Newsletter* 1, no. 1 (Spring 1984): 2-4.

Kaplan, Amy. *The Social Construction of American Realism.* Chicago: The University of Chicago Press, 1988.

Karcher, Carolyn. "Male Vision and Female Revision in James's *The Wings of the Dove* and Wharton's *The House of Mirth*." *Women's Studies* 10, no. 3 (1984): 227-244.

Kerkes, John. "The Great Guide of Human Life." *Philosophy and Literature* 8, no. 2 (Oct. 1984): 236–249.

Lawson, Richard. *Edith Wharton*. New York: Frederick Ungar, 1977.

Leach, Nancy. "Edith Wharton's Unfinished Novel." *American Literature* 25, no. 3 (Nov. 1953): 334–353.

Leavis, Q. D. "Henry James's Heiress: The Importance of Edith Wharton." *Scrutiny* 7 (1938–1939): 261–276.

Lewis, R. W. B. *Edith Wharton: A Biography*. New York: Harper and Row, 1975; Fromm International Publishing, 1985.

——. and Nancy Lewis. *The Letters of Edith Wharton*. New York: Charles Scribner's Sons, 1988.

Lidoff, Joan. "Another Sleeping Beauty: Narcissism in *The House of Mirth*." *American Quarterly* 32 (1980): 519–539.

Lindberg, Gary H. *Edith Wharton and the Novel of Manners*. Charlottesville: University Press of Virginia, 1975.

Logue, Marie Theresa. "Edith Wharton and the Domestic Ideal." Ph.D. diss., Rutgers University, 1983.

Lubbock, Percy. *Portrait of Edith Wharton*. New York: D. Appleton-Century, 1947.

Lyde, Marilyn. *Edith Wharton: Convention and Morality in the Work of a Novelist*. Norman: University of Oklahoma Press, 1959.

Malcolm, Janet. "The Woman Who Hated Women." *The New York Times Book Review*, 16 Nov. 1986, 11.

Maynard, Moira. "Moral Integrity in *The Reef*: Justice to Anna Leath." *College Literature* 14, no. 3 (Fall 1987): 285–295.

McDowell, Margaret B. *Edith Wharton*. Boston: Twayne, 1976.

——. "Edith Wharton's *The Old Maid*: Novella/Play/Film." *College Literature* 14, no. 3 (Fall 1987): 246–262.

——. "Viewing the Custom of Her Country: Edith Wharton's Feminism." *Contemporary Literature* 15 (1974): 521–538.

McManis, Jo Angew. "Edith Wharton's Hymns to Respectability." *Southern Review* 7 (1971): 986–993.

Morrow, Nancy. "Games and Conflict in Edith Wharton's *The Custom of the Country*." *American Literary Realism* 17 (1984): 32–39.

Murad, Orlene. "Edith Wharton and Ethan Frome." *Modern Language Studies* 13, no. 3 (Summer 1983): 90–103.

Nevius, Blake. *Edith Wharton: A Study of Her Fiction*. Berkeley and Los Angeles: University of California Press, 1953.

Olin-Ammentorp, Julie. "Edith Wharton's Challenge to Feminist Criticism." *Studies in American Fiction* 16 (Autumn 1988): 237-244.

Petry, Alice Hall. "A Twist of Crimson Silk: Edith Wharton's 'Roman Fever.'" *Studies in Short Fiction* 24, no. 2 (Spring 1987): 163-166.

Poirier, Richard. "Edith Wharton's *The House of Mirth*." *American Novel* 34 (1965): 117-132.

Price, Alan. "Lily Bart and Carrie Meeber: Cultural Sisters." *American Literary Realism* 13 (1980): 238-245.

Radden, Jennifer. "Defining Self-Deception." *Dialogue* 23, no. 1 (March 1984): 103-120.

Rose, Alan Henry. "'Such Depths of Sad Initiation': Edith Wharton and New England." *New England Quarterly* 50 (1977): 423-439.

Saunders, Judith. "Becoming the Mask: Edith Wharton's Ingenues." *Massachusetts Studies in English* 8 (1982): 33-39.

———. "A New Look at the Oldest Profession in Wharton's *New Year's Day*." *Studies in Short Fiction* 17 (1980): 121-126.

———. "Ironic Reversal in Edith Wharton's *Bunner Sisters*." *Studies in Short Fiction* 14 (1977): 241-245.

Schriber, Mary. "Convention in the Fiction of Edith Wharton." *Studies in American Fiction* 11, no. 2 (1983): 189-201.

Sensibar, Judith L. "Edith Wharton Reads the Bachelor Type: Her Critique of Modernism's Representative Man." *American Literature* 60 (December 1988): 575-590.

Showalter, Elaine. "The Death of a Lady (Novelist): Wharton's *House of Mirth*." *Representations* 9 (1985): 133-149.

Schulman, Robert. "Divided Selves and the Market Society: Politics and Psychology in *The House of Mirth*." *Perspectives on Contemporary Literature* 11 (1985): 10-19.

Stein, Allen. "Wharton's *Blithedale*: A New Reading of *The Fruit of the Tree*." *American Literary Realism* 12 (1979): 330-337.

Tintner, Adeline. "Mothers, Daughters, and Incest in the Late Novels of Edith Wharton." *The Lost Tradition: Mothers and Daughters in Literature*, ed. Cathy N. Davidson and E. M. Broner, 147-156. New York: Frederick Unger, 1980.

———. "Mothers vs. Daughters in the Fiction of Edith Wharton and Henry James." *A. B. Bookman's Weekly* 6 (June 1983): 4324, 4326-4329.

———. "An Unpublished Love Poem by Edith Wharton." *American Literature* 60 (March 1988): 98-103.

Trilling, Lionel. "The Morality of Inertia." *Great Moral Dilemmas,* ed. R. M. MacIver. New York: Harper and Row, 1956.

Tuttleton, James. "The Feminist Takeover of Edith Wharton." *The New Criterion* 7 (March 1989): 6-14.

Tyler, William. "Personal Memories of Edith Wharton." *Proceedings of the Massachusetts Historical Society* 85 (1973): 91-104.

Walker, Nancy. " 'Seduced and Abandoned': Convention and Reality in Edith Wharton's *Summer.*" *Studies in American Literature* 11 (1983): 107-114.

Walton, Geoffrey. *Edith Wharton; A Critical Interpretation.* Rutherford, N.J.: Fairleigh Dickinson University Press, 1970; East Brunswick, N.J.: Associated University Presses, 1982.

Wershoven, Carol. "The Divided Conflict of Edith Wharton's *Summer.*" *Colby Library Quarterly* 21, no. 1 (1985): 5-10.

_____. "Edith Wharton's Final Vision: *The Buccaneers.*" *American Literary Realism* 15, no. 2 (1982): 209-220.

_____. *The Female Intruder in the Novels of Edith Wharton.* Rutherford, N.J.: Fairleigh Dickinson University Press, 1982.

Westbrook, Wayne. "Lily—Bartering on the New York Social Exchange in *The House of Mirth.*" *Ball State University Forum* 20, no. 2 (1979): 59-64.

White, Barbara. "Edith Wharton's *Summer* and 'Women's Fiction.' " *Essays in Literature* 11, no. 2 (Fall 1984): 223-235.

_____. *Growing Up Female: Adolescent Girlhood in American Fiction.* Westport, Conn.: Greenwood Press, 1985.

Winner, Viola Hopkins. "Introduction." In *A Novelette by David Olivieri.* Charlottesville: University Press of Virginia, 1977.

Wolff, Cynthia Griffin. "Edith Wharton and the 'Visionary' Imagination." *Frontiers: Journal of Women's Studies* 2, no. 3 (1977): 24-30.

_____. *A Feast of Words: The Triumph of Edith Wharton.* New York: Oxford University Press, 1977.

_____. "Lily Bart and the Beautiful Death." *American Literature* 46 (1974): 16-40.

_____. "The Women in My Life." *Massachusetts Review* 24, no. 2 (1983): 438-452.

Worby, Diana. "The Ambiguity of Edith Wharton's 'Lurking Feminism.' " *Mid Hudson Language Studies* 5, no. 1 (1982): 81-90.

Zilversmit, Annette Clair Schreiber. "Mothers and Daughters: The Heroines in the Novels of Edith Wharton." Ph.D. diss., New York University, 1980.

RELATED SOURCES

Abel, Elizabeth. "(E)merging Identities: The Dynamics of Female Friendships in Contemporary Fiction by Women." *Signs: Journal of Women in Culture and Society* 6, no. 3 (Spring 1981): 413–435.

Abel, Elizabeth, Marianne Hirsch, Elizabeth Langland, eds. *The Voyage In: Fictions of Female Development.* Hanover, N.H.: University Press of New England, 1983.

Bauer, Dale M. *Feminist Dialogics: A Theory of Failed Community.* New York: State University of New York Press, 1988.

Baym, Nina. "Melodramas of Beset Manhood: How Theories of American Fiction Exclude Women Writers." *American Quarterly* 33 (Summer) 1981: 123–139.

———. *Women's Fiction: A Guide to Novels by and about Women in America, 1820–1870.* Ithaca, N.Y.: Cornell University Press, 1978.

Benjamin, Jessica. *The Bonds of Love: Psychoanalysis, Feminism, and the Problem of Domination.* New York: Pantheon Books, 1988.

Benstock, Shari, ed. *The Private Self: Theory and Practice of Women's Writings.* Chapel Hill & London: The University of North Carolina Press, 1988.

———. *Women of the Left Bank: Paris, 1900–1940.* Austin: University of Texas Press, 1986.

Bettleheim, Bruno. *The Uses of Enchantment: The Meaning and Importance of Fairy Tales.* New York: Knopf, 1976; reprint Vintage Books, 1977.

Brownstein, Rachel M. *Becoming a Heroine: Reading About Women in Novels.* New York: Viking, 1982.

Chevigny, Bell Gale. "Daughters Writing: Toward a Theory of Women's Biography." *Between Women: Biographers, Novelists, Critics, Teachers, and Artists Write about Their Work on Women,* edited by Carol Ascher, Louise DeSalvo, and Sara Ruddick, 356–379. Boston: Beacon Press, 1984.

Chodorow, Nancy. "Family Structure and Feminine Personality." *Women, Cutlure, and Society,* edited by Michelle Rosaldo and Louise Lamphere, 43–66. Stanford, Calif.: Stanford University Press, 1974.

———. *The Reproduction of Mothering: Psychoanalysis and the Sociology of Gender.* Berkeley and Los Angeles: University of California Press, 1978.

Cott, Nancy. *The Bonds of Womanhood: 'Women's Sphere' in New*

England, 1780–1835. New Haven: Yale University Press, 1977.

Davidson, Cathy, and E. M. Broner, ed. *The Lost Tradition: Mothers and Daughters in Literature*. New York: Unger, 1980.

Degler, Carl. *At Odds: Women and Family in America from the Revolution to the Present*. New York: Oxford University Press, 1980.

Dinnerstein, Dorothy. *The Mermaid and the Minotaur: Sexual Arrangement and the Human Malaise*. New York: Harper and Row, 1976.

Donovan, Josephine. *New England Local Color Literature: A Women's Tradition*. New York: Frederick Ungar, 1983.

_____. "The Unpublished Love Poems of Sarah Orne Jewett." *Frontiers* 4, no. 3 (1978): 26–31.

Eakin, Paul John. *The New England Girl: Cultural Ideals in Hawthorne, Stowe, Howells and James*. Athens: The University of Georgia Press, 1976.

Faderman, Lillian. *Surpassing the Love of Men: Romantic Friendships between Women from the Renaissance to the Present*. New York: Morrow, 1981.

Flax, Jane. "The Conflict between Nurturance and Autonomy in Mother/Daughter Relationships and Within Feminism." *Feminist Studies* 4 (Feb. 1978): 171–189.

Frankfort, Roberta. *Collegiate Women: Domesticity and Career in Turn-of-the-Century America*. New York: New York University Press, 1977.

Freud, Sigmund. "Creative Writers and Daydreaming," in *The Freud Reader*, edited by Peter Gay, 436–443. New York: W. W. Norton, 1989.

Gardiner, Judith. "The (US)es of (I)dentity: A Response to Abel on '(E)merging Identities.'" *Signs: Journal of Women in Culture and Society* 6, no. 3 (Spring 1981): 436–442.

Gilbert, Sandra, and Susan Gubar. *Madwoman in the Attic: The Woman Writer and the Nineteenth-Century Literary Imagination*. New Haven, Conn.: Yale University Press, 1979.

Gilligan, Carol. *In a Different Voice: Psychological Theory and Women's Development*. Cambridge, Mass.: Harvard University Press, 1982.

Haller, John S., and Robin W. Haller. *The Physician and Sexuality in Victorian America*. Urbana: University of Illinois Press, 1974.

Hirsch, Marianne. "Mother and Daughters." *Signs: Journal of Women in Culture and Society* 7, no. 1 (Autumn 1981): 200–222.

Kolb, Harold H. *A Field Guide to the Study of American Literature*. Charlottesville: University Press of Virginia, 1976.

Lears, Jackson. *No Place of Grace: Antimodernism and the Transformation of American Culture, 1880–1920*. New York: Pantheon, 1981.

Lewis, R. W. B. *The American Adam: Innocence, Tragedy, and Tradition in the Nineteenth Century*. Chicago: University of Chicago Press, 1955.

Leverenz, David. *Manhood and the American Renaissance*. Ithaca, N.Y.: Cornell University Press, 1989.

Lorber, Judith, Rose Laub Coser, Alice S. Rossi, and Nancy Chodorow. "On *The Reproduction of Mothering*: A Methodological Debate." *Signs: Journal of Women in Culture and Society* 6, no. 3 (Spring 1981): 482–514.

Miller, Nancy. *The Poetics of Gender*. Boulder: Colorado University Press, 1986.

———. *Subject to Change: Reading Feminist Writing*. New York: Columbia University Press, 1988.

Miner, Valerie, and Helen E. Longino, eds. *Competition: A Feminist Taboo?* New York: Feminist Press, 1987.

Olney, James, ed. *Autobiography: Essays Theoretical and Critical*. Princeton, N.J.: Princeton University Press, 1980.

Pascal, Roy. *Design and Truth in Autobiography*. Cambridge, Mass.: Harvard University Press, 1980.

Perry, Ruth, and Martine Watson Brownley, eds. *Mothering the Mind: Twelve Studies of Writers and Their Silent Partners*. New York: Holmes and Meier, 1984.

Pratt, Annis, with Barbara White, Andrea Loewenstein, and Mary Wyer. *Archetypal Patterns in Women's Fiction*. Bloomington: Indiana University Press, 1981.

Ragland-Sullivan, Ellie. *Jacques Lacan and the Philosophy of Psychoanalysis*. Urbana: University of Illinois Press, 1986.

Rich, Adrienne. *Of Women Born: Motherhood as Experience and Institution*. New York: Norton, 1976.

Rowbotham, Sheila. *Woman's Consciousness, Man's World*. London: Penguin, 1973.

Russ, Joanna. "What Can a Heroine Do? Or Why Women Can't Write." In *Images of Women, in Fiction: Feminist Perspectives*, edited by Susan Koppelman, 3–20. Bowling Green, Ohio: Bowling Green University Popular Press, 1972; reprint 1973.

Ryan, Mary P. *The Empire of the Mother: American Writing about Domesticity*. New York: Harrington Park Press, 1985.

Sahli, Nancy. "Smashing: Women's Relationships before the Fall." *Chrysalis* 8 (Summer 1979): 17–27.

Showalter, Elaine. "Feminist Criticism in the Wilderness." *Critical Inquiry* 8, no. 2 (Winter 1981): 179–205.

_____. *A Literature of Their Own: British Women Novelists from Brontë to Lessing.* Princeton, N.J.: Princeton University Press, 1977.

Smith, Sidonie. *A Poetics of Women's Autobiography: Marginality and the Fictions of Self-Representation.* Bloomington: Indiana University Press, 1987.

Smith-Rosenberg, Carroll. *Disorderly Conduct: Visions of Gender in Victorian America.* New York: Alfred A. Knopf, 1985.

_____. "The Female World of Love and Ritual: Relations between Women in Nineteenth-Century America." *Signs: Journal of Women in Culture and Society* 1 (1975): 1–29.

Stein, Allen F. *After the Vows Were Spoken: Marriage in American Literary Realism.* Columbus: Ohio State University Press, 1984.

Thorne, Barrie, ed., with Marilyn Yalom. *Rethinking the Family: Some Feminist Questions.* New York: Longman, 1982.

Todd, Janet. *Women's Friendship in Literature.* New York: Columbia University Press, 1980.

Welter, Barbara. "The Cult of True Womanhood: 1820–1860." *American Quarterly* 18 (Summer 1966): 151–174.

Winnicott, D. W. *Human Nature.* New York: Schocken, 1988.

_____. *Playing and Reality.* London: Tavistock Publications, 1971.

Winston, Elizabeth. "The Autobiographer and Her Readers." In *Women's Autobiography,* edited by Estelle C. Jelinek, 93–111. Bloomington: Indiana University Press, 1980.

Ziff, Larzer. *The American 1890's: Life and Times of a Lost Generation.* New York: Viking, 1966.

INDEX